MW00380326

RIFFS

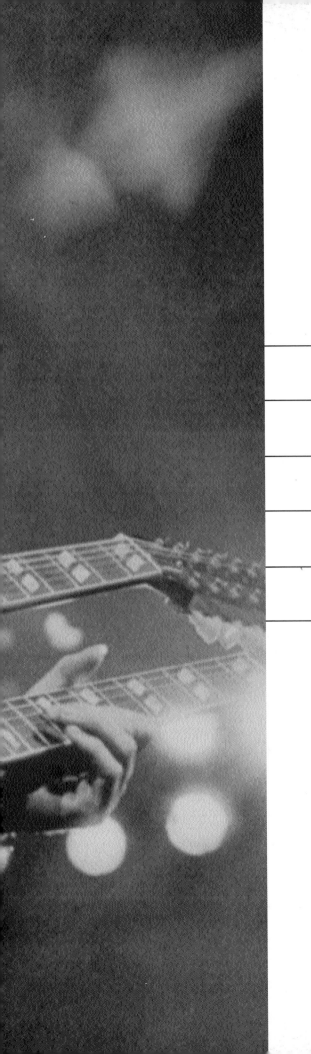

RIFFS

How to create and play great

GUITAR RIFFS

By **RIKKY ROOKSBY**

Backbeat
Books

RIFFS

How to create and play great GUITAR RIFFS

A BACKBEAT BOOK
First edition 2002
Published by Backbeat Books
600 Harrison Street,
San Francisco, CA 94107
www.backbeatbooks.com

An imprint of The Music Player Network United
Entertainment Media Inc.

Published for Backbeat Books by Outline Press Ltd,
115J Cleveland Street, London W1T 6PU, England.
www.backbeatuk.com

ISBN 0-87930-710-2

Copyright © 2002 Balafon. All rights reserved. No part of this book covered by the copyrights hereon may be reproduced
or copied in any manner whatsoever without written permission, except in the case of brief quotations embodied in
articles or reviews where the source should be made clear.
For more information contact the publishers.

Art Director: Nigel Osborne
Design: Paul Cooper
Editorial Director: Tony Bacòn
Editor: Paul Quinn
Production: Phil Richardson

This book is dedicated to Marc Bolan (1947-1977)

Printed by Colorprint (Hong Kong)

02 03 04 04 06 5 4 3 2 1

Contents

Introduction

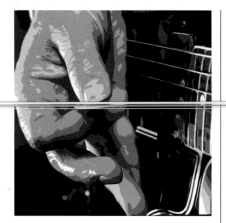

From Johnny Kidd & The Pirates' 'Shakin All Over' (1960) to Limp Bizkit's 'Rollin' (2001), there is no escaping the riff – that short, super-charged musical phrase that gets under your skin and sets your pulse racing. Riffs have been a central feature of rock music for over 40 years. Many great rock numbers depend on them. For decades guitarists have spent many an hour (and many a rehearsal) playing their favourite riffs. They have bent their ears working out favourite riffs from scratched LPs, stretched tapes, and shiny CDs.

Riffs get people excited, whether they are musicians or listeners. Advertising agencies use riffs on television and in film trailers. Riffs sell songs, concert tickets, and guitars. Millions have mimed playing riffs on 'air guitar'…

So, how do you define a riff? How many kinds of riff are there. What makes them work? How do you write one? And how do you make better use of the riffs you write…?

WHAT IS A RIFF?

The word 'riff' entered the language as musical slang way back in the 1920s. The *Little Oxford Dictionary* describes a riff as a "short repeated phrase in jazz and similar music". In jazz its function was to provide a static harmonic part for soloists to improvise over – it's easier to improvise over a repeated short riff than over a whole chord progression. A riff is therefore instrumental. In rock music it moved to the foreground, becoming a hook, something that sticks in the memory after only a single hearing. It has been a central part of rock music almost since rock'n'roll was invented, but gained ground from the mid-1960s onward.

There's no water-tight definition of a riff. But for the sake of this book, and for inventing your own riffs, let's take this as a working description:

A riff is a short, repeated, memorable musical phrase, often pitched low on the guitar, which focuses much of the energy and excitement of a rock song.

We'll examine this description in more detail and qualify its terms.

First, 'short'. The majority of riffs are between one and four bars in length. Any longer than that and they can sound more like a melody or a solo. Parts of a riff may be repeated with slight variations to last eight, 12 or 16 bars, for example, but that doesn't change the fact that the basic material of the riff is usually about four bars.

Second, 'repeated'. All riffs are repeated. This is an essential element of how they fix themselves in the mind of the listener. A well-constructed riff will make you feel you want play it over and over. In rock music the repetition of the riff fuels the energy of the song – like shovelling coal into a steam-train's furnace.

Third, 'memorable'. A good riff has certain rhythmic, harmonic or melodic qualities that make it lodge in the mind. If it has these it may rival even the sung chorus as the most interesting part of the song. Many famous rock numbers – think of 'Layla', 'Smoke On The Water', 'Enter Sandman', 'Smells Like Teen Spirit', 'Whole Lotta Love' or 'Sultans of Swing' – are known as much for their riffs as their melodies.

Fourth, 'pitched low on the guitar'. The bulk of guitar riffs are played on the lower three strings. Why? The E, A and D strings have the power and authority generally associated with bass notes (the bass part in any music usually defines the harmony above it). As the strings themselves are denser they give out more volume. In the 1950s, when the electric guitar was a new instrument, players fell in love with the 'twang' of the lowest strings. It was this particular guitar tone – epitomised by Duane Eddy, then developed by The Shadows and The Ventures – that pushed the instrument to the centre of popular music through recordings of guitar instrumentals. By the mid-1960s 'twang' gave way to distortion, and the rock guitar riff as we know it was born.

Some riffs, of course, are played on the higher strings: this is true of a player like The Edge who has written fine riffs on the higher strings for U2 songs such as 'With Or Without You' and 'Sunday Bloody Sunday'. In his case, echo thickens and sustains these phrases, allowing them to combine with the bass guitar more effectively.

Lastly, the term 'rock song'. This book is primarily concerned with riffs in rock guitar music. The use of guitar riffs is probably more

"a good riff has certain rhythmic, harmonic or melodic qualities that make it lodge in the mind"

characteristic of rock than any other style of popular music, but riffs can be found in soul, R&B, blues, funk, pop, disco, reggae, and so on. They are also found on other instruments, such as bass guitar and keyboards.

WHY ARE RIFFS IMPORTANT?

Riffs are central to rock music of all kinds (and all degrees of ferocity). The strong rhythmic element of a good riff makes a big contribution to the energy of a rock performance. Riffs get audiences up and dancing. They also fill sections of a song where there aren't vocals. Instead of a simple progression of chords as the link between verse and chorus, the riffs in a song allow an arrangement to go quiet when the singer delivers the verse, then let rip instrumentally with a loud riff.

Riffs not only have a rhythmic function but also a harmonic and a melodic function. A riff can replace a chord progression during a verse or chorus, or under a solo. It can also be something you can hum because of its melodic qualities. Think of this as a creative formula when writing riffs:

Riff = RHM – rhythm, harmony, melody.

Check a riff for all three.

Riffs are popular because they're often easy to play. They usually don't necessarily involve much guitar technique, which is why beginners plague music shops with their initial stabs at 'Sweet Child O' Mine' or 'Whole Lotta Love'. Musicians love riffs because once you've got a riff together the whole band can get behind it and there's an instant feeling of musical unity. Riffs are great for jam sessions: for instance, the guitar plays a riff in unison with the bass and then breaks away to solo while the bass keeps the riff going. Jamming is also a good way to come up with new riffs. In a live context they offer an opportunity to look up from what you're doing, or move away from the mike if you're singing *and* playing guitar, to interact with the audience and take in the vibe of the gig itself.

A BRIEF HISTORY OF THE RIFF

In its myriad forms, rock music has been around for about 50 years. During that time it's not only the technology of rock that has changed. Its musical language has undergone some developments and additions. Rock remains a music about assertion and complaint, rebellion and outsiders, about living on the edge or in the fast lane (choose your own cliché). It still has a big beat at the centre of the performance, and it is still in love with the sound and spectacle of loud guitars and what can be said with a handful of chords. But rock's harmony has grown and changed, and this moulds the riffs heard today. At the heart of this process is rock's relationship to one of its musical parents, the blues.

Riffs ended up in rock because they were already present in jazz and blues in the years before Elvis, often in the left-hand of boogie-woogie piano parts. Rock began with rock'n'roll, which was based on the blues format of the 12-bar and blues scales. The influence of scales like the pentatonic minor and major can be heard on riff-based 1950s songs like Duane Eddy's 'Peter Gunn' and Jimmy McCracklin's 'The Walk'. The influence of the 12-bar format meant that in the Beatles' early music you hear riffs played first where the key chord (chord I) would be, and then moved up or down to begin on the roots of the other two chords of the 12-bar sequence.

In some ways, year zero for the riff was 1964. The Beatles had a vice-like grip on the upper positions of Top 20 charts the world over with the melodic, vibrant pop of songs like 'She Loves You' and 'I Wanna Hold Your Hand' (despite the fact that they'd started out playing rock'n'roll, and still enjoyed raving in concert through 12-bar-based 1950s classics like 'Long Tall Sally'). Their success meant things would never be the same again for instrumental groups like the Shadows, where the guitar had been both melody instrument and soloist. The Beatles had broken down a door, and in their wake came guitar-plus-vocal groups who sought commercial impact with a 'dirtier', more raw sound – bands like The Rolling Stones, The Who, The Kinks, The Animals, and Them – with music often driven by aggressive guitar riffs. These bands recorded some of the first, definitive riff-based songs, where guitar chords were no longer supporting the harmony but were the focus of interest because the riffs fused harmony to a punchy rhythm. Think of The Kinks' 'You Really Got Me' and 'All Day And All Of The Night', The Kingsmen's 'Louie Louie', The Who's 'I Can't Explain', and Them's 'Gloria'.

In the early 1960s the electric guitar and its portable (usually valve) amplifier were still new technology. The modernity of the electric guitar is nowhere more convincingly expressed than by composer/arranger John Barry's decision to give the 'James Bond 007' theme to Vic Flick's electric guitar (even if the guitar in question was not a solid-body), rather than a more traditional instrument. So it was that millions across the world who went to see *Dr No* in 1962 heard the electric guitar claim its place in the world of film soundtracks.

As ever, technology and music-making went hand-in-hand. The kind of instrument you play has a substantial effect on the kind of music you write. Back then, guitarists were literally left to their own devices, because there was almost no tutorial material (such as this book and CD) available in the early 1960s. Learning guitar was a hit-and-miss mixture of word-of-mouth, lucky insights, hard work, listening to records, and watching other players. Amps were turned up to compete with drummers and loud audiences, valves distorted, speakers were damaged, but in the process a

"in some ways, year zero for the riff was 1964"

key sound accessory of the rock riff was discovered: distortion. Distortion, with its saturation of over-tones, made the guitar sound more dangerous. It gave the notes more sustain. Chords seemed less like harmony and more like battle-cries. Distortion encouraged a different kind of song. By the mid-1960s inventors figured out how to take that sound and bottle it up in a small metal box with an input, an output, and an on/off switch. The 'fuzz-box' was born, and offered distortion at any volume desired.

During the 1964-66 period a significant number of hit singles featured guitar riffs and a more primitive rhythmic urgency (often matched, as in the case of the Troggs' 'Wild Thing', with lyrics of matching sexual directness). The riff was to play an important role in the defining of a heavier 'rock' music, which had artistic and counter-cultural aspirations. Rock jettisoned the 'n'roll' and had long since cast off the Teddy Boy drapes. Now it wanted to take on the world. Pop could keep the Top 20. Rock wanted to make a Big Statement. Its main vehicle for this was the album, the long-player, not the increasingly despised 45rpm single. Songs started to get lengthier. Instrumental prowess was looked to for revelation. Bigger amps provided the means of delivery. The riff held it all together.

Bigger amps and more distortion meant that one or two notes in a riff could sound huge. Think of 'Sunshine Of Your Love' or 'Foxy Lady'. Technology and rock's changing sense of itself combined to popularise riff-based guitar music in the second half of the 1960s. Improved amplification and effects pedals offered greater sustain, which meant more noise could be achieved with fewer musicians. The quartet line-up of the Beatles (two guitars, bass and drums) was for a time eclipsed in popularity by the power trio. Groups like Cream, Jimi Hendrix, post-1968 Who, and Free, started writing material based around single-note riffs instead of chord progressions.

This went hand-in-hand with the way rock's musical vocabulary became more linear, with the influence of the fascination with static, trance effects (copied initially from Indian music) in contrast to the sequential 'goal-oriented' tonality of pop. Single-note-sequence riffs were easy for audiences to remember, and often allowed players to improvise more easily than over more elaborate chord sequences.

In musical terms, during the blues boom and the heyday of progressive/heavy rock (1966-75), the pentatonic minor was the most popular scale. There was an increase in the use of bare fifths as opposed to whole chords, especially in riffs. Eventually guitarists began to exploit the darker possibilities of the dissonant tritone interval (two notes, six semitones apart, eg E-Bb) that had always lurked in the blues scale (E-G-A-Bb-B). A notable exponent was Tony Iommi on Black Sabbath's debut

LP in 1969. In 1970 several heavy rock riffs became unlikely hit singles – Free's 'Alright Now', Deep Purple's 'Black Night' and Black Sabbath's 'Paranoid', to name three. But that wasn't the only style to take riffs back into the charts. In 1971, glam-rock raised its glittery head.

Glam was always electric guitar-based, and at the bottom of glam's wardrobe (beneath the satin and lurex) is the riff. Glam's best moments are often built around great riffs. Think of T.Rex's '20th Century Boy', 'Telegram Sam' and 'Get It On'. Think of the Stones-based raunch of Bowie's 'Rebel Rebel', and the Esus4 riff in 'Jean Genie'. Think of the opening riff of Alice Cooper's 'School's Out', or the phrase that runs throughout Roxy Music's 'Street Life'. Or the droning detuned guitar on Gary Glitter's 'Rock'n'Roll', and any one of a number of Slade hits.

Punk guitar was always more chord-based. The guitar riff as such was despised by most punk bands because they associated it (like guitar solos) with either glam or heavy rock or the excesses of the progressive era – though exceptions occasionally cropped up at the more experimental edge of punk, with bands like The Banshees and Magazine. After punk and new wave, the guitar momentarily lost its place centre-stage to keyboards and synths during the 'new romantic' early 1980s. Riffs were still written, but in chart acts they were more likely to be found on keyboards – for example the octave riff in Gary Numan's 'Are Friends Electric'.

The next significant musical step for the rock riff came in the mid-1980s. Two guitar music movements conspired to draw the musical vocabulary of heavy rock away from its former pentatonic/blues-based habits. Players like Vai, Satriani, Gambale, Malmsteen, Morse, Johnson *et al* were united by a quest for a new musical bag of tricks with which to define themselves against the overshadowing guitar greats of the past. They played faster, and sought out new scales and new techniques with which to reinvent the guitar hero. Much of this was inspired indirectly by Eddie Van Halen, whose mastery of the 'tapping' technique had suggested that more could be done with rock guitar. The new scales and techniques of the late 1980s speed merchants inevitably led to new riffs. At the same time a new wave of heavy metal bands like Metallica, Megadeth, Anthrax and Slayer found ways to be heavier than their predecessors. One method was to base riffs not on blues-based scales but on those less common scales known as modes. The phrygian, with its lowered second (E-F-G-A-B-C-D), and the locrian, with lowered second and fifth (E-F-G-A-B♭-C-D), were vital in this.

Some of this approach to riffs then re-combined with a pop sensibility in some of the grunge bands like Nirvana. The use of modes continued throughout the 1990s and into the 21st century. Another significant feature has been the widespread use of detuning and altered tunings to increase the 'heaviosity' of riffs. Seven-string guitars and five-string basses also offer new sonic possibilities. The rumble factor of rock has increased dramatically.

HOW MANY TYPES OF RIFF ARE THERE?

This question involves asking what musical materials go into a riff. Remember the RHM formula – riffs can be sorted according to their rhythmic, harmonic and melodic elements. Riffs have a rhythm, they imply or use certain chords (harmony), and intervals (melody). The RHM formula is used in this book to separate riffs into three main groups, dealt with in the book's first three sections. **Section One** includes riffs based on fundamental **intervals** between single notes, as found in a major or natural minor scale; the second group (**Section Two**) gathers together the types of riff that draw on **scales** like the popular pentatonic major and minor; **Section Three** deals with riffs that use or are based on **chords**. The three groups add up to **30 basic riff types**. Riffs could be classified in others ways, but this will help identify riffs you hear or learn or write, so you can relate like with like.

It's in the last group – riffs using chords – that some of the problems of defining a riff become evident. Sometimes there is a fine line between deciding whether a chord change constitutes a riff or a chord progression. Take the chorus of Boston's hit 'More Than A Feeling', which has a circling G-C-Em-D sequence. Is it a progression or a riff? My feeling is it counts as a riff, for two reasons. Firstly because of the repetition, and secondly because of its accented rhythm. If a chord change is repeated often enough and with a defined, punchy rhythm, it can be usefully be described as a riff.

HOW THIS BOOK WORKS

Whether you write riffs, play riffs or just like listening to them, this book is an all-purpose, encyclopedic compendium of rifferama – nothing less than a guided tour of the riff in all its foot-stomping, head-shaking, bone-crushing glory. It explains all the main types of riff and the musical ingredients that go into their creation. Each riff type is illustrated by discussion of famous bands and songs from four decades of rock history. Read about the techniques that will improve the riffs you write, and make better arrangements and recordings of them. On the specially recorded accompanying CD you can even hear original examples of each riff type.

Each of the 30 types of riff has its own sub-sections, where you can read how the riff is derived from the basic musical material. Tips are given on where to find each riff on the guitar and how to fit it into a song's harmony. There are musical examples in notation and TAB. Scale patterns are given for the riffs in Section Two – the patterns have been

"sometimes there's a fine line between a chord change and a riff"

chosen to be those most useful for writing riffs, so they do not go high up the neck, and there is an emphasis on the lower octaves. The frequent **Riff Galleries** provide detailed analyses of selected famous riffs: these descriptive entries give information about the kind of riff used on the selected track, how it works musically, and even how it was recorded and arranged. Many of these famous songs could be fitted into more than one category, because some have more than one type of riff. So don't consider the placing of these songs as exclusive.

Many of these songs belong to the first wave of hard rock, between about 1967-1980, when the bands who wrote the rule book for riffs were recording. These are songs that have established themselves as classics, so it's safer to assume that readers have heard them rather than a riff by a death metal band from the 1990s (though some of these are mentioned too). For as long as someone, somewhere, wants to plug an electric guitar into an amplifier and play a distorted riff, they will look to The Who, Hendrix, Cream, Black Sabbath, Deep Purple, Led Zeppelin, Free, Queen, Van Halen, Metallica and the like for inspiration.

Section Four of the book deals with techniques and tips for presenting riffs – in other words, what do you do with it once you have it? This covers topics such as writing riffs in unusual time signatures, how to arrange riffs on a multi-track recording, using detuning and open tuning, using harmony parts, and how guitar effects change the kind of riff you write. You can use these ideas to improve riffs that come to you in creative moments and through jamming.

Section Five is a masterclass with John Paul Jones, former Led Zeppelin bass player/multi-instrumentalist and in-demand producer, and is full of insights into riffs, past and present. A great chance to hear about the writing, arranging, and recording of riff music from a player's perspective.

Section Six provides notation and a guided tour to the 30 riffs that have been specially recorded on the CD accompanying this book. For more information about the songs from which some of these riffs are taken visit my website, *rikkyrooksby.com*. (If you want to explore the wider territory of songwriting in general, seek out a copy of *How To Write Songs On Guitar*, this book's companion volume; and for more information about recording and arrangement ideas, see *Inside Classic Rock Tracks*.)

Once you have a good awareness of the 30 riff types, you'll be able to work out riffs more easily, understand how they function, and perhaps be inspired to write the kind of riffs you like and that fit your musical style.

So now, let's have a look at 30 ways to riff heaven... Rock on.

Rikky Rooksby, 2002

Interval-based RIFFS

This section explores riffs based on a particular interval – meaning the distance between one note and another, be it a semitone, tone, third, fourth, fifth, octave etc – and we look in general at how intervals are used in riffs.

The riffs in this first section illustrate the use and sound of the interval – the distance between two notes. We will look at these as they occur either as single notes or pairs of notes, or even chords – the thing that matters is the underlying movement of the root note. The intervals are derived from the major scale, which arranges the notes in this pattern: tone-tone-semitone-tone-tone-tone-semitone.

Here's the scale of C major:

C major

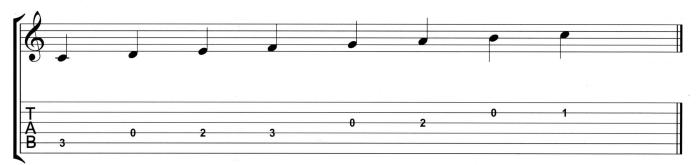

The table at the top of page 15 shows the names of all the intervals in an octave from the first note of this scale – the seven notes that make up the *major scale* are marked with asterisks*.

Notes	Distance in semitones	Interval name
C-Db	1	minor second
C-D	2	major second*
C-Eb	3	minor third
C-E	4	major third*
C-F	5	perfect fourth*
C-F#/Gb	6	augmented fourth/diminished fifth
C-G	7	perfect fifth*
C-Ab	8	minor sixth
C-A	9	major sixth*
C-Bb	10	minor seventh
C-B	11	major seventh*
C-C	12	perfect octave*

1. THE SEMITONE RIFF

The semitone riff is the simplest of all riffs. It uses two notes that are next to each other. On the guitar this means any adjacent frets on the same string. Doesn't seem promising, does it? But there is more here than meets the eye, or the ear.

Take two notes a semitone apart – say A and G# on the bottom string:

Semitone riff

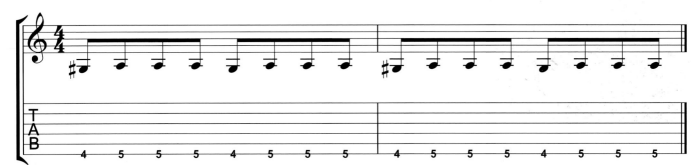

This type of riff was immortalised in rock'n'roll by Eddie Cochran, who used it to drive hits like 'Summertime Blues' and 'Something Else' at the end of the 1950s. It enjoyed a revival in 1976-78 during the heyday of punk with songs like The Damned's 'New Rose' and the Sex Pistols' 'Holidays In The Sun'. In their songs it often crops up in the bass guitar and sometimes in a chord form on the guitar. You will also hear it in 1990s neo-punk bands like Green Day. David Bowie's 'Hang On To Yourself' uses it in a similar rock'n'roll fashion, combining an F#-G single-note riff for six beats with accented D and C chords, making two bars in all.

The semitone riff often has a 'delinquent' quality. A little musical analysis will show why. First, let's imagine that the higher note of the pair G#-A is the key note. So we're in the key of A major, whose scale consists of the notes A-B-C#-D-E-F#-G#. Notice that G# is the seventh note. In music theory this seventh note has a special function and name: it's called the *leading note*. Every major scale ends with a semitone step from the leading note to the key note. This movement, especially when supported by the right chords, has the effect of re-establishing the key and the primacy of the key note, or 'tonic'. So if we have a riff that repeatedly moves from G# to A, spending longer on the A than the G#, then the note A is re-stated as the key centre. In musical terms this is a perfectly normal, conservative idea. So how do you get this feeling of delinquent teenage rebellion?

Strange things happen if this G#-A single-note riff is given an upper note. In rock the most direct way of doing that is by using fifths (nicknamed 'power-chords'). A perfect fifth is an interval of three-and-a-half tones. So the fifth G#-D#

would then move up to the fifth A-E. (Fifths have a sub-section all to themselves later in this chapter.) Here's what this fifth change looks like when it's notated:

Semitone shift (fifths)

But wait a minute, there's a problem. If we're in A major we ought to take these upper notes from the scale of A major. Look at its fourth note: D natural, not D#. But if we put D above the G# in this riff we have an augmented fourth (three tones), not a perfect fifth. It's true that the augmented fourth is an important interval for heavy rock, as we'll see later, but here we want parallel perfect fifths for our G#-A change. So for that we are committed to using a D#, which is off-scale. The ear, which is deeply accustomed to the major key system and all its laws, hears this D# as a 'foreign' note, a note that breaks the rules. In other words, hey presto, a delinquent note. So as you thrash your guitar, with the amp on 11, at 154bpm, singing that the modern world is rubbish, the music *on its own terms* is backing you up.

This 'delinquent' effect is magnified if we go a step further and put not just a fifth above our G#-A change but a whole major chord. In this instance that means a chord of G# (G#-B#-D#) moving to a chord of A major (A-C#-E). Again compare the notes in these chords with the scale of A-major. The notes in the A chord blend perfectly with the scale. But the G# chord not only has D# instead of the proper D but B# instead of B, so it contains *two* delinquent notes, which reinforces the effect:

Semitone shift (chords)

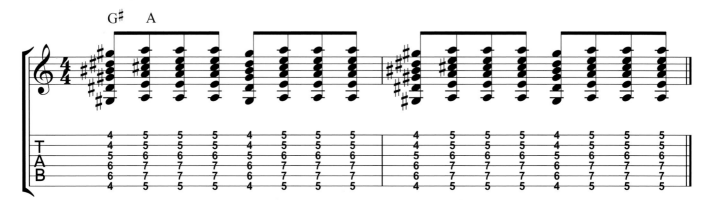

The chords of a key are generated by using the seven notes of the major scale. To create basic three-note chords (triads), start with each note in turn, and miss every other note until you have a group of three. For instance, the first note would be combined with the third and the fifth note of the scale (I-III-V) to create the first chord of the key; the second note would be joined by the fourth and the sixth (II-IV-VI), after which come III-V-VII (3-5-7), IV-VI-I (4-6-1), V-VII-II (5-7-2), VI-I-III (6-1-3), and VII-II-IV (7-2-4). In the key of A this produces the chords: A major, B minor, C# minor, D major, E major, F# minor and – wait for it – G# diminished (G#-B-D), as you can see on the stave at the top of page 17.

The diminished chord is neither major nor minor, and is used very little in

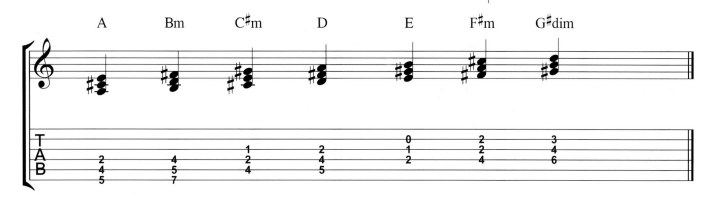

rock. Chord seven (VII) in any major key should be diminished. Our G#-A chord change has substituted a G# major for this diminished chord. The ear recognises the G# major chord as not in key. In fact, no major key normally permits two major chords to occur a semitone apart, anywhere – there is no major key in which that would naturally happen. So if we have two major chords a semitone apart we step outside the boundaries of the harmony of the major key.

In other words, the semitone riff, as a fifth or a chord shift, breaks the rules. Instant musical rebellion.

More can be done with this idea. We can develop this semitone riff into a song structure – imagine a punk rock 12-bar progression using the chords A, D and E. To get the punk style we would preface each of the chords with the major chord or fifth a semitone lower: G#-A, C#-D, D#-E. Whether as fifths or full major chords, the C# and D# chords will include other 'delinquent' out-of-key notes.

From a playing aspect, semitone shifts on the guitar are easy with barre chords because it only involves moving a fret up or down. The barre shapes for F and B are both equally useful for doing this. Double the delinquent element with two semitone shifts, one after the other – as in Elvis Costello's stomping 'Pump It Up' with its relentless B, B♭, A chords. Gomez's 'Whippin' Piccadilly' does the same thing in A♭ going in the opposite direction. Terrorvision made a riff out of an A♭-A7 shift in 'Perseverance'.

In recent years the semitone shift, either as single notes or as fifths, has become significant in rock styles like nu-metal. Where the traditional Eddie Cochran-inspired semitone shift is from the seventh note to the root note, more recently rock songs take the semitone shift from the root note upward – the first to the second of the scale. Linkin Park's 'With You' and 'Points Of Authority', Limp Bizkit's 'Counterfeit' and 'Clunk', The Offspring's 'Pretty Fly For A White Guy', Fear Factory's 'Self Bias Resistor', and Machine Head's 'Old', all have examples of the semitone shift.

In bands like Metallica and Pantera this happens when a song uses the Phrygian or Locrian modes, where the step from the first note of the scale to the second is a semitone. These modes are discussed in Section Two. The Queens Of The Stone Age's 'Feel Good Hit Of The Summer' uses a semitone move downward from the flattened second (♭II) to the key note, whereas 'Quick And To The Pointless' does a 1950s move from a semitone beneath the key note, changing E-F (and can be compared with the riff on T.Rex's 'Jupiter Liar').

So far we've talked about the semitone riff as it is used in a rock'n'roll/punk context. But this does not exhaust its possibilities by a long way. Played as a single note riff, the semitone can be made to sound sleazy or exotic, particularly if a bend is used – as we'll see when we go through the first of our Riff Galleries, starting over the page.

Triads of A major

"the semitone shift has become significant in rock styles like nu-metal"

Artist	David Bowie
Title	'The Man Who Sold The World'
Writer	Bowie
Released	album: *The Man Who Sold The World*, RCA 1971

Here's a very original riff composed out of almost nothing. The first chord you hear is an A major, which goes to Dm, F, then Dm again. The key is D minor (the A chord is the traditional chord V of D minor). The riff consists of an A bent up a semitone to B*b* and an open G. In D minor these notes are scale degrees IV, V, and VI. The B*b* sounds exotic because of the bent approach, and is dissonant against the A major chord. If you want to hear how different these three notes could sound, play the riff against a G minor or F major. During the coda the riff is heard against a number of different chords; listen for the varied colouring each one gives the riff.

Mick Ronson's distinctive guitar tone (probably the front pickup of his Les Paul Custom) adds to the mystery. In this song the riff is not a rabble-rousing incitement to bang heads but a sinister portrait of the twisted intent of Bowie's misanthropic character. Rarely have three notes sounded so much like the end of the world.

Artist	T.Rex
Title	'Chariot Choogle'
Writer	Bolan
Released	album: *The Slider*, T.Rex Wax Co/EMI, 1972

'Chariot Choogle' is the great 'lost' T.Rex single of 1972 (Bolan considered putting it out but changed his mind). The main riff is a semitone fifth from B-C, in the key of C, and is supported by bass and cellos. When the vocal begins the melody is not placed where you would expect it, so there is a fascinating tension between the riff's rhythm and the melody.

No-one thinks of Bolan much as a guitar player – which is a hangover from the judgement made back in the early 1970s by rock critics sold on the prog-rock ethic of technical prowess and 'serious' music. He may have only known a small number of chords and a few lead licks, but what magic he created with them. If you're unfamiliar with Bolan's guitar playing, check out the albums *Beard Of Stars*, *T.Rex*, *Electric Warrior* or *The Slider*: they're full of raunchy rhythm, great riffs and simple but inspiring lead, all played with classic, lusted-after guitar tones. (Bolan's main guitars were a Gibson Les Paul and white Fender Strat – he revered Hendrix – though he was seen on TV with a Tele, Les Paul Custom, and a Flying V; his amps were mostly transistor types like Vampower and H/H, and FX included Arbiter Rangemaster treble boost, fuzz/wah and WEM Copycat echo.)

Artist	Sex Pistols
Title	'God Save The Queen'
Writer	Rotten/Jones/Matlock/Cook
Released	single: Virgin 1977
	album: *Never Mind The Bollocks Here's The Sex Pistols*, Virgin, 1977

The Pistols' sardonic punk anthem had all the ingredients that made *Bollocks* one of the 1970s best rock albums. The riff itself takes eight bars and is used for the verse. There is a two-bar phrase of an A chord going to a D-C#-D change. If you count the first bar's rhythm 1&2&3&4&, the second bar is groups 123, 123, 12.

Experiment playing the D-C#-D change as fifths and then as major chords and compare the two. After three of these phrases the riff is completed by two bars of a G#-A change. The emphasis in the guitars is on what sounds like fourths played on the top two strings (a fourth is a fifth inverted, as will be explained in a few pages). Extra colour is gained by the damping of the A chord, taking the damping off for the D-C#-D change.

Other semitone chord shifts can be heard during the bridge. The 'delinquent' effect of major chords shifting in semitones is also heard on the "No future" coda. If this were a pop song the descending chords would follow those of the key: D-C#m-Bm-A. But what it actually sounds like is D-C#-B-A – all majors. Elsewhere on the same album, semitone shifts can be heard at the end of the verse of 'No Feelings' and the chorus of 'EMI'.

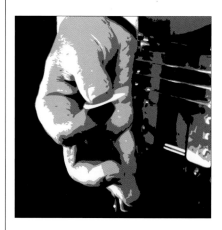

Artist	**Led Zeppelin**
Title	**'Kashmir'**
Writer	**Page/Plant/Bonham**
Released	**album: *Physical Graffit*i, Swansong, 1975**

'Kashmir' is built on a powerful but steady drumbeat, a bass which moves in octave Ds, and a four-note riff. The guitar, in DADGAD tuning, is not particularly prominent: it has the intro riff, two verses, a bridge section on A, a chorus that moves restlessly from Gm to A, two more verses, the chorus, and the coda where an ascending scale of G-A-Bb-C-D-E-F-G-A-B-C# appears, replete with Middle Eastern trumpet flourishes.

The main riff is D5-Daug5-D6-D7. This could be classified in a number of ways – for example as a chordal riff – but I've chosen to include it here because it's really the semitone movement of the notes A-Bb-B-C that is its most defining characteristic. This clever riff has the quality of a picture by RC Escher: every time you get to the end of the riff it sounds as though it's a bit higher, but it isn't. This is made even more pronounced by the descending sequence of Mellotron orchestra effects laid over the top of it. Sing and tap out the main riff when it disappears behind the descending sequence and you'll be amazed how it emerges. This arrangement effect makes it unique among the hundreds of riffs in this book.

In this instance the semitone steps are made against a single chord, but you could create a riff that moved in semitones in which each note had a different chord to harmonise it. The chord changes would probably distract from the individual notes but it might prove a colourful effect.

Artist	**Siouxsie & The Banshees**
Title	**'Nightshift'**
Writer	**Budgie/McGeoch/Sioux/Severin**
Released	**album: *Ju Ju*, Polydor, 1981**

'Nightshift' is a doom-laden, gothic epic that quickly became one of the highlights of the Banshees concerts. Normally, no major key has two major chords a semitone apart; it's also true that it usually never has two minor chords a semitone apart either, as is the case here. This riff grew out of Steve Severin's unorthodox approach to playing bass. It's made up of a minor third on the top two strings (A-C) over the open A-string. After two bars the minor third slips down a fret to G#-B, creating a strange chord – an implied Am9 with a major 7th in it. Severin's picked, flanged bass continues on this riff throughout the verses, with McGeoch's guitar re-stating the Am-G#m chord change. The tip is to try writing a chord riff on bass and work over that.

"you could create a riff that moved in semitones in which each note had a different chord to harmonise it"

2. THE TONE RIFF

Almost as simple as the semitone riff is the tone riff – for instance using two notes a tone apart, say A and G on the bottom string at the third and fifth fret. The one-tone change is probably the primordial riff, and was immortalised in rock in the mid-1960s by records like The Kinks' 'You Really Got Me' and The Who's 'My Generation'. It has always been a staple of hard rock and heavy metal. A more recent use of it would be on U2's 1991 hit 'The Fly', where echo and a wah-wah pedal gave it additional intensity. The tone riff has a slightly different effect to the 'delinquent' semitone riff.

Let's imagine again that we're in the key of A. As we saw earlier the seventh note should be G#, but to get a tone shift we lower it to G.

Tone shift

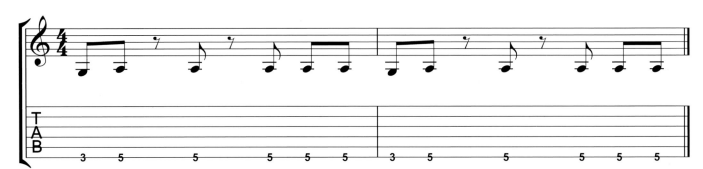

This particular tone shift, moving onto the key note, is more striking than the tone shifts that normally occur on the major scale (A-B, B-C#, D-E, E-F#). This is because lowering the seventh note undermines the major key by removing the 'leading note' of traditional harmony. The scale that results – A-B-C#-D-E-F#-G – is an example of the mixolydian mode. (You'll find out about modes when we get to the next group of riffs in Section Two.)

This lowered seventh is found throughout popular music. As soon as any blues influence creeps in the seventh gets lowered, whether it's in an instrumental part on the guitar, the bass, or in a vocal melody. When this 'flattened seventh' (*b*VII) is heard *against* the usual chords of A major it is heard as a 'blue' note. This is a different effect to when it is used on its own as single notes or as fifths.

If this G-A single-note riff is turned into perfect fifths we get G-D going to A-E.

G⁵   A⁵

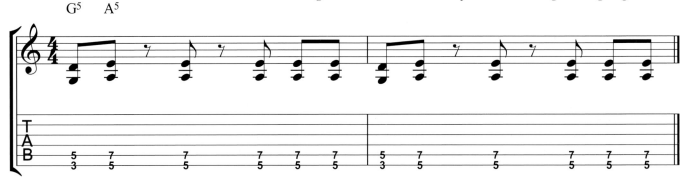

Tone shift (fifths)

The upper notes are already on the scale of A major, so they don't produce the 'delinquent' sound of the semitone fifths. Similarly, if these notes are turned into major chords a tone apart we get G major and A major. The G major chord thus replaces the G# diminished chord that would normally be chord VII in the scale of A major. This chord can, however, be built from the mixolydian mode by taking the flattened seventh, the second and the fourth of the mode (G-B-D). You can see what this looks like notated at the top of page 21.

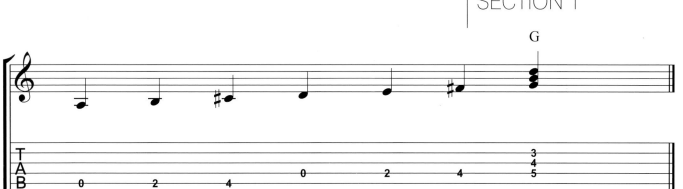

Mixolydian scale, chord VII

The tone riff is usually found not on its own but mixed up with a few other intervals. Remember that each of the riffs in Section One is often found combined with other elements from Section Two and Section Three. The riff for the bridge of Blind Faith's 'Presence Of The Lord' takes A pentatonic minor and entirely uses tones: G-A, C-D, D-E, G-A.

Tone riffs are also heard in Eric Clapton's 'Cocaine', The Troggs' 'Night Of The Long Grass' (which has an interpolated bar of 6/4 in the verse just to keep things interesting), Madonna's 'Erotica', Thin Lizzy's 'Johnny The Fox Meets Jimmy The Weed' (with a ♭3), Jimi Hendrix's 'If Six Was Nine' (with a ♭7), Deep Purple's 'Child In Time' (played in octaves), and Bad Company's 'Feel Like Making Love' (chorus). An A5 and G5 tone shift drives the verse of the Stooges' '1969', and tone changes A-G, E-D, D-C feature in their 'No Fun'.

The tone shift is essential to the MC5's 'Teenage Lust' and 'Looking At You', the Pretenders' 'Message To Love', and the Vines' 'Highly Evolved'. On 'A House Is Not A Motel', Love insert a high single-note E-D tone-shift riff as a link from the last vocal section to the guitar solo – it's played by two electrics at 2.17 on either side of the stereo image, which then break away into their solos. Tears For Fears' 'Everybody Wants To Rule The World' has a tone-shift chord riff over an E♭ pedal.

RIFF GALLERY:
tone riffs

Artist	**The Kinks**
Title	**'You Really Got Me'**
Writer	**R Davies**
Released	**single: Pye, 1964**
	album: *The Kinks*, Pye, 1964

'You Really Got Me' is a must for any history of riffs. The brutal simplicity of the opening riff stood in marked contrast to much of pop at the time from other guitar bands. This was, after all, the heyday of first-generation 'jangle' from the like of The Searchers. Unlike later heavy rock, the riff here is chordal. It's the rhythm that turns it from a chord change to a riff. Notice the way the snare drum smacks down in the space between the riffs – this rhythmic arrangement detail is vital to the sense of power. Then, as the verse develops, the riff is transposed upward several times.

The Kinks re-visited this riff on 'All Day And All Of The Night' and 'Tired Of Waiting For You', making it slightly more complicated by adding a third chord based on the flattened third chord of the key. Another song from the same period which makes similar use of the one-tone riff is the Who's 'My Generation', which also develops the part by transposing it upwards. Don't forget Van Halen's swaggering version of 'You Really Got Me' on their first album.

Artist	Atomic Rooster
Title	'Devil's Answer'
Writer	Cann
Released	single: B&C, 1971

Atomic Rooster were a minor progressive band of the early 1970s who had a couple of chart hits: their keyboardist Vincent Crane played with The Crazy World Of Arthur Brown, and they had Carl Palmer, later of super-group ELP, on drums. 'Devil's Answer' is carried on a single riff. The first phrase is a two-bar change from C-B♭ and back, the second phrase goes C-B♭-F-C (a mixolydian I-♭VII-IV). The placing of an F in the bass under the B♭ each time gives the riff a bit more variety. The rest of the song depends on the arrangement, with the guitar playing a single-note idea.

Artist	Mountain
Title	'Mississippi Queen'
Writer	West/Laing/Pappalardi/Rea
Released	single: Windfall/Island, 1970

'Mississippi Queen' is a riff that has unfairly slipped through the cracks of rock history. In terms of heaviness, it was a milestone. Mountain were originally dismissed as a Cream clone, but this obscured some genuine strong points. The inclusion of keyboards gave Mountain a harmonic advantage over Cream's power trio line-up: no more big holes in the mix when the guitarist takes a solo.

The riff is delayed by a four-bar intro moving B-A-G, as if we have entered at bar 9 of a 12-bar. This enhances the entrance of the riff when it does come in – a hammering D5-E5 change with various answering phrases after it. Transposition is used during the verse: the riff occurs four times on E, two on A, two on E, one on B, one on A, and then a different E phrase polishes off the 12-bar derived form. A famous adage states, "brevity is the soul of wit". Heavy rock is not known for either brevity or wit, so this is a timely reminder of how exciting it can be to focus your musical efforts into a truly dynamic couple of minutes: the studio version of 'Mississippi Queen' clocks in at only 2.30...

Artist	Free
Title	'Fire And Water'
Writer	Fraser/Rodgers
Released	album: *Fire And Water*, Island, 1970

Here's a classic example of the 'tone-shift fifths' riff that's the blueprint for so much hard rock. Free also used tone-shift fifths on tracks like 'Catch A Train'. It's often the case that these fifths will start with the first one being slid to the upper, so the higher of the two fifths is not struck initially but is heard after. The verse here starts with an A5-B5 shift and also uses D5-E5, implying a I-IV B to E chord change. There's far more to Paul Kossoff's guitar parts than is often recognised: famous for his inimitable vibrato and wailing lead, careful study of his rhythm parts and riffs reveal that he found interesting sonorities on the guitar to suit the essential power-trio instrumentation of Free. What sound like only movements of fifths often turn out on closer inspection to include other intervals, such as sixths, and combinations of fretted with open strings. The aim of these is to give more weight and/or colour. In a quartet with no keyboard and only one guitar, every string counts.

"in a quartet with no keyboard and only one guitar, every string counts"

Artist	**Black Sabbath**
Title	**'Paranoid'**
Writer	**Iommi/Butler/Ward/Osbourne**
Released	**single: Vertigo, 1970**
	album: *Black Sabbath*, Vertigo, 1970

In 1970, Led Zeppelin, Deep Purple and Black Sabbath were immediate heirs of the high-volume blues-rock of Cream and Hendrix. Of the three, it's Sabbath who have had the greatest influence on grunge and metal. Black Sabbath gave heavy metal its doomy atmosphere, its occult imagery, and the sludgefest of Tony Iommi's guitar riffs. Their steady eighth-note rhythm became a hallmark of later rock (which was a pity, because some of the best rock of the early 1970s had some syncopation and swing).

'Paranoid' has several riffs. The first is heard on the intro and is an E5 up at the seventh fret with a couple of hammer-ons on the E pentatonic minor scale. The guitars then settle into a chugging eighth-note rhythm on E and then D, finished off with a quick Dsus4 to D, and then an implied G. So the verse riff isn't simply a tone-shift fifth, but there's no doubt the essence of it is the tone-shift.

Artist	**Queen**
Title	**'Tenement Funster'**
Writer	**Taylor**
Released	**album: *Sheer Heart Attack*, EMI, 1974**

'Tenement Funster', written and sung by drummer Roger Taylor, uses full arpeggiated chords for its first verse, with a strong emphasis on Em and Am, and an unexpected Cm7 further on. The tone-shift riff consists of fifths going from D5-E5 and G5-A5, giving the chorus's first lines a slightly funky feel. But this tone-shift riff is set in a highly musical context. Listen for the way the harmony 'opens out' when a G chord appears, closely followed by G7, C, Cm7, D and then Em-G for the start of the solo. An extra dimension is brought to the solo by an unexpected chromatic shift from G to G#m and Bm. This allows May to construct an elegant, colourful solo in echoed phrases.

'Tenement Funster' suggests that tone-shift riffs in fifths can be more powerful when placed in a musical context that offers contrasting, fuller harmony.

Artist	**REM**
Title	**'The One I Love'**
Writer	**Stipe/Berry/Mills/Buck**
Released	**single: IRS, 1987**
	album: *Document*, IRS, 1987

REM have never been what you would think of as a 'riff band'. From the outset they showed a healthy distaste for many of rock's hackneyed gestures, and this was certainly true of Peter Buck's approach to the guitar. But when they did use a guitar riff in a song it was almost always noteworthy. Buck is more renowned as a rhythm player, and for the 'jangle' guitar arpeggios of REM's classic early period. But the main guitar figure of 'The One I Love' has sufficient force and definition to count as a riff. It exploits the open-string resonance of an E-minor chord moving to a Dsus2 (a chordal tone-shift), where the top E is still sounding. It does this via a low G, and a slide from D to E on the second string with the top E sounding at the same time. It's almost a blues riff, though played at a greater velocity than most blues riffs. Guitarists should also listen for the way the song ends, with a slowing up that adds dramatic weight to the highly dissonant chord which consists of the Em shape one fret back (E-B♭-D#-G-B-E), just before the final E minor.

Artist	**The Cult**
Title	**'Wild Flower'**
Writer	**Astbury/Duffy**
Released	**album: *Electric*, Beggars Banquet, 1987**
	single: Beggars Banquet, 1987

With Rick Rubin in the producer's chair, The Cult's album *Electric* set out to bang heads in an old-fashioned, 1970s sort of way. Nothing could be simpler than 'Wild Flower', a fine example of a riff that comes from an idiosyncrasy of the guitar. If you hold down a B chord (x2444x), the open string A is now the flattened seventh so beloved in hard rock/blues riffs. To get it you only have to lift that finger off the A string while hitting the rest of the chord. Play to a mildly syncopated rhythm and repeat over a four-square no-frills drum beat. During the chorus and verse Billy Duffy develops the riff by finding versions of it on the D and E chords.

Artist	**Haven**
Title	**'Let It Live'**
Writer	**Briggs/Wason/Gronow**
Released	**album: *Between The Senses*, Radiate, 2002**
	single: Radiate, 2002

Haven are a new UK rock band whose powerful and poignant debut album was produced by ex-Smiths guitarist Johnny Marr. 'Let It Live' comes in on a tone-shift riff based on B5, with the bass playing variations on this, and a Gail Force Ten lead guitar also playing a tone-shift figure through a wah-wah. This riff is felt throughout the verse, despite the fact that the harmony changes as it is adjusted to whatever the chord is. It also returns for the two-note guitar solo.

'Let It Live' is a classic English pop/rock song in which 1960s group The Casuals (of 'Jesamine' fame) collide with Soundgarden. Listen for the guitar octaves on the chorus, the hints of vocal harmony, and the sizzling, splashy hi-hat eighths. The yearning hook-line is one of the loveliest I've heard in a long time. A band to watch.

3. THE OCTAVE RIFF

Our third type of riff is arrived at by taking a single note and playing it at different octaves. This is an economical way of writing a riff because it creatively deploys pitch to get more out of the single note. A semitone-shift or tone-shift idea could be thickened by playing the note in octaves. An octave drop or jump can also lend a bit of unpredictability to a riff.

The octave riff works independently of keys and scales because you're not actually changing the note by adding another different one above or below. In this way octaves offer flexibility: because they're neither major nor minor, you can put a major or a minor chord over them, and if soloing you can use either major or minor scales.

The use of instruments with octave stringing – such as 12-string guitar or eight, ten and 12-string bass – will automatically add a new dimension to a single-note riff. Bass players often use octaves, which creates a more dynamic effect than sticking on a single-note bassline, without altering the harmony. A riff where both bass and guitar move in octaves can have a propulsive effect. The most effective octave riffs are those that lock in with the drums in some way – in other words, think carefully about where the notes are placed *rhythmically*.

Here are the finger patterns for octaves on the guitar:

Octaves

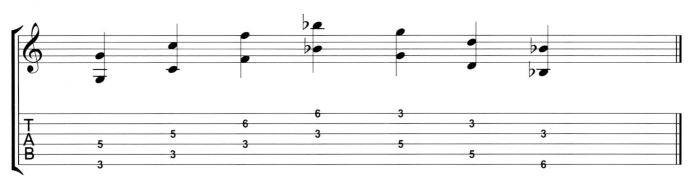

Octave riffs can be heard on the intro riff of Television's 'Friction', in the bridge of Gun's 'Word Up' and Deep Purple's 'Woman From Tokyo', and played by synthesiser on the intro and during the verse of Gomez's 'Get Miles'. David Bowie's 'TVC15' has a bridge and coda with a fierce octave riff running from top down, and using a tone shift.

RIFF GALLERY:
octave riffs

Artist	**Spencer Davis Group**
Title	**'Gimme Some Lovin'**
Writer	**S Winwood/M Winwood/S Davis**
Released	**single: Fontana, 1966**

The Spencer Davis Group were an R&B-influenced combo blessed with the vocals of one of the UK's best singers of the 1960s, Stevie Winwood. The riff here is an inverted octave on G, with the low G coming on the fourth beat of the bar. On the intro you can hear the bass and, just faintly, a guitar doubling the figure, and a piano is struck on the fourth beat G. The riff is then used as the harmonic base for smoky thirds on the organ, but also features throughout the song. The rhythmic significance of riffs is clearly demonstrated here. There's a similar riff in their hit 'Somebody Help Me'.

Artist	**The Knack**
Title	**'My Sharona'**
Writer	**Aaverre/Berrios**
Released	**single: Capitol, 1979**
	album: *The Little Girls Understand*, Capitol, 1979

The Knack's brief career as purveyors of commercial US new wave commenced with this catchy single built on a sharp-dressed octave riff. This is a good example of the 'jumpy' quality you can get in an octave riff as it goes up and down, with the bass playing the same figure as the guitars. Listen for the slide from F# back to the G octave at the end of bar two (a throwback to Cochran-type semitone-shift 1950s riffs) and the way bar four is finished off with C5 and Bb5. These fifths have a refreshing effect for the listener in contrast to the bare octaves. They also imply a blues harmony (a IV-bIII I change). The pentatonic minor scale G-Bb-C-D-F supplies the fifths and later on in the song it also provides some of the chords.

Artist	**Led Zeppelin**
Title	**'The Immigrant Song'**
Writer	**Page/Plant**
Released	**single (US): Atlantic, 1970**
	album: *Led Zeppelin III*, Atlantic, 1970

On a rising tide of tape-echo hiss, Zep's third album charged in with this Viking battle-hymn. Over Page's octave F# riff, Plant pitched an octave C# falling back a semitone to C (the flattened fifth). Tremolo guitars add a watery shimmer to the E-A chord changes on the verse, and the rising A-B-C chorus is underpinned by some rapid bass scales from Jones. The chorus ends suddenly on the C chord, which is in a false relation to F#, an example of dissonant chord relationships in heavy rock. A similar dissonant chord can be heard repeatedly inserted into the octave riff on the outro.

Zep revisited this Viking theme and poked about in the scorched ruins in 'The Wanton Song' on *Physical Graffiti*, which is built on a terrific G octave riff with battering intermissions by John Bonham. Octaves are also crucial to 'Trampled Underfoot', which is discussed in the section on thirds.

Artist	**Jimi Hendrix**
Title	**'Dolly Dagger'**
Writer	**Hendrix**
Released	**single (US): Reprise, 1971**
	album: *First Rays Of The New Rising Sun*, MCA, 1997

There was a late flowering of Hendrix's songwriting in the last two years of his life. Had he finished his intended album *First Rays Of The New Rising Sun* it would have shown some important cross-breeding between rock and soul. 'Dolly Dagger' was slated to be the first single from it. It starts with a three-phrase riff consisting of two bars of 6/4 and a bar of 4/4. Unlike the previous examples, this is an instance of octave doubling. The opening riff is based on B pentatonic minor but each note is doubled at the octave – listen for the fuzzy synth or bass off to one side. The first four notes are then transposed down for a repeat, and the riff concludes with a five-note blues run. On the coda Hendrix alters the riff by extending the first phrase. Also listen for the bent thirds under the word 'Dolly' on the chorus.

For a rock guitarist Hendrix was uncommonly found of octaves for doubling. Playing in a power trio they helped him thicken the band's live sound. So 'Fire' and 'Ezy Rider' both open with octaves, and in 'Third Stone From The Sun' he put them to their traditional jazz use of thickening a melody. 'In From The Storm' and 'Gypsy Eyes' both feature tone shift phrases repeated at different octaves in rapid succession. 'Foxy Lady' depends on an octave jump for its riff, but you'll find that song under Fourths in this book.

"the opening riff is based on B pentatonic, but each note is doubled at the octave"

4. THE PERFECT FIFTH

This interval, especially played as a series of fifths, is essential to the sound of rock. As already mentioned, a perfect fifth – colloquially known as a 'power-chord' – consists of two notes three-and-a-half tones apart.

Here are the usual ways of playing them on the guitar:

Fifths

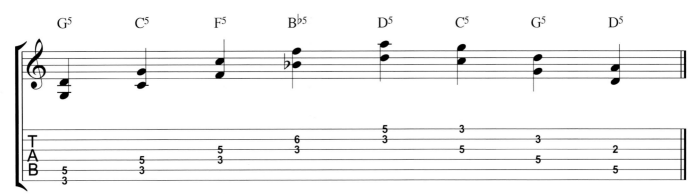

The fifth has a tough but slightly cold, 'hollow' sound. The reason for this is evident if you take A5 – a perfect fifth on A – and compare it with the triads of A major and A minor:

Major, minor, neutral

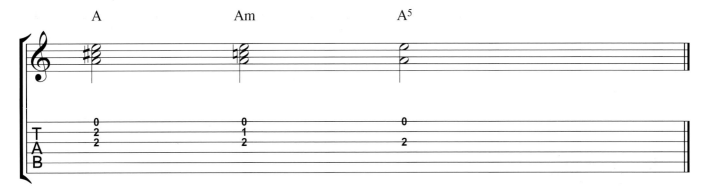

Both chords have a perfect fifth in them. The only note that differentiates them is the one in the middle (the so-called 'third' of the chord), which is C# in A major and C in A minor. It's this note in the middle, the third, which carries the emotional content, the feelings associated with major chords and minors. In comparison with majors, minors sound sad. But if the third is omitted, this happy/sad element is removed. Like octaves, fifths are neither major nor minor, so they combine with major and minor chords on a second instrument, and major and minor scales can be used over them. But if the fifth moves up or down, it will need to move to the same notes of the scale used by the lead guitar. This will often be the pentatonic minor, as we'll see in Section Two of the riffs. Fifths are the simplest way of 'harmonising' a scale for rock purposes.

Perfect fifths infiltrated rock in the mid-1960s as technology changed the sound of rock bands: amps increased in power, rock bands got louder, and the first fuzz/distortion boxes went into wider circulation. Unlike major and minor chords, perfect fifths will tolerate large amounts of distortion/overdrive and still be effective (this has to do with the 'overtones' boosted by distortion).

We've already seen how the semitone and tone riffs can be expressed as fifths. The sound of a fifth can in turn be thickened by adding the octave above the root note. The fifth moving onto the key note from the flattened seventh is a classic rock riff – in the key of E, D5 to E5 is an example. Fifths are most frequently heard on the lowest two strings of the guitar (they are also effective on the bass guitar). Some guitarists have constructed memorable figures by using fifths on the higher strings, as in the case of The Edge of U2. For an insight into what happens when you put two perfect fifths together (AE + EB = AEB), see the discussion on suspended chords in Section Three.

Fifths can be heard in tracks like Black Sabbath's St Vitus's Dance' and 'NIB' (on an E natural minor scale), Iron Maiden's 'The Number Of The Beast', The Jam's 'Billy Hunt', and Blur's 'Song 2' (the guitar on the verse). In terms of which intervals the fifths themselves are moved between, the minor third has always been very popular in rock. You can hear it in Public Enemy & Anthrax's 'Bring The Noize' where the chorus riff moves from F# to A (I to bIII).

RIFF GALLERY: perfect fifths

Artist	**Led Zeppelin**
Title	**'Whole Lotta Love'**
Writer	**Page/Plant/Jones/Bonham/Dixon**
Released	**single (US): Atlantic, 1969;** **single (UK): Atlantic, 1997** **album: *Led Zeppelin II*, Atlantic, 1969**

Rock music was never the same after this. 'Whole Lotta Love' may have owed a lyrical debt to Willie Dixon, but the musical result was something else entirely. Zep took a simple blues phrase of three notes (B-D-E), added an E5 and amplified it into a gargantuan riff, undeniably raw and exciting. I heard a blast of it on the radio this morning during a polite interview broadcast, and 30 years after release it still comes on like a wolf at a vicarage tea-party.

The first statement of the riff consists of two bars of E5 with the single notes added in-between. The single note D, fretted on the fifth string, is doubled by the open D-string – a neat trick. The riff is then shortened to a bar just before the vocal enters. Note Page's harmony on the riff on the outro where the last two notes D and E have A and G# over them. The extended version on *The Song Remains The Same* (1976) ends with Page playing a number of variations on the basic riff.

Artist	**Derek & The Dominoes**
Title	**'Layla'**
Writer	**Clapton/Gordon**
Released	**single (UK): Polydor, 1970, 1972, RSO 1982;** **(US) Atco, 1971, 1972** **album: *Layla And Other Assorted Love Songs*, Polydor 1971**

Familiarity has perhaps chipped off some of its lacquer, but 'Layla' remains one of the all-time great rock riffs. Rarely has a guitar riff been used with such emotional force to make a statement about a situation between a man and a woman, as opposed to the staple heavy rock lyric's litany of death, doom and despair... and trolls, of course. 'Layla' is also an object lesson in guitar orchestration.

The opening hail of notes (on several guitars, at different octaves) is D pentatonic minor (A-C-D-F-D-C-D). This is a blues lick with new fire in its belly. The D is left sustaining while another guitar comes in with a sequence of fifths from D to C to Bb, which then ascend back to D. The neat touch is that the lower note of each of these fifths descends to a note on the sixth string, making excellent use of the fifth shape on the guitar. This could be compared with Dire Straits' 'Expresso Love', a quicker, extended version of the same idea.

The high riff in 'Layla' takes the form a1, a2, a1, a3, where bars 1 and 3 are the same D pentatonic minor phrase that opened the song, but bars 2 and 4 provide a different 'answer' – bar 4 bending G up to A instead of F up to G. What is often overlooked is the wonderful counterpointed guitar phrase that lies midway in pitch between the extremes of the lower string riff and the very audible high part. This accentuates the sad minor-key feel because it uses the first three notes (D-E-F) of the D natural minor scale. This guitar can be heard on the left. Its first and third bars are the same as the other guitars.

Artist	**Be Bop Deluxe**
Title	**'Sister Seagull'**
Writer	**Nelson**
Released	**album: *Futurama*, EMI/Harvest, 1975**

Be Bop Deluxe were a British band who came through in the twilight of glam rock on its more arty flank. Their music was defined by the vocals and fastidious guitar arranging of Bill Nelson. Like his contemporary Brian May, Nelson was an enthusiastic orchestrator of multiple lead guitars, often harmonised. The songs tend to teem with ideas, sometimes seeming too fussy. The band never quite managed to focus itself sufficiently to go for the commercial 'jugular' in the way that Queen did, though 'Ships In The Night' and the truly marvellous 'Maid In Heaven' were chart singles.

'Sister Seagull' features a four-bar opening riff that links chorus to verse. Bar 1 is a slid fifth from D to E heard in the centre. Bar 2 answers this with a stereo lead phrase using a 'cascade' figure on E pentatonic minor at the 12th fret. Bar 3 repeats bar 1. Bar 4 is a variation in which the scale cascade is terminated with a bend. Throughout the song the D5-E5 is constant but the 'answers' are subject to variation. It's a fine riff precisely because it welds together fifths and lead notes. Sometimes a riff can have its constituent parts given to more than one guitar.

Artist	**Thin Lizzy**
Title	**'Jailbreak'**
Writer	**Lynott**
Released	**album: *Jailbreak*, Vertigo/Mercury, 1976**
	single: Vertigo/Mercury, 1976

The title track from Thin Lizzy's breakthrough album is not one of their more complicated riffs. It's a good example of the significance of F# as a key centre in heavy rock. The F# major scale consists of the notes F#-G#-A#-B-C#-D#-E#. In rock it is much more common to find this scale in the form known as the mixolydian mode, where the seventh note – here E# – is flattened to E. E, of course, is the bottom string on the guitar, which means riffs in the key of F# have the benefit of an open-string flattened seventh as the lowest note, which then moves up a tone to F# at the second fret. The 'Jailbreak' riff uses this idea with fifths in the sequence A5-E5-F#5. The riff runs all the way through the verse, as well as serving as a link back from a chorus to the next verse. Fifths can also be heard on the chorus.

Many Lizzy songs had riffs in fifths, including 'The Boys Are Back In Town' (A5-B5-D5 intro), 'Southbound' (verse) and 'Waiting For An Alibi', where half the verse is played as fifths and half in unmistakeable minor chords.

"sometimes a riff can have its constituent parts given to more than one guitar"

Artist	**U2**
Title	**'With Or Without You'**
Writer	**U2**
Released	**single: Island, 1987**
	album: ***The Joshua Tree*****, Island, 1987**

Among all the hard rock and heavy metal low fifths, here's an example of what you can do with a high-pitched fifth. 'With Or Without You' is founded on a simple four-chord turnaround of D, A, Bm, G, though you won't hear these chords stated outright because they are simply implied. Over this sequence, a couple of verses in, the Edge's high, echoed guitar is heard playing a riff consisting of two two-bar phrases. In each case the first half of the phrase is a G5 at the eighth fret which 'opens' into the harmonically expressive minor sixth of F#-D. Remember that fifths are harmonically neutral, so G5 is in itself neither major or minor. But with a thumping D in the bass, an F#-D sixth on the guitar implies a D major chord (D-F#-A). The clever thing is that the repeat of this sixth takes place over a B in the bass, which makes us hear those notes as belonging to a B minor chord (B-D-F#). Each phrase is completed by either an open fourth string D and open third G, or open fourth string D and the D an octave above on the third string. It's the manner in which this riff is coloured two ways that makes it so beautiful.

Tip: it can be interesting, creatively, to try repeating a riff with different chords underneath.

---

5. THE PERFECT FOURTH

Turn a perfect fifth upside-down – in other words reverse the order of the notes – and you get the interval called a perfect fourth. For instance A-E becomes E-A. Although not as popular as perfect fifths, fourths have also been important in riff history. A perfect fourth consists of two notes two-and-a-half tones apart, the distance between C and F. On all the strings except the second and third, a fourth can be held down with a single finger. Here are the usual ways of playing them on the guitar:

Fourths

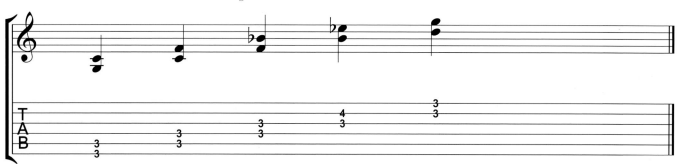

Fourths also have a tough but slightly cold, 'hollow' sound. They sometimes feature in lead guitar breaks on the top two strings to give an 'oriental' sound. Pulp's 'A Little Soul', the Cranberries' 'Zombie', The Vapors 'Turning Japanese' and The Beatles' 'Don't Let Me Down' are good examples of exploiting fourths for their oriental feel, and there are some tasty fourths on the intro of Wings' 'Band On The Run', where Dmaj7 helps them fit in, and for the main riff of Television's 'Marquee Moon'. Chuck Berry's famous guitar break at the start of tracks like 'Johnny B Goode' incorporates fourths. T.Rex's 'Get It On' has a Chuck Berry-derived fourth riff at the top, and the same can be heard in the second verse of the Offspring's 'Pretty Fly For A White Guy'. The chunky quality of fourths is heard on the main riff of Supergrass's 'Time'.

Like fifths, fourths are neither major nor minor, so the same rules apply about chords, scales, and distortion. If they are less popular than fifths for riffs it's because they are slightly harder to use, being more musically ambiguous. Often the root note in a fourth is the upper note of the pair – in other words, in a fourth such as D-G, G would be treated as the root note, not D.

Let's look at why fourths are not as straightforward as either fifths or thirds. Here is the scale of G major on the top string harmonised with a fourth on the second string.

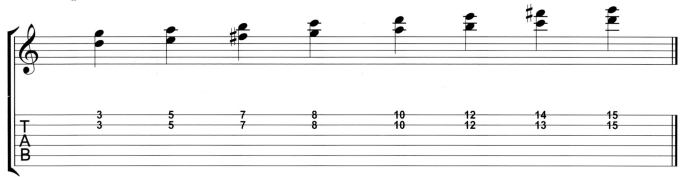

Fourths, G major

Listening to this, you may notice that the scale in fourths sounds OK until you get to the 14th fret, which doesn't sound so good. This is even more noticeable if you play that fret position over a record in G major or a recording of yourself strumming a G, C, D chord sequence. Why does it sound wrong? The top note at the 14th is F#, which is in the scale of G, so that's fine. The lower note, however, is C# which is the correct note for the interval but doesn't belong to G-major (it should be a C). To be in key, the seventh note of the scale (F#) needs a C under it. C-F# is an augmented fourth, not a perfect fourth.

If you slide these fourths around over a G major chord sequence, that 14th fret position (or the second fret, the same fourth one octave down) will sound horrible. It's because of that 'rogue' note, C#. It clashes with chord I (G, making an augmented fourth), chord II (A minor, making a major third), chord IV (C, another minor second), and chord V (D, making a major seventh). It's tolerable, if exotic, over chord III (B minor) and chord VI (E minor), provided the context allows. If chord VII is present in its flattened form (F), as is common in rock, the C# will also clash with that.

This unpredictability is one of the reasons why guitarists have been wary of using fourths in riffs beyond certain tried and tested patterns. One way around this is to use only certain fourths within the key. If you hit both strings at frets three, five, seven, ten, and 12 you get G pentatonic major on the top string (the first of these pairs): G-D, A-E, B-F#, D-A, and E-B:

Fourths, G pentatonic major

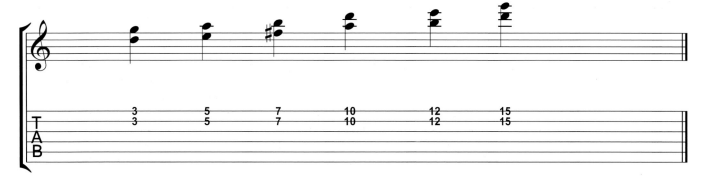

Notice that the seventh (F#) has come into the picture, so we've actually used more than the normal five notes (G-A-B-D-E) of the pentatonic. If we turn this into a fret/interval pattern we get a movement of 2-2-3-2-3, finishing at the 15th fret, where G-D is an octave above the first one. The practical application of the 'gap' formula 2-2-3-2-3 is this: whatever key you're in, locate the root note on the top string and just move up by that formula and you'll get the same sequence of fourths. For riffs you must work out the same sequence on the lower strings.

Here it is on strings two and three for D pentatonic major:

Fourths, D pentatonic major

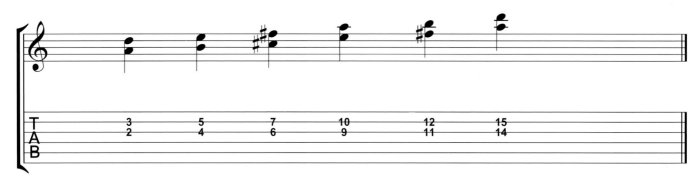

A semitone shift on fourths is quite rare. Even the tone shift is not especially common. The standard arrangement trick for the 'fourth riff' is to have the bass guitar play the root note or for the guitar to play the fourths over a pedal note – an open lower string on the guitar (we'll be looking at drones and pedals in Section Three). Low-to-middling fourths over a bass pedal note are especially typical of a band like ZZ Top. This will tend to put the fourths over either the open E or A-string, though in 'dropped D' tuning, fourths over a low D are available. T.Rex's 'Children Of The Revolution' uses a B-E fourth at the second fret, going on and off the open A and D strings, with an E pedal note underneath. Van Halen's 'You're No Good', 'Bottoms Up!' and 'Light Up The Sky' all put the guitar riff in fourths over a pedal root note, with the riff transposed up a tone in 'Light Up The Sky'. Ozzy Osbourne's 'I Don't Know' features fourths ascending over an A pedal played in bursts of 16th-notes, and rounded off with a G-D chord change, and similar fourths in A for 'Suicide Solution'. There is a great run of high fourths in Wings' 'Let Me Roll It', over E and F#m chords. The 'oriental' quality of high fourths is heard on the main riff of Robert Plant's 'Slow Dancer'.

Fourths combine well with fifths and sixths. In the Cult's 'American Horse' there is a tone-shift riff played first in fourths and later in fifths. For the neat trick of using fourths on the bottom strings to make your guitar sound detuned even when it isn't, see the entry on Hendrix's 'Spanish Castle Magic' in Section Two.

**RIFF GALLERY:
perfect fourths**

Artist	**Deep Purple**
Title	**'Smoke On The Water'**
Writer	**Blackmore/Gillan/Glover/Lord/Paice**
Released	**album: *Machine Head*, EMI/Purple (US Warners), 1972**
	single: (US) Warners, 1973; (UK) Purple, 1977

Deep Purple were formed in 1968 in the mega-watt blues-rock rumble started by Cream and Hendrix, and stoked by The Who, among other bands. As a five-piece with keyboards they always had musical avenues open which a power trio couldn't go down.

One of the all-time favourite rock riffs, 'Smoke On The Water' is the definitive hard rock use of fourths. On this track the bass guitar supplies a string of eighth-note Gs. Listen for the two quicker bursts of fourths in the chorus under "a fire in the sky". The fourths are based on the G pentatonic minor scale: D-G, F-B*b*, G-C; and A*b*-D*b* (D*b* being the flattened fifth of the scale). To hear just what fourths give the riff, try turning it into fifths and play it that way. The difference is considerable. Fourths are something of a musical fingerprint for guitarist Ritchie Blackmore, who put fourths into a number of other songs, including 'Burn', the Rainbow hit 'All Night Long', and (in 12/8) 'Strange Kind Of Woman'.

Artist	**Alice Cooper**
Title	**'School's Out'**
Writer	**Cooper/Bruce/Buxton/Dunaway/Smith**
Released	**single: Warners, 1972**
	album: *School's Out*, Warners, 1972

The concentration on Alice's ghoulish imagery and Rocky Horror stage antics tends to obscure the fact that Cooper albums like *School's Out* and *Billion Dollar Babies* contain some fine rock guitar, especially in the lead department. In 'School's Out' delinquency is signalled from the outset by the strident garage quality of the riff, which uses *high* fourths (as opposed to the low fourths of 'Smoke On The Water'), each riff finished off with the sulky ciggies-behind-the-bikeshed E-E*b*-D phrase. Notice how the riff changes its sound when the bass guitar settles down, going into the verse. The choice of bass guitar note can always add extra colour to a riff. The riff carries the song through most of the verse before a series of heavily accented on-the-beat chords lead into the chorus with its melodramatic triplets. The band found a nice variation on this with the intro riff to 'No More Mr Nice Guy', in which fourths also feature.

> "the choice of bass guitar note can always add extra colour to a riff"

Artist	**U2**
Title	**'Pride (In the Name Of Love)'**
Writer	**U2**
Released	**single: Island, 1984**
	album: *The Unforgettable Fire*, Island 1984

U2 have a special place in rock history. In the early 1980s they helped to show that guitar music in rock was not exhausted, as some thought. They did this with an experimental approach born of necessity from (at that time) a self-confessed lack of technique. At the core of U2's new approach was the Edge, a guitarist who once tellingly remarked that he found little solace in standard blues-based pentatonic guitar. This compelled him to look for new guitar figures, which he found with the crucial stimulus to his imagination of a delay unit. This ensured that the riffs which drove U2's early music sounded like nothing else.

One technique central to U2 is the *implied* chord, as discussed in the entry on 'With Or Without You'. In most rock bands guitars and bass function together. Wherever the chords go, the bass follows, making sure it hits the correct root notes. U2 exploited the fact that the bass can change under a static guitar chord and create the *illusion* there has been a chord change. 'Pride', Bono's homage to 1960s civil rights leader Martin Luther King, is built on an implied four-chord turnaround of B, E, A, F#m.

Listen to the first two bars of the guitar riff. The bass moves from B to E, but Edge keeps playing the same echoed figure on the top three strings. This is how it goes: the fourths form part of the high guitar figure, a B-F# combination and then C#-G#. Edge's B-F#-E notes are I, V and IV over B but they become V, II and I over E. He then moves up and plays A-G#-C# over A (I, VII and III) which become III, II and V over F#. The delay is set so there are always two of each note-pair sounding, with the guitar and the echo rhythms in sync. The band use the same trick in the middle-eight, when a single guitar lick is played over a rising B-D-E bassline. The other advantage of U2's high guitar riff/low bass is that it creates a space in the middle of the arrangement for the vocals.

Artist	**Jimi Hendrix Experience**
Title	**'Foxy Lady'**
Writer	**Hendrix**
Released	**album: Are You Experienced, Track (UK)/ Reprise (US) 1967**
	single: (US) Reprise, 1967

It's amazing how fresh *Are You Experienced* sounds on close listening. With Hendrix there's always the danger that we *think* we know what he sounds like, and forget to listen. Nuances are forgotten, and Hendrix's guitar palette is reduced to a noisy E7#9 chord. But this LP is the real deal, the sheer imagination that delivered guitar herodom to your ears, unburdened by the crippling self-consciousness it now carries. Transforming the Fender Stratocaster, from which only a few years earlier Hank Marvin had produced his glassy, clean playing, Hendrix combined and filtered blues, R&B, soul, Dylan, pop and the new hard rock through his own sci-fi/psychedelic vision. After Hendrix there could be no doubt in anyone's mind that the electric guitar was far more than merely an amplified version of the acoustic.

'Foxy Lady' is not a pure fourths riff. The reason I've included it in this section is the sheer stridency of the fourth, E-A, on the top two strings, which gives the riff its power. One of the great examples of feedback on a rock record establishes, from the start, a raw, dangerous sexuality. The riff is based on an F# octave and the bare fourth on the top two strings, with a B chord interpolated every other bar. The implied chord is F#m7, not F#7#9 as many think. In songs where it seems Hendrix is using the 7#9 chord of 'Purple Haze' fame, check it isn't a minor 7.

Listen for the second guitar that doubles the fourth, sometimes adding a double-stop A-F# and other decorations. Two first inversions on F# and E chords add spice to chorus two. The feedback returns at 2.24 and it all ends with a pick slide.

Artist	**ZZ Top**
Title	**'Tush'**
Writer	**Gibbons/Hill/Beard**
Released	**album: *Fandango*, London, 1975**
	single: (US) London, 1975; (UK EP) Warners, 1985

When it comes to writing riffs in fourths, ZZ Top are in a Texan league of their own. 'Tush' uses fourths on strings three and four over a 12/8 shuffle in G, with a G pedal note, and a little syncopation. Riffs like this are effective in a power trio because they make a lot of noise.

The intro to the song is worth mentioning. The riff is heard once only placed in the centre of the stereo mix, then the band enter (earlier than expected) and the riff splits into two guitars panned left and right. The riff is played only three times before the vocal starts the verse, rather than the usual four times. The verse itself is a standard 12-bar with the riff occurring in bars 1-4 and 7-8. When the chords change to C and D the guitars play a standard rock'n'roll shuffle figure rather than transposing the fourths riff. This means the riff's return after the first guitar solo is fresh.

In 'La Grange' (from 1973's *Tres Hombres*) the same fourths are played in A, but without a predominant pedal note on the intro – that's saved for the verse. A is probably the most popular key for this type of riff because it means the open A-string provides the root note, as in Bon Jovi's 'Always Run To You'.

6. THE TRITONE

Between the perfect fifth (C-G) and perfect fourth (C-F) lies another interval of great importance to rock. This is the flattened fifth (C-Gb), which could also be called the augmented fourth (C-F#), depending on how you want to look at it. Its other name is the tritone, referring to the fact that it's an interval of three full tones. A tritone naturally occurs on the major scale only between the fourth and the seventh notes (F-B in C major).

In harmonic terms the flattened fifth is a subversive force because it undermines the perfect fifth between the key note and the fifth of the scale on which stable harmony is maintained. In church music of centuries gone by it was known by the Latin phrase *diabolus in musica* (the devil's interval) and its use in sacred music was prohibited because it was felt to have an evil quality – precisely the effect that makes it popular in heavy rock. So the tritone has always had a 'bad press', though it is capable of wider musical effects than evoking a 'black magic' vibe. Even in rock it can express erotic feelings rather than satanic ones.

The tritone makes a vital contribution to styles of music with a more complex harmony than rock, such as the symphony. If you play a G7 chord and then a C chord you have what is known as a 'perfect cadence' or V-I change. This chord change has been used for hundreds of years whenever composers wish to establish a new key or finish a phrase, a section, or a whole piece, with a powerful assertion of the home key (in this example C major). The G7 comprises the notes G-B-D-F. Notice the B-F? Yes, it's the tritone, hiding right in the middle of this apparently most traditional of chord changes. In other words, by a profound musical paradox, the tritone is actually part of the 'glue' that binds traditional harmony together. The diminished seventh chord, rare in rock but common in jazz, which is also used for key-changing, actually has *two* tritones in it. G diminished is G-Bb-C#-E. The note pairs G-C# and Bb-E make tritones.

The other musical source for the tritone is the blues. Popular scale patterns in blues music often include a flattened fifth alongside the normal fifth. We will see more of this in Section Two.

Here are some tritone shapes on the fretboard:

Tritones

When it comes to making up tritone riffs there are several methods. It would be unusual to try to string a sequence of tritones together played as intervals, though it is effective to hit a tritone in the middle of single notes or other moving intervals such as fourths and fifths. You can also make a riff that moves in single notes by a tritone. These are described in the famous songs in the Riff Gallery coming up.

Led Zep's use of the tritone can be heard in the violin bow solo in the live 'Dazed And Confused', which is littered with tritones from E-Bb and F-B, and in 'Dancing Days'. Tritones occur in Limp Bizkit's 'Stuck' (tritone on the chorus riff), Soundgarden's 'Outshined', Stone Temple Pilots' 'Down', and Korn's 'Pretty'. Ozzy Osbourne's 'Revelation (Mother Earth)' has several riffs that use an E-Bb change, on the intro backed up by the unsettling effect of a run based on E diminished. On the chorus of The Strokes' 'Soma' a C# in octaves is played against a G chord, followed by a contrasted C in octaves over an F chord. It's a long way from heavy metal, but the tritone does its job of introducing 'edginess'.

**RIFF GALLERY:
tritones**

Artist	Black Sabbath
Title	'Black Sabbath'
Writer	Iommi/Butler/Ward/Osbourne
Released	album: *Black Sabbath* (Vertigo/Warners 1970)

This slice of pre-*Exorcist* Gothic horror scared many a 14-year old silly when they pinched the album sleeve (overgrown graveyard, figure in cloak) from their elder brother's bedroom for a surreptitious play. When I interviewed him in the 1990s, Toni Iommi explained that the occult imagery of Black Sabbath's songs had come about almost by accident. Ozzy needed words that would fit Iommi's evil-sounding riffs. You can't sing about flowers and love in the air over the trilled tritone riff of 'Black Sabbath'.

Sabbath songs often have lots of riffs. Iommi never seems to be stuck for one. He produces them like an endless stream of one-ton black rabbits from a hat, to be recorded with his own unique guitar tone: the photograph on the inner sleeve of the fourth album shows his Gibson SG with what looks like a non-standard pickup, and there was also the Rangemaster Treble Booster unit to push his valve amps into more distortion.

Iommi must take some credit for the introduction of the tritone into the Grimoire Of Ye Heavy Ryffe. 'Black Sabbath', with its famous thunder, rain and tolling bell intro, is almost entirely built on a tritone riff, G-D*b*. Hendrix had, of course, stuck one on the front of 'Purple Haze', but 'Black Sabbath' is probably the defining early use of the tritone in the realms of metal. The riff to Sabbath's 'Children Of The Grave' is also tritone-based (D5-A5-A*b*5), as are 'Wheels Of Confusion' (the F#-A-C-B idea at about 3.40) and 'Under The Sun'.

Apart from the tritone, what's hugely influential about the riff in 'Black Sabbath' is its slow tempo – almost glacial by rock'n'roll standards. Little Richard this ain't. As for the erotic quality of the tritone, Sabbath weren't that interested. It would take Jimmy Page's musical sex-magic to nail that one

Artist	REM
Title	'Feeling Gravity's Pull'
Writer	Berry/Buck/Mills/Stipe
Released	album: *Fables Of The Reconstruction*, IRS, 1985

REM's third album opens with the most angular riff they ever recorded. To emphasise the fact, the track starts with Buck's guitar on its own. What's fascinating is that here the tritone so beloved of metal bands is transferred to the top two strings and given a different slant. The first three notes are B, F# and F. The riff starts with a fourth on the top strings and then moves back a fret, creating a tritone between B and F. This is repeated with a few extra lower notes to extend the phrase. Then Buck hits a B on the bottom string and intersperses this with harmonics in a sort of mutant funk rhythm.

Only when the drums come in is the sense of uncertainty about beat and time signature cleared up – notice that the drum entry indicates that the riff doesn't quite start where you think it does.

This riff carries on throughout the verse, creating a remarkable, doomy backdrop to Stipe's mournful vocal. Perhaps it's the dark influence of the tritone that made me think for years that Michael Stipe was singing, 'It's a mandrake kind of sky', instead of Man Ray.

Artist	**T.Rex**	
Title	**'Rock On'**	
Writer	**Bolan**	
Released	**album: *The Slider*, T.Rex Wax Co/EMI, (USReprise), 1972**	

At a time when pretension was cutting rock off from its fundamental energy, Bolan took rock music back to its roots: the 1950s 12-bar based rock'n'roll of Presley, Berry and Cochran filtered through a 1960s post-Dylan, post-Hendrix sensibility.

You will have to listen closely to this one to hear the tritone, but that's kind of the point. The examples looked at so far have all been strident expressions of this interval, placing its unmissable dissonance right at the front of the music. But it can be used in a subtle way to add a dark, sexy undertone to a chord change. This riff begins in G major with a high G-D fourth, and then lands on a pungent B*b* as the chord changes from G to B*b*. This change is, of course, a I-*b*III blues change. At the back of the mix there are several acoustic guitars, and as they strum on the Bb an open top E-string is audible. B*b*-E is a tritone.

Artist	**Jimi Hendrix Experience**			
Title	**'Purple Haze'**			
Writer	**Hendrix**			
Released	**single: (UK) Track, 1967; (US) Reprise, 1967**			
	album: *Are You Experienced*, Track/Reprise, 1967			

One of the earliest examples of the dramatic use of the tritone is on this, Jimi Hendrix's ground-breaking, ear-bending second (UK) single. It is a truism of commercial music designed for radio play that you need to do something in the first five seconds to get the listeners' attention and make your record stand out. Hendrix has Noel Redding play an E octave on bass. Over the top of it he places a Bb octave, thus creating a tritone.

I can't think of another chart single of the time that in musical terms is so nakedly confrontational. The tritone's unrest expresses the psychological distress of the lyric.

The song itself features an E pentatonic minor-based riff (starting in bar three), which is unusual because it covers two octaves and a minor third – riffs don't usually spread out that much. It's a riff that makes you aware of the big jumps between the notes. The main chord change is based on E, G and A (a classic blues-derived I-*b*III-IV progression). The song also features the E7#9

"the tritone so beloved of metal bands is transferred to the top two strings and given a different slant" chord, which has become known as the 'Hendrix chord' because of his fondness for it. Its notes are E G# D G, and its dissonance caused by the tritone G#-D and the major seventh G#-G.

Artist	**Metallica**
Title	**'Enter Sandman'**
Writer	**Hetfield/Ulrich/Hammett**
Released	**single: (UK) Vertigo, 1991; (US) Elektra, 1991** **album: *Metallica (The Black Album)*,** **Vertigo/Elektra, 1991**

Anthrax, Slayer, Megadeth and Metallica were leaders of a generation of bands that arose in the mid-to-late 1980s playing a new brand of heavy rock. Their often detuned riffery owed less to the blues-based hard rock of the late 1960s/1970s and was played initially at lightning speed, prompting the label 'thrash metal'. When the dust settled, Metallica emerged as kings of the pack. Playing up the existential despair, they popularised a new harmonic vocabulary for metal, using a *b*V and *b*II in the minor scale (E-F-G-A-B*b*-B-C-D). In came a new guitar tone to disembowel your speakers: the 'mid-scooped' power-chord with its thumping top and bottom-boosted EQ.

'Enter Sandman' soon joined the pool of famous guitar riffs to play in music shops, augmenting a select group that includes 'Smoke On The Water' and 'Sweet Child O' Mine'. A cleanish guitar arpeggio and one cat-spit of wah-wah start the song before drums and bass enter, and then the riff appears. Listen for the guitar on the opposite side to the riff, which initially is changing from an E5 to A5 chord. Both guitars play the riff at the end of this long build-up. 'Enter Sandman' is constructed on variations of a riff built on the tritone of E-B*b*, in which there is an octave leap from E up to E, a fall back to B and an immediate semitone slip to B*b*. The verses use a semitone E-F shift, and the chorus goes up a tone to F# C-B (another tritone) for "exit light, enter night", where fifths are also used.

There is a masterful arrangement stroke with the unexpected re-entry of the rhythm section at 4:28, two riffs earlier than you expect. Along with the carpet-bombing riffage, Metallica had a maniacal sense of arrangement. In rock and pop, four of anything is very predictable – so make a cut. For another Metallica track with tritone and strong minor seconds, see 'Of Wolf And Man' from the same album.

7. RIFFS IN THIRDS

So far we have covered semitone and tone-shift riffs, octaves, fourths, fifths and the tritone. These are the most important intervals for riff-making – this by no means exhausts the intervals within an octave, but the others are not used as much. Major and minor seconds (two notes a tone or semitone apart) are too close together to be played as pairs in the way that fifths are. Similarly, major and minor sevenths are too discordant to be played together. So that leaves thirds and sixths.

Thirds are notes either three or four semitones apart: three semitones for a minor third (C-E*b*), and four for a major third (C-E). Thirds have a characteristically 'sweet' effect, which is to say they are harmonious and pleasing to the ear if they are fully in key. Thirds are an essential feature of vocal harmony singing, especially in duets. Their use in rock riffs is therefore limited, since they don't project a tough, aggressive quality without a little help. Where they are important in rock is as the basis of the rock style known as 'twin lead', where two guitarists in a band play melodic phrases largely in thirds. This style was pioneered by bands like Wishbone Ash, Thin Lizzy and Queen, and can be heard to famous effect on the guitar coda to The Eagles' 'Hotel California'. Thirds provide the lead break for The Beatles' 'Twist and Shout', melodic interest in Van Morrison's 'Brown-Eyed Girl', and there's a smooth thirds riff in Suede's 'Asbestos' over a G#m-C# chord change. Thirds sound great on strings one & two or three & four, and then progressively less effective down the strings. (They can also work well on the high strings of a bass.)

Turning away from the guitar for a second, Tori Amos' 'Girl' (from her debut *Little Earthquakes*) has a remarkable one-bar piano riff in thirds that runs hauntingly throughout the intro and verses of the song. The thirds in question are drawn from the scale of G natural minor. Around this hypnotic re-iteration, Amos' vocal melody and piano make a texture of great beauty. Unlike fifths or fourths, this use of thirds emphasises the tonality, be it major or minor. A comparable instance on guitar would be the thirds over the A minor and F chords in Fleetwood Mac's 'Rhiannon'.

Before tackling thirds as riffs, let's look at how they occur on a major scale. Let's take the scale of D major (D E F# G A B C#), and have the same scale overlaid two notes out of alignment, so F# goes over the D, and so on:

Thirds, scale of D major

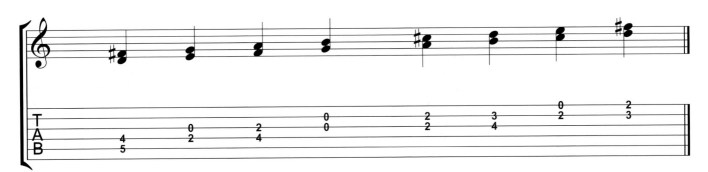

So we now have a scale in thirds. This sounds harmonious because it is a sequence of major and minor thirds. This sequence goes major, minor, minor, major, major, minor, minor. If you were to try and have a sequence all major or all minor the result would sound obviously wrong, because to do so would require introducing notes not on the original scale. Try playing the following D major scale harmonised in major thirds and you'll hear what I mean.

Major thirds

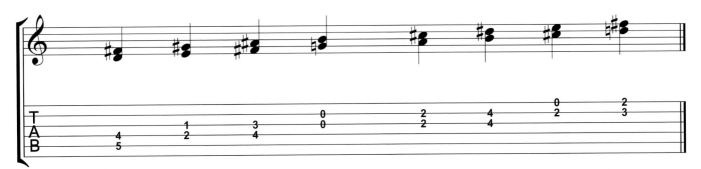

Even this could be used to creative effect. Jimmy Page exploited the sound of consecutive out-of-key major thirds in 'Friends', using an open C tuning.

At the top of page 40 you'll see the finger patterns for thirds on the guitar: minor third first, then major third.

Thirds do sometimes occur as riffs when they're played on the top two pairs of strings – take the classic Chuck Berry bent thirds on the G and B strings. Thirds on

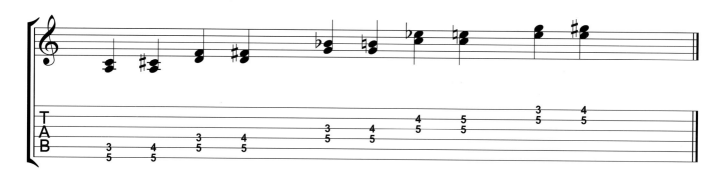

Minor and major thirds

these strings can be heard in the main riff of Cream's 'SWLABR' and 'Outside Woman Blues', Rory Gallagher's 'Public Enemy No1', the intro of Bowie's 'Station To Station' (accompanied by a tone-shift riff), the Stones' 'Can You Hear Me Knocking', REM's 'Letter Never Sent', and the Who's 'Young Man Blues'. Guitarists like Steve Cropper and Johnny Marr have made fills out of thirds on the top two strings.

If you want to give them a bit more 'edge', try chromatic (off-key) shifts up or down a semitone. If you want to make a riff from thirds lower in pitch, try putting them over the open bottom E or A-string (see the section on pedal notes in Section Three). Something like this occurs on the intro and verse of the Police's 'Don't Stand So Close To Me'. Therapy's 'Nowhere' has a good example of thirds played rapidly over an A-E-F#m-D chord sequence.

So far we've spoken of thirds as pairs of notes, but the interval of a flattened (minor) third (C-Eb) is crucial to riff-writing, because this is a 'blue' note. A vast number of guitar riffs use the flattened third. The most common keys would be A (C instead of C#) and E (G instead of G#). The effect of a riff where there is a minor third is strengthened if the key and the underlying chords are majors.

You can hear this in a song like T.Rex's 'Twentieth Century Boy', where the opening riff uses the notes E and G over an E major chord, and in Springsteen's 'Adam Raised A Cain', where the blues influence is even more noticeable, and in the Groundhogs' 'Cherry Red'. The Stone Roses' 'Driving South' makes hay with a riff that uses both the major and minor third through an extended 12-bar and transposes that riff up a fourth.

The ambiguity of using both major and minor third is easily produced when the riff is played on slide with an open tuning, as in the Roses' 'Love Spreads'. Other riffs that mix the two thirds are the Offspring's 'Pay The Man' and Gomez's 'Shot Shot'.

Less commonly you may find riffs that create a three-note idea with the flattened seventh, first and major third (G, A and C# in A). An example is Nirvana's 'Breed'. Queen's 'Tie Your Mother Down' has a main riff on A with a C# added rather than the blues C that would be more common (as heard on Led Zep's 'Rock And Roll'). There are plenty of riffs where the blues third is followed by the usual major third, as in Led Zep's 'Houses Of The Holy' (notice the funky accented A6 chord). Thirds can also combine with fourths, as on the riff of Television's 'See No Evil'.

Other songs where the third is a crucial interval in the riff include Free's 'Woman', which has B-B-D-B from the pentatonic minor then slides a third D-F# up to E-G#. The Jam's 'The Place I Love' has a riff using low slid thirds from E-G# to D-F#.

Artist	Howlin' Wolf
Title	'Smokestack Lightning'
Writer	Burnett
Released	single: (US), Chess, 1956; (UK) Pye, 1964
	album: *Moanin' In The Moonlight*, Chess, 1965

Chester Burnett, better known as Howlin' Wolf, was a leading figure of electric Chicago blues. 'Smokestack Lightning' – covered by the Yardbirds in 1965, and a key song of the British Blues Boom – is a one-chord number based on a two-bar riff, dominated by Burnett's famous wolf-howl falsetto. At the core of this famous blues riff is the first change of notes: the open E and B strings (making a fourth) going onto G and D (another fourth). The two pairs are a minor third apart. The riff is then completed with another third as B and D are heard in close succession, and the G-E is heard again as the scale moves downward. Apart from the dark majesty of the vocal, much of the track's power comes from the tension created by the way the melody rides across the riff and not with it, setting up a counter-rhythm.

The blues third can be heard in other Wolf songs like 'Wang Dang Doodle', 'Spoonful' (later covered by Cream, who did a number of Wolf's songs), 'Little Red Rooster', and mutated in 'I Asked For Water'.

Artist	Chuck Berry
Title	'No Money Down'
Writer	Berry
Released	single: (US) Chess, 1956; (UK) London, 1956
	album: *After School Sessions*, Chess 1958

'No Money Down' is a fine example of contrasting a riff with vocals. After a brief intro in which guitar and piano briefly tussle over the riff, the riff carries the whole verse. It's one of the most famous of all blues riffs, and comprises a five-note figure in 12/8 that starts on the last eighth-note of the third beat and ends on the first beat of the following bar. In its original blues form (on songs like Muddy Waters' 'I'm A Man') it occurs as a pure pentatonic riff using notes I-bIII-IV (in G: G-C-Bb). But Berry would often play it with a quick hammer-on that converted the blues flattened third to the normal third (G-C-G-Bb-B-G), as he does here, and the C and B notes both lend themselves to having thirds added above them.

Similar thirds mix with fourths for the main B riff of Berry's 'Around And Around'. Check out the MC5's 'Tonight' for another example of the minor third/major third interplay derived from Chuck Berry.

Artist	Motorhead
Title	'Ace Of Spades'
Writer	Kilminster/Taylor/Clarke
Released	single: (UK) Bronze, 1980; (US) Mercury, 1980
	album: *Ace Of Spades*, Bronze/Mercury, 1980

Possibly rock's noisiest-ever three-piece, appealing to heavy metal fans and punks alike, Motorhead didn't so much plays songs as pummel them into submission. At the core of the band's assault was Lemmy's chordal approach to bass guitar, coupled with a vocal style that made Joe Cocker sound like Cliff Richard, and drummer Taylor's double bass-drums.

The frenetic 'Ace Of Spades' riff is introduced by an initial phrase of E-Eb-D over an open E. The main riff is then superimposed over this at the end of the

> "the track's power comes from the tension created by the way the melody rides across the riff and not with it"

first couple of lyric lines. It consists of thirds played on the second and third strings and bent up in what most guitarists know as a Chuck Berry-type lead idea. These thirds are often used to spice up fast passages of minor pentatonic playing. They can also be heard in other Motorhead songs like 'Metropolis' and 'Bomber', and at a slower tempo on the Alex Harvey Band's 'Swampsnake'.

Artist	**Led Zeppelin**
Title	**'Trampled Underfoot'**
Writer	**Page/Plant/Jones**
Released	**single: (US) Swan Song, 1975**
	album: *Physical Graffiti*, Swan Song, 1975

On their sixth album, Led Zeppelin spliced their own brand of hard rock with a slight funk influence. 'Trampled Underfoot' is a staggering display of monolithic power, complete with relentless drumming from Bonham, nimble clavinet from Jones, and another classic Page riff. The keyboard part makes consistent use of octaves on G; over this Page plays two major thirds – A-C# and Bb-D – followed by a seven-note G pentatonic minor run. The C# makes a tritone against G but is softened a little by being in harness with the A. At the end of each verse the riff is punctuated either with a Bb-C change or Bb-C-Eb-F, followed by a variation on the riff an octave higher.

I've never counted just how many times the riff is played during the track, but it must be a record for Zep. Such an unremitting focus on the riff is part of what gives the track its power, but it's a difficult thing to pull off without boredom setting in.

Artist	**Nirvana**
Title	**'Come As You Are'**
Writer	**Cobain/Nirvana**
Released	**album: *Nevermind*, Geffen, 1991**
	single: Geffen, 1992

This riff (played on a guitar detuned by a tone) consists of a minor third moving in steps into a perfect fifth, the two notes of each pair alternating rather than being struck together. The riff is played for the intro, verse and under the guitar solo. What's unusual about it is the fact that it uses a third pitched so low. Notice how the vocal sits well above it. You can also hear that the riff guitar has some kind of chorus effect applied to it. A fuller guitar texture starts at 1.38 for the bridge, before the riff leads into the guitar solo. The two chords on the chorus are also a minor third apart.

Artist	**Jimi Hendrix**
Title	**'In From The Storm'**
Writer	**Hendrix**
Released	**album: *The Cry Of Love*, Track/Capitol, 1971**

As mentioned earlier, Hendrix's later songs show him widening his compositional forms and harmonic vocabulary. 'In From The Storm' is a fine example, with thirds helping to fill out a single-note riff. The main riff is based on F# pentatonic minor: it starts with a tone shift E-F#, followed by thirds on the second and third strings (A-C# and B-D#), and then a pentatonic run which unexpectedly drops onto the flattened third of the scale, an A at the fifth fret.

The riff is placed by Hendrix as an 'answer' to the first two lines of lyric, which themselves are sung over a single chord. Having a vocal phrase over a single chord followed by a busier riff makes a good contrast: the static chord won't distract attention away from the vocal.

After a couple of verses Hendrix starts the instrumental bridge section with a descending riff on the A blues scale at the fifth fret, which again runs down to the flattened third at the eighth. He then transposes this riff twice to reach the guitar solo. (The version of 'In From The Storm' that Hendrix played at the *Isle Of Wight Festival* is worth seeking out.)

In a power trio context, such as Hendrix often worked in, thirds take on a special significance because they so easily sketch out the harmony without the guitarist having to play block chords. If you have a riff that consists of single notes, it's a good idea to look for opportunities to add major and minor thirds to some of those notes in order to suggest chords. This works best when neither of your notes is the root note, which can be left to the bass player to handle.

---

8. RIFFS IN SIXTHS

Turn a third upside down (reverse the notes) and it becomes a sixth. Sixths are notes either eight or nine semitones apart. Eight semitones make a minor sixth (C-Ab); nine make a major sixth (C-A).

Like thirds, sixths have a harmonious quality, though the distance between the notes reduces the 'sweetness' compared with thirds. The use of high sixths in rock riffs is also limited for the same reasons: they don't, by themselves, sound tough enough. Van Halen used low sixths for the opening riff of 'Women In Love' and Jimmy Page has low sixths in the main riff of 'The Only One' on his solo album *Outrider*. There is a riff in sixths in REM's 'Binky The Doormat'. They are also a trademark of guitarist Steve Cropper on his many 1960s soul recordings with Booker T & The MGs, and are often found in twin lead guitar playing – listen to the opening of Wishbone Ash's 'Throw Down The Sword'.

Here's how they occur on the scale of D major harmonised in sixths:

Sixths, scale of D major

As with thirds, there is a pattern of finger movements you can learn: 2-2-1-2-2-1-1. Harmonise a major scale with the right notes and you get major, major, minor, major, major, minor, minor, in sixths.

In hard rock styles sixths are more likely to be found in conjunction with fifths and/or fourths. They can be highly effective in this way, introducing variety into a sequence of the tonally neutral intervals, because the sixth (like the third) will usually imply a major or a minor chord in a way that bare fourths and fifths do not.

Consider the sequence at the top of page 44...

Sixths with other intervals

A-E moves down to G-D (A5 to G5), then to G-C (a fourth) and then F#-D (a minor sixth). In such an instance the sixth clearly implies the chord of D major, though it could also be harmonised with a B minor. As with thirds, this makes sixths significant in any band where a single guitar is the harmony instrument.

RIFF GALLERY: sixths

Artist	**Dire Straits**	
Title		**'Where Do You Think You're Going'**
Writer		**Knopfler**
Released		**album: *Communique*, Vertigo, Warners, 1979**

This is a highly-charged gem of a track, the stand-out of the Straits' second album. It begins with a progression of Am, F, G, E to form the verse. The riff functions as a link between verses, and the coda over which the second guitar solo is played. Like the more famous 'Sultans Of Swing', it's a riff that was probably shaped by Knopfler's right-hand picking technique, since it uses two strings at a time. It's built over a four-chord, four-bar sequence of Am, F, Dm, F. The first bar has thirds on strings two and three, resolving onto an F triad; the second bar has complementary sixths on strings one and three, resolving onto a D minor triad; sixths occur again in bar three, resolving onto F in bar four. Knopfler plays these with a sensitive touch, utilising the Strat's neck/middle and, later, middle/bridge pickup positions.

After the last verse, the drums enter with a crescendo, the tempo increases, and more guitars play the riff than earlier. It's an exhilarating moment. 'Where Do You Think You're Going' is an object lesson in what you can do in a song with thirds and sixths, and with dynamics.

9. MIXED INTERVAL RIFFS

Now that we've surveyed the important intervals for rock guitar riffs, we can conclude Section One with a look at how to get extra mileage out of these intervals by using more than one type in a riff. The famous songs that follow in the Riff Gallery provide examples of this. With creativity it's possible to combine any intervals in a riff, either playing them as single notes or together. Octaves, fifths, fourths, thirds and sixths will combine easily and be comfortable to finger. Seconds and sevenths are more awkward and don't sit so well under the hand. There are mixed intervals in The Offspring's 'The Kids Aren't Alright', where there's a sequence with thirds, fourths and fifths. Wishbone Ash's 'Persephone' combines thirds and fourths on the top strings over an Em-D chord change. On the coda the riff is lengthened in a dynamic variation.

Artist	Dire Straits
Title	'Money For Nothing'
Writer	Knopfler/Sting
Released	album: *Brothers In Arms*, Vertigo/Warners, 1985
	single: Vertigo/Warners, 1985

Although *Brothers In Arms* famously featured a silver resonator guitar on the sleeve, tracks like 'Money For Nothing' featured Knopfler applying his guitar skills to a cranked-up Les Paul. The result is an interesting hybrid tone, caused by the blend of his technique and a traditional rock guitar sound.

'Money For Nothing' comes on initially with enough dirty guitar to appeal to those who liked a good head-banging riff, though the song also has enough sweeteners, in the way of a catchy chorus, synths and Sting's guest vocals, to appeal beyond the heavy rock audience. It's also one of the longest riffs in the book (eight bars), is in G pentatonic minor (G-Bb-C-D-F), and mixes single notes with fourths and fifths. The first four-bar phrase ends with the Bb-C change; the second mirrors that with an F-G change. It's harder to play than it seems, because Knopfler's finger-style means it's rhythmically varied, and harmonics pop and squeak from the strings. To get the tone his Les Paul was played through a wah-wah pedal fixed open at just the right angle to create the distinctive 'honky' EQ boost.

Artist	Led Zeppelin
Title	'Good Times Bad Times'
Writer	Page/Jones/Bonham
Released	album: *Led Zeppelin*, Atlantic, 1969
	single: (US) Atlantic, 1969

Zeppelin's recording career blasted off with the double-crunch E chord of this intro. Right from the lift-off, dynamics were top of the band's musical agenda. Long songs were not yet the order of the day. The whole compositional approach here is to get as many different thrills as possible into less than four minutes. 'Good Times Bad Times' is the final maturing of the type of concise rock song which bands like The Who and The Kinks started in 1965, with clearly defined verses and choruses, as well as a riff.

'Good Times Bad Times' has several identifiable riffs: Riff 1 is a couple of E5s, a fast arpeggio on D followed by a slinky chromatic C#-D-D# approach to the tonic E. The underlying harmony is mixolydian: E-D-A and back to E. At the end of the first chorus, instead of returning to the verse, Zep pull a surprise by tumbling into a contrasted section on F# with a riff made up of fifths and fourths. Page would use this combination of F# as a tonal centre and fourths underneath the guitar solo in 'Over The Hills and Far Away' in 1973.

Artist	Golden Earring
Title	'Radar Love'
Writer	Kooymans/Hay
Released	single: (UK) Track, 1973; (US) Track, 1974
	album: *Moontan*, Track, 1973/1974

Golden Earring were a Dutch band who formed in 1961, went through many line-up changes, toured with The Who in 1972, signed to the English band's label Track, and in late 1973 to early 1974 scored an international hit with 'Radar Love'. The riff here functions as a fill after each line of the lyric during verse one, almost as a musical comment on the lyric (see 'Walk This Way' in this regard). The bass guitar plays a steady F# and above it the guitar riff plays a third (A-C#) and two fourths, F#-B and E-A, hence its selection here as a mixed interval riff. The riff is a distant relative of a typical Chuck Berry double-stop but filtered through an early 1970s hard rock sensibility. Notice the effect of the riff pausing on the E-A, rather than F#-B, the former implying an F#7 chord. The riff guitar is panned to the left. A higher variant of this riff follows the first two lines of verse 2, before the riff is heard an octave higher, and finally at the original pitch. This track also has a splendid drum break, a menacing middle-eight, and above all an atmospheric intro with a killer guitar tone.

Artist	The La's
Title	'There She Goes'
Writer	Mavers
Released	single: (UK) Go! Discs, 1990; (US) London, 1991
	album: *The La's*, Go! Discs, 1990

'There She Goes' is a wonderful example of a high guitar riff with various intervals in quick succession, and of a riff occurring in a song that isn't hard rock. The riff is a stereo chiming figure based on a D-G fourth, with other notes above and below it added and taken away. The D stays constant and lends a drone-like quality to it, along with the chiming effect of E-D-E-D-E-D on the top two strings, one open, one fretted – an example of getting a major second by using an open string with a fretted note. At first the riff is heard on its own without a harmony, but notice how its harmonic value changes when the chords (G, D, Cadd9) enter underneath. The riff is extended when the Am chord appears.

"notice how the riff's harmonic value changes when the chords enter underneath"

Artist	Whitesnake
Title	'Still Of The Night'
Writer	Coverdale/Sykes
Released	single: (UK) EMI, 1987; (US) Geffen 1987
	album: *Whitesnake* 1987, EMI/Geffen, 1987)

Heavy rock enjoyed a revival of commercial fortunes in the late 1980s. The pendulum that had swung against guitar music at the start of the decade swung back, and at the same time there was a re-evaluation of Led Zeppelin's music – all of which led to numerous attempts to profitably fill the Zeppelin-sized hole in the market. Cue shrieking blonde singers, a guitar hero or two, mega-watt heavy riffs, and ponderous drumbeats served up in a canyon of reverb. Which brings us rather neatly to Whitesnake and 'Still Of The Night'.

This track features four distinguishable riffs. The first and most important is a four-bar riff using the F# blues scale (F#-A-B-C-C#-E), which has two phrases: a1 ends with E5-B5; a2 ends with B5-E5. The first two beats of bars two and four have an octave leap on F#, making the riff sound like a welding together of Zep's 'Black Dog' and 'Immigrant Song'. Riff number two is shaped by an octave, on E, with a couple of fourths at the end of it. Listen for this riff's return, after the chorus, when it is played twice in time with the drums, and twice across a continuous drum beat.

Riff three comes during the instrumental bridge, over an Em-C change, and consists of a four-bar set of phrases derived from the E natural minor scale. Riff four follows with triads moving downwards over an E pedal. 'Still Of The Night' crams a whole lotta riffology into a short space.

Scale-based RIFFS

Riffs can also be built on a scale – a set pattern of notes related to the key of a song – which could be a major, minor, or blues scale, or a mixolydian, dorian or other mode. Don't worry, it's not as complex as it sounds...

A scale is a fixed sequence of notes dividing an octave into a pattern of intervals based on the semitone and the tone. From the scale a sense of key and that key's harmony is derived. Riffs can also be built from a scale – in rock it's usually the pentatonic major and minor, with the blues scale, and the addition of extra chromatic notes if you want to get slinky. Often riffs are drawn from the same fretboard patterns that players use for lead guitar – the emphasis simply falls on the lower-pitched areas of those patterns.

In the selected examples in the Riff Galleries, the grouping of songs and their riffs under the heading of a scale does not imply that the riff has *all* the notes of the scale. It means that the riff draws *most* of its notes from that scale; it may only be a partial expression of the scale.

10. THE PENTATONIC MINOR RIFF

The most important scale for rock music is undoubtedly the pentatonic. This is the scale heard most frequently in lead guitar solos and in riffs, in both its major and minor form. Pentatonic means 'five notes' (the major scale has seven), and this type of scale is found in the folk music of many cultures. It can be heard when the five black keys on a piano octave are played, and is the scale most people first learn on the guitar.

The pentatonic minor can be played from any note provided you move up the neck using the intervals of 3, 2, 2, 3 and 2 semitones (or frets) on a single string. The stave at the top of page 49 shows what it looks like in A and E.

The notes are A-C-D-E-G. What makes it a minor scale is the distance between the first two notes: three semitones make a minor third. In comparison to a major scale, minor scales sound sad. Normally, a minor scale can only be played in a minor key, and a major scale in a major key – but rock and soul share a particular

A pentatonic minor   *E pentatonic minor*

musical practice, derived from the blues, which involves singers and instrumentalists using flattened 'blue' notes against a major chord backing where such notes would not normally be in key. The arising tension creates a musical effect most associated with the blues. Played over a major chord backing the pentatonic minor gives a distinctive 'tough' sound. This colours any riffs written on the scale so they share that 'tough' quality.

When writing your own songs, try experimenting with a riff in A pentatonic minor over an A major chord backing. Then play the same riff over an A minor chord. Hear the difference? In the first instance two of the scale's notes – C and G – are functioning as blues notes, because in A major they should be C# and G#. But over the A minor chord they don't function in this way because the scale of A minor features C and G. So the A pentatonic minor riff sounds perfectly OK but blends in, rather than having the assertive quality it has in the major key.

Pentatonic minor riffs are the most common in rock. AC/DC's 'Whole Lotta Rosie' uses a classic blues phrase speeded up as a rock'n'roll idea (A pentatonic minor, the notes A, C and D). Stevie Wonder's 'Superstition' is an E pentatonic minor riff. Deep Purple's 'Fireball' verse is based on B pentatonic minor single notes (with a two-part four-bar riff), while 'Highway Star' uses G-Bb-C-Bb as chords, not single notes, on the first part of its verse.

Other pentatonic minor riffs include Soundgarden's 'Spoonman', Reef's 'Naked', Van Halen's 'Outta Love Again', the MC5's 'Kick Out The Jams' (E5-G-A is I-bIII-IV of the pentatonic minor scale), Ocean Colour Scene's 'Riverboat Song' (just with B, D and E notes), and Extreme's 'Rest In Peace', with its Hendrixy intro. Hendrix's 'Little Miss Lover' has a riff using I-bIII-bVII.

Artist	**Johnny Kidd & The Pirates**
Title	**'Shakin' All Over'**
Writer	**Heath (Kidd)**
Released	**single: (UK) HMV, 1960; (US) Capitol, 1960**

'Shakin' All Over' was ahead of its time in both its use of a riff and its sense of space, which was unusual in the chart at that time when many records featured syrupy strings and female backing vocals in choirs. The main riff is a straight run down an E pentatonic minor scale, taking advantage of the fact that all the notes of this scale (E-G-A-B-D) are open strings on the guitar. The riff is played in first position, with pull-offs from fretted notes onto open strings. After the first burst, a chugging lower pentatonic riff takes over. This in turn is played high up with heavy muting once the vocal gets under way.

The song was memorably covered by The Who on their *Live At Leeds* album.

RIFF GALLERY:
pentatonic minor riffs

Artist	The Temptations
Title	'Get Ready'
Writer	Robinson
Released	single: (UK) Tamla Motown, 1966; (US) Gordy, 1966

Taken as a bass guitar riff, 'Get Ready' seems straightforward: a D pentatonic minor riff with the bass sometimes doubled by brass. But the song has a strongly contrasting verse and chorus: the verse has the riff, while the chorus has a four-chord sequence in F major (F, B*b*, Gm, C), with James Jamerson switching to a bassline on the F major scale (F-G-A-B*b*-C-D-E) in running eighths. Things get a little more complex when the arrangement of the riff is scrutinised. The riff is accompanied by a piano part that appears to be hitting a D major chord over much of the riff, and adding major thirds above some of its notes. This leads to the notes F# (the major third of D) and the blues third F sounding in close proximity. The bridge (at 1.41) brings in the D blues scale by using an A*b*.

Artist	Free
Title	'Wishing Well'
Writer	Rodgers/Kirke/Yamauchi/Kossoff/Bundrick
Released	single: (UK) Island, 1972
	album: *Heartbreaker*, (UK) Island, (US) A&M, 1973

Taken from Free's last studio album, 'Wishing Well' was one of the heaviest tracks the band recorded. By now guitarist Paul Kossoff was in poor health and did not play on the track, although he received a writing credit. It was Rodgers who did a very passable imitation of Kossoff's patented lead wail, running a guitar through what sounds like a Leslie speaker. The riff itself is a descending E pentatonic minor scale, divided into two parts: E-D-B-A, B-A-G-E. The first four notes are repeated before it comes to rest on a G5 chord. Later in the song the riff is transposed to A pentatonic minor, by shifting the fingering across one string.

Artist	Free
Title	'The Stealer'
Writer	Fraser/Rodgers/Kossoff
Released	single: (UK) Island, 1970; (US), A&M, 1970
	album: *Highway*, Island/A&M, 1970

'The Stealer' is an excellent example of an A pentatonic minor single-note riff. It breaks into three parts: there's A-G-A in the bass, then a C-A and up an octave to A, and finally a C slid to D, with the open D-string also hit. Doubling a fretted note with an open string was one of Paul Kossoff's guitar trademarks. The riff has effective rhythm (punctuated by Fraser's typically loping bass), unexpected changes of direction, and resonance. It's recorded in stereo or double-tracked. Listen for the overdubs during the verse. The riff continues but its effect is altered by the high guitar chords on top, which add a new dimension. The second chord riff on this song uses the chords I-IV-*b*VII-IV. Other pentatonic minor Free riffs include 'Mr Big', with its memorable Em7 chord.

Artist	**Free**
Title	**'Heartbreaker'**
Writer	**Rodgers**
Released	**album: *Heartbreaker*, Island/A&M, 1973**

From the same album as 'Wishing Well', the title track (not to be confused with Led Zeppelin's 'Heartbreaker') makes fine use of a heavy, multi-tracked D pentatonic minor scale. The interesting point about the notes is the way the riff starts not on D but on A and works up the scale, A-C-D-F-G-A, before dropping back to D. In other words, the key note is displaced into the middle of the riff. The timing also plays a significant role: the riff starts on the second beat of a slow 4/4 time and arrives on D in the second bar, but the phrasing makes the riff sound more like a bar of 3/4 and one of 5/4 rather than two bars of 4/4. The slow groove is typical Free, though the thickened guitars and ambient sound give it more impact than their earlier songs.

Compare this with Ten Years After's 'Love Like A Man' (B-D-D#/E-D-B-D*b*-G-E) which is a tone higher and has the same finger pattern with the root on the fifth fret and in the middle. The riff is used throughout the verse. Other relevant Free songs here are 'The Hunter' – which has a G pentatonic minor riff with a G major chord on the third beat of each bar of G from time to time, which makes it sound like Cream – and 'I'll Be Creeping', in which the first part of the riff is in B pentatonic minor but the second part is a major chord with a D-D# hammer-on.

Artist	**The Temptations**
Title	**'Ball Of Confusion'**
Writer	**Whitfield/Strong**
Released	**single: (UK) Tamla Motown, 1970; (US) Gordy, 1970**

Much of this book concentrates on rock riffs, but riffs are also a big feature in soul, funk and R&B. 'Ball Of Confusion' gives a profound insight into what can be done with the idea of a pentatonic minor riff contrasting with major harmony. It's a typical Norman Whitfield 'groove' song, with a repetitive two-bar C pentatonic minor bass riff churning beneath the C major harmony. On top, guitars add strange licks with echo, notably on the dramatic intro with Dennis Edwards' arresting count-in (listen on headphones and you can hear the amps buzzing), and the brass section has the occasional jazzy flourish. Every now and again there's an arpeggiated bridge using C, F and G, with a punchy James Brown-type link — but the rhythmic drive of the riff is relentless. The music can be simple because of the clever division of the lyric among the Temps' contrasting voices.

The lesson here is that a riff placed in the bass doesn't quite collide with the vocal in the way that it would if it were higher-pitched on guitar. Whitfield & Strong used similar riff ideas, drawing on the I, III, IV, and bVII of the pentatonic minor, in songs such as 'Psychedelic Shack', 'You Make Your Own Heaven And Hell Right Here On Earth', and 'Papa Was A Rollin' Stone'. A distant relative of this type of pentatonic minor riff on the bass occurs (improbably) on Gomez's 'Get Myself Arrested', the Stone Roses' 'Daybreak' (on bass), Black Rebel Motorcycle Club's 'White Palms', and Living Colour's 'Middle Man', which is in C minor but with B as well as B*b* in the riff.

"a riff placed in the bass doesn't quite collide with the vocal in the way it would if it were higher-pitched on guitar"

Artist	Black Sabbath
Title	'The Warning'
Writer	Iommi/Butler/Ward/Osbourne
Released	album: *Black Sabbath*, Vertigo/Warners, 1970

Tony Iommi found his own variations on the pentatonic minor riffs common in late 1960s hard rock. The Sabs' debut album has 'The Wizard' (A pentatonic minor, semitone A5-Bb5 change for the verse), 'Behind The Wall Of Sleep' (A pentatonic minor, A5-B5 riff on bridge), 'Evil Woman' (centred on G with the blues derived flattened seventh and flattened third notes), and 'The Warning' with its D-F/I-*b*III riff. 'The Warning' uses a popular structure of the time: take a 12-bar sequence, play four riffs on the key note, two riffs transposed up a fourth, two riffs on the key note and then, where chord V would have been in bar nine, add something else. Occasionally riffs are transposed up a fourth or, in 'Evil Woman', a sixth.

Artist	The Strokes
Title	'Alone, Together'
Writer	Casablancas
Released	album: *Is This It*, Rough Trade 2001

As you might expect from The Strokes, here's an A pentatonic minor riff presented in a very different musical style to hard rock. This is spiky New York new millennium new wave. The one-bar riff is played a mere four times, which takes all of ten seconds, and then we're into verse 1. It crops up twice after two lines of lyric, and then four times after the next two lines of lyric. During the chorus the guitar that was playing the riff follows the vocal melody, while the other guitar plays chords in straight eighths. When the riff is playing it isn't doubled by either the second guitar or the bass, so the arrangement has more breathing space.

At about 1.45 the riff is heard with an A minor chord, making the minor tonality explicit. Listen out for the minimalist guitar solo toward the end. At the three-minute mark the riff makes two more appearances before the song suddenly finishes. There's no attempt to use the riff for any serious head-banging.

Artist	The White Stripes
Title	'Expecting'
Writer	J White/M White
Released	album: *White Blood Cells*, Sympathy For The Record Industry/V2, 2001

Another band who were getting a good deal of press in 2001 were Detroit duo The White Stripes, possibly rock's first ever power-duo – since they don't have a bass player. Jack White is a man obviously in love with the sound of an electric guitar. 'Expecting' comes across as a garage band trying to do Black Sabbath. The main riff, played in fifths, uses the I, *b*III and *b*VII of the pentatonic minor (D-F-C) and transposes it down a fourth onto A (A-C-G). The Stripes' idea of recording as live as possible is evident in the delightful fluctuations in the tempo. No click tracks here...

11. THE BLUES SCALE RIFF

There's an important variation on the pentatonic minor, known as the blues scale. This is created when the flattened fifth is added between the fourth and fifth. This is the note that was discussed in the section on the tritone in Section One of the riffs.

Here are two blues scales:

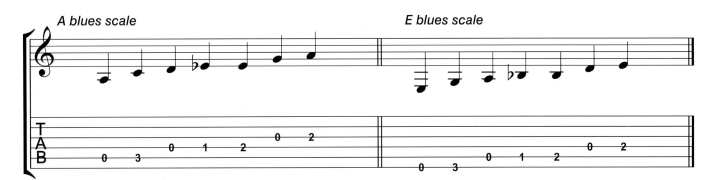

The notes in A are A-C-D-E*b*-E-G. In lead playing the extra note (E*b*) is often heard when the D is bent up a semitone, but it can also be fretted as a note in its own right. Add it to the pentatonic minor if you want a riff to have a bit more colour, and to have more step-wise movement. The flattened fifth is an example of what's known as a chromatic passing note. The word chromatic literally means 'colour', which in musical terms means a note that does not usually belong to the scale (of A pentatonic minor in this instance).

Along with the pentatonic minor, the blues scale is found everywhere in rock. Mountain's 'One Last Cold Kiss' has an A blues scale riff, structured a1, a2, a1, a3, with the flattened fifth achieved via a bend. The Queens Of The Stone Age's 'Leg Of Lamb' has a bend from A*b* up to A, with a low D sounded underneath the A*b* (a tritone), and then finishes off with the lower part of the D blues scale. Black Sabbath's 'Rat Salad' is a kind of 'Moby Dick' drum solo/riff number based on a G blues scale (G-B*b*-C-D*b*-D). The Eagles' 'Life In The Fast Lane' starts with an E blues riff that makes good use of variation of the initial idea.

Artist	**Cream**	
Title	**'Sunshine Of Your Love'**	
Writer	**Bruce/Brown/Clapton**	
Released	**album: *Disraeli Gears*, Reaction (UK)/Atco (US), 1967**	
	Single: (US) Atco, 1968; (UK) Polydor, 1968	

RIFF GALLERY:
blues scale riffs

Cream were rock's original power-trio, linking high-volume blues-influenced riffing with live improvisations and Pete Brown's poetic lyrics. The riff to 'Sunshine' became one of the most-played rock riffs: it's based on a D blues scale (D-F-G-A*b*-A-C) and terminates with a D-F-D phrase which is either above or below the riff, depending on where in the song it is. After its initial statement in single notes the first D-D-C-D is turned into dominant seventh chords. This is a good example of how a single-note riff can be partially harmonised. During the verse the D riff is played four times before the whole thing is transposed onto G. Clapton's mellow front-pickup distortion is the icing on the cake.

Cream were one of Hendrix's favourite bands. The *Live At The Winterland* album has Hendrix lamenting, in his best stoned drawl, that Cream are splitting up, by way of introducing his version of 'Sunshine'. "It's not saying that we're better than them [amused smirk] but we'd like to do it in our own way, which is an instrumental loose jam-type scene..." At which point the Experience plough into 'Sunshine', faster than the original, with Jimi performing his usual minor miracles in keeping the riff going and interjecting scraps of the melody. Seek it out...

Artist	**Led Zeppelin**
Title	**'Heartbreaker'**
Writer	**Plant/Page/Jones/Bonham**
Released	**album: *Led Zeppelin II*, Atlantic, 1970**

Originally blasting off the second side of the vinyl album of *Led Zeppelin II*, 'Heartbreaker' is a classic example of how to get the most out of a riff by transposition. It uses an A blues scale riff of two one-bar phrases; the second has four 16th-note As instead of a single A. The riff is then transposed to B and back to A, and for the middle-eight transposed to C, D and E in turns. The effect of these transpositions in quick succession is mounting excitement culminating in the sudden stop on E. The riff is reinforced with Jones playing a bass distorted through a Leslie speaker.

'Heartbreaker' is very inventive hard rock. If you put it alongside comparable material on *Physical Graffiti* it's noticeable how many more ideas are crammed into this earlier song. For example, there are several other riffs *after* the guitar solo, one of which is based on the scale A-C-C#-G-F#-E, before the original riff returns.

Artist	**Led Zeppelin**
Title	**'Bring It On Home'**
Writer	**Page/Plant/Dixon**
Released	**album: *Led Zeppelin II*, Atlantic, 1970**

Sometimes it's not just how good a riff you have, but how well it's introduced. 'Bring It On Home' may be a bit of a steal from the blues repertoire, but they don't owe a debt to anyone else for the sheer drama with which the central section is kicked off with a blast of harmonica and the explosive first few plays of this E blues scale riff. The basic notes are E pentatonic minor, with the blues flattened fifth coming in as a bend from A. The riff also cleverly contrasts the blues flattened third G with the major third G#. It's also a great example of harmonising a riff, since Page doubles two octaves up – in the film *The Song Remains The Same* you can quite clearly see Page harmonising the riff several octaves plus a third above the bassline.

The vocal sections use a *b*III-IV-I progression. For other examples of a I-*b*III-IV chord riff listen to Rory Gallagher's 'Cradle Rock', Red Hot Chili Peppers' 'Higher Ground', Black Rebel Motorcycle Club's 'Spread Your Love', and Norman Greenbaum's 'Spirit In The Sky'.

Artist	**Fleetwood Mac**
Title	**'Oh Well (Part 1)'**
Writer	**Green**
Released	**album: *Then Play On*, Reprise, 1969**
	Single: (UK) Reprise, 1969; (US) Reprise, 1970

Before they metamorphosed into mid-1970s AOR icons with West Coast harmonies and platinum hooks, there was another Fleetwood Mac, spoken of in

"sometimes it's not just how good a riff you have, but how well it's introduced"

more reverential tones by people who bought their records in the late 1960s – when, at one point, it was said they were out-selling the Beatles and rivalling Led Zeppelin in the polls. This was the band's first incarnation, a triple-guitar blues-oriented line-up led by Peter Green.

It was Green that made Fleetwood Mac a band to be remembered. Not only did he have a fine voice for the blues, his lead playing had a finesse to match anything by Beck, Clapton, Kossoff or Page. His distinctive sensitivity can be heard on tracks like 'Need Your Love So Bad', 'Love That Burns', the minor-key 'Black Magic Woman' (later popularised by Santana), and the hit 'Albatross'. Few rock bands have played so poetically as the Mac on these numbers.

Their best album is *Then Play On*, from which 'Oh Well' is taken. The shuffley rhythm suggests it might have been initially written on acoustic guitar, and then arranged for the band. The somewhat African feel of the rhythm is something Mac were good at, and recalls The Who's exotic percussion on 'Magic Bus', as well as Santana. Riff 1 enters on acoustic guitar and is then doubled by lead guitar and bass. It's made of four phrases drawing on the E blues scale, starting with E pentatonic minor, and then bringing in additional notes to the scale. Riff 2 is a tone-shift single-note riff D-E. Riff 3 is a I-bIII-bVII which culminates in an ascending scale. There is considerable doubling of the guitars throughout.

Artist	**Aerosmith**
Title	**'Walk This Way'**
Writer	**Tyler/Perry**
Released	**album: *Toys In The Attic*, CBS/Columbia, 1975**
	single: CBS/Columbia, 1975

The virtues of this classic riff, later recycled by Run DMC for their version in the late 1980s, are not so much the choice of notes (E blues scale: E, G, A, Bb and B) or the octave drop from E down to E, but its rhythm (quick little bursts) and the rude flickers of damped guitar strings that punctuate it. The most telling feature of the song from the harmonic point of view is that the chorus is in C major and uses a C-F change, but the riff and choruses are in E. The first solo is in C as well, hence the shock of the abrupt shift back to E major at 1.23. Near the end of the song, at 2.43, there's another switch back to E. The riff itself is invested with extra innuendo because the lyric introduces the riff's appearance with the phrase, "like this".

Artist	**Van Halen**
Title	**'Jamie's Cryin''**
Writer	**E Van Halen/A Van Halen/Anthony/Roth**
Released	**album: *Van Halen*, Warners, 1978**
	single: (US) Warners, 1978

Van Halen's debut album is dominated by the guitar-playing of Eddie Van Halen, especially the lead dexterity and tapping demonstrated on tracks like 'Eruption'. But there are some mighty riffs present too: for instance, tons of bands had already covered 'You Really Got Me', but Van Halen provide a chunky take on the chord riff on their cover of that Kinks classic (also their debut single).

'Jamie's Cryin'' features a single-note riff descending the E blues scale (using the notes E, G, A and Bb) and a variation with a cleverly voiced E7 in which both D and B are fretted and doubled by an open string. The sonority of this chord is extended by Van Halen's amp distortion/phasing set-up. Notice how the descending four notes are shifted forward one eighth-note during the variation

"you can create variation in a riff by moving some notes backwards or forwards a beat"

(at 0.12), and the triplet arpeggio figure at 0.33 on the phrase "so sad". This type of triplet arpeggio always puts breadth into a single-note riff. You can create variation in a riff by moving some notes backwards or forwards a beat, or portion of a beat.

The riff is the basis for the guitar solo, around the two-minute mark, with Eddie supplying one outrageously 'vocal' bend at 2.02.

Artist	Jimi Hendrix
Title	'Fire'
Writer	Hendrix
Released	album: *Are You Experienced*, Track/Reprise, 1967

And now, another jewel of a riff from the Crown Prince of the Strat. Today's gem of wisdom from the guitar works of Jimi concerns visible guitar techniques and 'invisible' ones. A *visible* guitar technique is one people notice, like playing squillions of notes a second, grappling with the tremolo to get dive-bombing noises, or playing behind your back. An *invisible* technique is one people would only notice if you got it wrong, but they don't notice it when it's done correctly. Into this category falls string-damping. At the high volume levels at which he played, Hendrix had to be very good at string-damping. A highly amplified electric guitar is quite a beast to tame. He needed to be adept at positioning his fretting fingers so they would hold down notes *and* cut off unwanted strings at the same time.

This technique was necessary in a song like 'Fire' because the riff is a D blues scale at the tenth position, coming in on the flattened fifth (A♭), but played in octaves on strings five and three. By damping the other four strings, Hendrix was able to whack the whole lot and only get the octave pair to ring (the rest gave him a percussive noise). The riff itself is four bars long. The octave phrase occurs in bars 1 and 2; bars 3 and 4 use the notes A-C-D twice – this little phrase also supports the verse. (Hendrix was fond of octaves. You can hear them in 'Purple Haze' and '51st Anniversary'.) Notice that Hendrix transposes the chords on the chorus up a tone for the two guitar solos, but he doesn't transpose the riff itself.

Artist	Jimi Hendrix
Title	'Voodoo Chile (Slight Return)'
Writer	Hendrix
Released	album: *Electric Ladyland*, Track/Reprise, 1968 single: (UK) Track, 1970

Even in its shorter hard rock arrangement, 'Voodoo Chile' reveals its origins in the blues. Rock guitarists are familiar with the three-chord 12-bar format, but there are plenty of blues songs that never stray from their initial chord. It may not have the same definition as some of Hendrix's own riffs, but the basic idea of the guitar accompaniment can still be considered a riff.

Hendrix splits up the strings of the E chord, creating a bassline with a minor third E-G-E climb, a stab of harmony every time he hits the fretted notes of the chord, a strident fourth from the top two open strings, and a blues scale lead lick at the end of the bar. He makes many subtle rhythmic and tonal changes to this single-bar idea. The longer version of 'Voodoo Chile' makes the blues element more overt. If you like Hendrix in this vein, seek out what, in my opinion, is his deepest blues, 'Hear My Train A'Comin' – listen to the live version preserved on the *Jimi Hendrix Concerts* album.

The British Blues Boom produced plenty of songs with this kind of riff, for instance the Groundhogs' 'Mistreated', with its naked debt to Muddy Waters' 'Catfish Blues'.

Artist	**Lenny Kravitz**
Title	**'Are You Gonna Go My Way'**
Writer	**Kravitz/Ross**
Released	**single: (UK) Virgin, 1993**
	album: *Are You Gonna Go My Way*, Virgin, 1993

This may not be the world's most original riff, but it certainly hit the right spot for a lot of people, including guitarists, as 'Are You Gonna Go My Way' joined the list of 'must learn' riffs. There are some useful tips to gain from the arrangement here too.

The main riff is on the E blues scale, the Bb created by a bend from A. The riff is two bars, with bar 2 as an answering phrase that ends with a strident fourth (D-G) on the top two strings. Notice that since there isn't a G# anywhere to be heard, the implied chord is Em7, not the Hendrix chord of E7#9. When the vocal comes in that fourth disappears from the riff (it would have got in the way of the words). The first neat touch is a transposition of the riff from E minor up a minor third to G minor. The riff finds its way back down via some accentuated chromatic notes. The hook-line is supported by a short chord riff higher up the neck using a tone-shift E to D to E, and then a minor third E to G to E. A mixolydian chord sequence of E, D, A is used for the guitar solo.

When you have absorbed the guitar part, take time to listen to the rhythm section. The drums and bass provide just the right backing to give the riff maximum 'bounce', so listen for where the bass guitar leaves notes out, for example. Another Kravitz song, 'Rock And Roll Is Dead', has a riff using the A blues scale (A-C-D-Eb-E-G) and starts with a chromatic approach to the A by way of G and G#; and during the guitar solo the riff is transposed up a fourth to D.

"the drums and bass provide just the right backing to give the riff maximum bounce"

Artist	**Kingdom Come**
Title	**'Living Out Of Touch'**
Writer	**L Woolf/M Wolff**
Released	**album: *Kingdom Come*, Polydor, 1988**

Kingdom Come caused a ripple in heavy rock circles with this debut in the late 1980s, with its audacious attempt to recreate the sound of Led Zeppelin. 'Living Out Of Touch' is a half-decent hard rock number that starts with an A pentatonic minor riff structured a1, a2, a1, a3, with a3 bringing in the flattened fifth of the blues scale. Underneath, the bass moves from A to G. The verse mostly works an Am-F change with a well-placed four-note fill to wake up anyone in the back row. During the guitar solo the verse's chord change is transposed to Bm-G and later to C#m-A. Towards the end the first riff is transposed up a tone to B.

The best part is the second riff, which comes in the coda. This uses A, Bb, B and D from the E blues scale, with the flattened seventh D heavily weighted by repetition. Along with the Bonham-esque drums the effect is rather good, in a Zep-ish way. A similar riff in the same key can be heard on the Alex Harvey Band's 'Midnight Moses' (on *Framed*, 1973), and in Jeff Buckley's 'Last Goodbye'.

12. THE PENTATONIC MAJOR RIFF

There is also a *major* form of the pentatonic from which you can create riffs. In A its notes are A-B-C#-E-F#. Here it is in A and E:

A pentatonic major   *E pentatonic major*

Notice that the first three notes are each a tone apart. This scale is the first, second, third, fourth, fifth and sixth of the ordinary major scale. So when you play a riff based on the pentatonic major over a major chord backing you won't get the same 'tough' sound that the pentatonic minor gives. This is because none of these notes are 'blue' notes; they're all contained within the harmony and therefore blend in. If you try to use this scale over minor chords in A minor it sounds fairly horrible.

The pentatonic major scale is good for riffs that are bright and up-beat. It was popular in 1950s rock'n'roll, and lends itself to 12/8 or triplet-type rhythms, and also to an arpeggio-style riff using A-C#-E-F# and up to the octave A. Like the pentatonic minor, this scale has a blues variant where the flattened third (here C) is added to the scale, giving A-B-C-C#-E-F#. Suede used this variant for the riff of 'Elephant Man' in E (using E-F#-G-G#-B-C# and transposing the riff up a tone to F# for the last chorus). Other related riffs include T.Rex's 'Thunderwing' (in A), 'Beltane Walk' and 'Baby Boomerang' (both E), Dire Straits 'Walk Of Life', Jimmy McCracklin's 'The Walk', and Free's 'Ride A Pony' (E-G-G#-B-C#-E) where the blues riff is transposed onto A in the verse. David Bowie's 'TVC15' has a pentatonic major riff consisting of an upward run with a third hammer-on at the top, over a I-VI chord change.

RIFF GALLERY:
pentatonic major riffs

Artist	**Jimi Hendrix**
Title	**'Spanish Castle Magic'**
Writer	**Hendrix**
Released	**album: *Axis Bold As Love*, Track, 1967**

'Spanish Castle Magic' is a great piece of riff-writing, for several reasons. For a start, there haven't been as many great rock riffs written on the pentatonic major as the pentatonic minor. Hendrix wrote this in E, with the main notes being the bottom open E-string, C# and the E an octave above. He fills in the musical space by hitting a B-E fourth with the top two open strings, with the B possibly doubled on the third string at the fourth fret to get more resonance. For the chorus, instead of coming back to the E riff, Hendrix transposes up a fourth to A, twice, before returning to the E riff. This unexpected transposition creates a sunny, uplifting emotion. The riff has another transposition, up a tone to F#, where it's given a simplified form for the guitar solo.

This song's other riff feature is the use of fourths as inverted fifths during the verses, making it sound as though Hendrix has drastically detuned to get notes that seem so low. The first two chords of the verse are fifths, but the next two are fourths (at 0.17 and 0.26 in verse one). The choice of notes makes them seem lower than they really are.

Artist	**The Temptations**
Title	**'My Girl'**
Writer	**Robinson/White**
Released	**single: (US) Gordy, 1964; (UK) Stateside, 1965**
	album: *Temptations Sing Smokey*, Tamla, 1965

After several years simmering, 1964/65 was when Motown came to the boil in the charts. One of the company's biggest early hits was this gentle love song, penned by Smokey Robinson as a pairing to 'My Guy', and sung impeccably by David Ruffin, one great voice out of five in the Temptations. Motown records were not often arranged around guitar riffs, and where they do occur they have more of a supporting role than in rock. But occasionally the guitar does contribute a hook figure, as with the Four Tops' 'Something About You', and here in 'My Girl'. The verse works a I-IV chord change in C (C-F), and over this the guitar plays a C pentatonic major run (C-D-E-G-A-C) and then a similar pentatonic major run on F (F-G-A-C-D-F). For the last verse the song modulates to D major so the figure gets pushed up a tone. The guitar is remarkably clear and bright on the first verse, but pulled back for the second when the strings take over.

Artist	**Marmalade**
Title	**'Radancer'**
Writer	**Nicholson**
Released	**single: (UK) Decca, 1972; (US) London, 1972**

As well as a UK number one with their cover of The Beatles 'Ob-la-di-ob-la-da', and a US top ten with 'Reflections Of My Life', Marmalade also had the pleasure of knowing that their single 'I See The Rain' was one of Hendrix's favourite records of 1967. 1972's 'Radancer' sounds like an emulation of the then chart-dominating T.Rex, in particular 'Telegram Sam', which had been at number one in January that year, though the vocal delivery owes something to The Beach Boys. The riff is a two-bar figure using a I-VI-V (A-F#-E) sequence in A major on the bass strings. The second bar is a rhythmic variation of the first. During the verse the riff is transposed up a fourth to D, while another figure is used when the 12-bar derived verse reaches the obligatory E chord.

Unfortunately, the song itself doesn't live up to the riff, or the title. But those opening 15 seconds are exquisite, with a funky rock'n'roll guitar tone. Maybe one day someone will sample it.

T.Rex's 'Ride A White Swan' has a similar pentatonic major riff on the top two strings (in A♭, capo at fret IV). Van Halen's 'DOA' has a detuned, heavier version of the 'Radancer' idea. The intro of Badfinger's 'No Matter What' and Slade's 'Gudbuy T' Jane' reverse the direction of the V-VI-I idea on an A chord.

"the pentatonic major scale is good for riffs that are bright and up-beat"

Artist	**Roxy Music**
Title	**'Street Life'**
Writer	**Ferry**
Released	**single (UK): Island, 1973**
	album: *Stranded*, Island (UK); Atco (US), 1973

The early albums of Roxy Music were a far cry from the sophistication of their 1980s output, such as *Avalon*. Odd lyrics delivered by Ferry in a distinctly un-rockish quasi-crooning style were set to even odder structures and quirky parts supplied by Brian Eno and Phil Manzanera. Manzanera's guitar work was shaped by his lack of schooling in the typical blues-rock of the time, a lack he turned to his creative advantage.

The riff of 'Street Life' occurs throughout the verse. It consists of notes taken from a B♭ pentatonic major scale (B♭-C-D-F-G) played over the chord sequence B♭-E♭-A♭-F. The initial note B♭ of the riff is held over the first three chords and then the other notes are played over the F. Manzanera thus avoids distracting from the vocal because the run-up falls when Ferry is usually between phrases. Clever teamwork. On the fourth time there is an extra C note. At 1.25 Manzanera transposes and alters this run, starting on D♭, to lead into the next verse. It's a fine example of 'part-playing', where the guitar part complements the whole arrangement, rather than screaming for the spotlight. A riff can be an accompaniment and still be a hook.

COMPARING SCALES

Major, pentatonics and blues scale in E:

1	2	3	4	5	6	7
E major						
E	F#	G#	A	B	C#	D#
E pentatonic major						
E	F#	G#		B	C#	
E pentatonic minor						
E		G	A	B		D
E blues scale						
E		G	A B♭ B			D

This diagram reveals that all of these four scales have E and B. The pentatonic major is an abbreviated version of the full major, with notes four and seven dropped. The pentatonic minor, compared to the major, has the third and seventh flattened.

13. THE MAJOR SCALE RIFF

The major scale has been the basis for most Western music for about four centuries. It consists of *seven* notes arranged in a sequence of intervals: tone, tone, semitone, tone, tone, tone, semitone. In frets this is 2-2-1-2-2-2-1. Hold down any note on any string below the tenth fret (assuming you have a 22-fret electric guitar). Play it, then move up the string according to the 2-2-1-2-2-2-1 pattern, playing each note as you go, to hear a major scale.

The notes for a scale of C major are C-D-E-F-G-A-B. The semitone gaps between notes three and four, seven and eight, just happen to coincide with E-F and B-C, the two pairs of notes which need to be a semitone apart. If we start on any other note some in the scale must be lowered or raised to preserve this pattern. Thus in the scale of E major (E-F#-G#-A-B-C#-D#) four sharps are required to get the right 'gaps' (see below).

Though not as popular for riffs as the pentatonics, the blues scale or the mixolydian mode, the major scale is vital as a fundamental musical reference point. In fact, because it isn't used as much it offers an opportunity to make riffs sound different to the majority of those played by rock bands. For examples, listen to

tracks like The Offspring's 'Walla Walla', the intro riff to Sum 41's 'Fat Lip', or the Strokes' 'Barely Legal', where notes from the G major pentatonic scale are played on the intro over G and C chords. Springsteen's 'Born In The USA' has a three-note keyboard motif using E, F# and G# from the scale of B major (the fourth, fifth and sixth), which is then heard against an E chord. Another approach to the major scale, used by the Smashing Pumpkins on songs like 'Mayonaise', is to harmonise the major scale in fifths and make riffs out of those fifths. This creates interesting effects such as the occurrence of fifths on the major third and seventh instead of the blues flattened third and flattened seventh.

A major scale riff may well be easier to sing along with than other types of scale. Genesis made a four-note riff of the first four notes of G major in 'Follow You, Follow Me' which became the chorus melody.

RIFF GALLERY:
major scale riffs

Artist	**Them (featuring Van Morrison)**
Title	**'Here Comes The Night'**
Writer	**Berns**
Released	**single: (UK) Decca, 1965; (US) Parrot, 1965**
	album: *Them*, Decca/Parrot, 1965

Singer Van Morrison first came to fame with the band Them, lending his vocals to hits like 'Baby Please Don't Go', and 'Here Comes The Night'. Over the opening E-A chord change a five-note riff is played that owes something to Duane Eddy. It's pitched low on the guitar with a slightly 'woody' tone, and uses the notes B-E-B-C#-A (derived from E major). The fifth time, a variation is introduced in order to fit the underlying B chord that leads into the verse, with its change of rhythm. A distant relative of this riff crops up on Springsteen's 'Born To Run'.

Artist	**The Four Tops**
Title	**'I'm In A Different World'**
Writer	**Holland/Dozier/Holland**
Released	**single: (US) Motown; (UK) Tamla Motown, 1968**
	album: *Yesterday's Dreams*, (US) Motown, 1968;
	(UK) 1969

This Four Tops single, the last written for them by the H/D/H team, features remarkable changes of key and some beautiful guitar chords. But the aspect we're focusing on here is the two-bar guitar riff that crops up in the bridge section at 0.37, mostly doubled by the bass, and again at 1.47 and 2.20. The scale is Gb major with the seventh omitted, and the guitar tone is clear. The riff is supported by a I-IV-VI chord sequence in Gb (Gb-Cb-Db, or think of it in F# if you prefer, as F#-B-C#). The major scale is crucial to making this riff express the optimistic, joyful emotion in the lyric.

Artist	**Amen Corner**
Title	**'Bend Me Shape Me'**
Writer	**English/Weiss**
Released	**single (UK): Deram, 1968**
	album: *Around Amen Corner*, Deram, 1968

Amen Corner were a 1960s pop outfit whose songs were characterised by the feathery vocals of Andy Fairweather-Low. This bubble-gum song with a hint of Motown (which was a US hit for The American Breed in 1967, and paid homage to by Badly Drawn Boy on *The Hour Of Bewilderbeast*) is driven by a superb descending riff that occurs on the intro and through most of the verse. The first four notes are E-C#-B-G# – which could have come from a 1950s 'The Walk'-type riff. Instead, they're rounded off with an A and F#. The only note omitted from the E major scale is D#. The riff fits over a chord sequence of E, B, A, F#m. On both the E and B chords the riff moves to the note that implies the relative minor of these chords – C#m and G#m are relative to E and B. The riff is carried by the piano, bass and brass instruments to give a strong ensemble performance. At about 1.43 the riff is played by trumpets.

The tip here is to try writing a riff that can run through a strong chord sequence.

Artist	**Status Quo**
Title	**'Paper Plane'**
Writer	**Rossi/Young**
Released	**single: (UK) Vertigo, 1973; (US) A&M, 1973**
	album: *Piledriver*, Vertigo/A&M, 1973

Status Quo emerged riding the coat-tails of psychedelia, and reached the Top 20 with the mildly lysergic 'Pictures Of Matchstick Men'. But by the early 1970s they had turned into a blue-denimed, eight-armed, four-headed, hair-shaking, Telecaster-thrashing beast of 12-bar boogie. In the context of a Top 20 dominated by Donny Osmond, David Cassidy and the Sweet, Quo were a fresh breath of stale, sweaty air.

The Quo were not really a riffs band. They didn't believe in breathing spaces, for a start. Most of their songs featured that good old rock'n'roll 'V-VI' shuffle figure – alternating root note + fifth with root note + sixth – with precious few gaps. 'Paper Plane' earns its citation here because it includes a clever variation. The riff is a B*b* shuffle at fret six, lasting two bars. In bar two, from the third off-beat, three eighth-notes suddenly flash into view (Eb-D-C) and flow into the B*b* that starts the next bar. These notes imply the Bb major scale. The transition between the boogie shuffle pattern and these notes is seamless – a fine bit of guitar fingering.

Artist	**Queen**
Title	**'Bohemian Rhapsody'**
Writer	**Mercury**
Released	**single: (UK) EMI, 1975; (US) Elektra, 1975**
	album: *A Night At The Opera*, EMI/Elektra, 1975

This riff was famously immortalised in the first *Wayne's World* film, in a sequence where an outbreak of headbanging takes place in a car, but some readers will recall the winter of 1975 when 'Bohemian Rhapsody' took up what seemed like a permanent position at the British number one slot.

Sometimes with a riff, placing is everything. The riff here comes after the mock-operatic middle of the track, which climaxes with a B*b* chord topped with a note (sung by Roger Taylor) so high it can induce altitude sickness. With a crash the band re-enter playing a four-bar riff in E*b*. The key is unusual, since the guitar is not given to flat keys like B*b* and Eb, where most of its open strings are ineffectual. This was a consequence of 'Bo Rhap' having been composed by

"sometimes with a riff, placing is everything"

Mercury on piano. Writing a riff in a less-guitar friendly key may enable you to come up with something different, and to make unusual use of open strings.

Anyone who's worked the riff out on guitar will have found that it doesn't sit comfortably under the fingers. It's also unusual because it's based on the major scale and does not have the flattened seventh so often used in rock. The first bar drops from E♭ to G and then ascends the Eb major scale (the only note missing is an F). Bar two has a variant that stops halfway up on the fifth, B♭. Bar three repeats bar one. Bar four transposes the idea of bar two onto F major.

Artist	**The Jam**
Title	**'Going Underground'**
Writer	**Weller**
Released	**single (UK): Polydor, 1980**

The Jam were not a band for riffs. Because of his early Townshend fixation, Paul Weller's approach was always rhythmic and chord-based, and, after all, who feels like playing low-string, heavy riffs on a Rickenbacker? Like The Edge, though for different reasons, Weller rejected the blues/rock vocabulary of the 1970s guitar hero. It took him until the mid-1990s before his solo work drew selectively on British rock of the 1968-73 era. Yet, scattered through the Jam's output, there are some memorable guitar figures that count as riffs.

'Going Underground' starts with a multi-tracked riff that initially works the old rock'n'roll D5-D6 idea. The twist is that the riff culminates with a quick D-C#-B phrase – notes taken off the D major scale, when we might have expected a flattened seventh C natural. This riff is used for the first part of the verse before the sudden shift to B major for the rest. Alternation of keys (further developed by a lift to C# for the guitar solo and final chorus) is an important structural feature. The Jam's 'It's Too Bad' (from *All Mod Cons*) is another example of a major scale-based riff, on the chords G, C and D. Compare this with Supergrass' 'Tonight' where a rock'n'roll shuffle figure occurs with the major seventh instead of the blues flattened seventh.

14. THE MIXOLYDIAN RIFF

Having covered the major scale and the pentatonic minor and major, we come to a group of scales collectively known as *modes*. There are seven main modes, which date from ancient Greece and have always been present in Western music. Modes are simply scales that use a different pattern of intervals to the major scale. The Greeks called our major scale the Ionian mode, so we've already covered *that* one. To get the interval pattern for any mode, play from any 'natural' note (ie one of the white

A mixolydian   *E mixolydian*

keys on a piano – C, D, E, F, G, A or B) to its octave using no sharps or flats. This same interval pattern can then be generated from any starting note with the addition of the right sharps and flats.

Think of the mixolydian as being a variation on the major scale, because it is the same except for the seventh note, which is flattened by a semitone. Since rock music has flattened sevenths everywhere, the mixolydian mode is common. Rock singers habitually sing melodies in which the seventh note of the major scale is flattened, and it's also a common note alteration in riffs and lead guitar. It is easy to introduce into your playing: take any major scale pattern, locate the seventh note and move it back a semitone. This flattened seventh gives a mixolydian riff a 'harder' quality than the straight major scale riff, but the presence of the rest of the major scale makes for a more sophisticated scale than the pentatonic. If you want step-wise movement in a riff use the mixolydian.

For a funky E mixolydian riff, try Lenny Kravtiz's 'Always On The Run', where there are plenty of blues thirds added as well (in single notes and in the G chord on the chorus). In Bowie's 'Panic In Detroit', the verse chord change of D to E is threaded by a descending D mixolydian scale which stops on E; that note is treated as the root of an E major chord rather than the expected E minor. Led Zeppelin's 'Custard Pie' takes a classic rock'n'roll shuffle figure in A and extends it to the octave with a partial mixolydian run of E-F#-G-A over A. Smokey Robinson & The Miracles' 'Tears Of A Clown' is driven by a mixolydian bassline in D♭ using all the notes of the scale. Primal Scream's 'Rocks' and 'Jailbird', Green Day's 'Warning' (the complete mixolydian in A), and Ike & Tina Turner's 'Nutbush City Limits' all use mixolydian riffs.

RIFF GALLERY:
mixolydian mode riffs

Artist	The Animals
Title	'We've Gotta Get Out Of This Place'
Writer	Mann/Weil
Released	single: (UK) Columbia, 1965; (US) MGM, 1965

The Animals' most famous guitar moment is obviously 'House Of The Rising Sun', but that is an arpeggio accompaniment and lacks the rhythmic definition that turns a chord sequence into a riff. Instead, I've chosen 'We've Gotta Get Out Of This Place', propelled by a C mixolydian bass riff (C-D-E-F-G-A-B♭) in which only the D isn't used. The riff carries much of the first verse with only a cymbal and the voice. Other instruments come in but the bass just keeps going all the way to the first chorus at 1.11, where the chord changes to F. Notice also the second riff that comes in as a link to verse two, after chorus one, which goes I-♭VII-IV-V, twice. The lesson of the arrangement is: keep a riff going with different things happening on top to create tension.

Bass player Chas Chandler went on to manage a guitarist who had quite a flair for riffs – see under 'Hendrix, Jimi'...

Artist	Rolling Stones
Title	'(I Can't Get No) Satisfaction'
Writer	Richards/Jagger
Released	single: (UK) Decca, 1965; London, 1965
	album: (US) *Out Of Our Heads*, London, 1965

The riff for 'Satisfaction' came to Keith Richards in the middle of the night – he just managed to get it down before falling asleep again. It was originally conceived as a Stax-type horn line, but played on guitar over a stomping four-to-the-bar drumbeat, with sardonic little flickers of tambourine, it provided the perfect accompaniment for one of the 1960s' seminal tales of teenage frustration. The riff itself consists of only three notes – B, C#, and D – the fifth, sixth and flattened seventh of E major. Its innovation lies in starting on an E chord with a B rather than the root E. Secondly, the sound of the riff is defined by the supporting chords: D major under the D and A under the C#. The guitar line also stuck out at the time because of the fuzz tone used. A similar figure with a clean guitar sound can be heard on the Four Tops' 'Something About You'.

Artist	The Beatles
Title	'Taxman'
Writer	Harrison
Released	*Revolver*, (UK) Parlophone; (US) Capitol, 1965

'Taxman' has a vintage bass figure consisting of the notes I-VIII-IV-V-*b*VII, in this case starting in D major: D-D-G-A-C. During the verse this figure is transposed to the chords of C and G. In this song the guitar doesn't double the riff (as it would with such a riff in later heavy rock) but instead plays pungent slashing chords. In the absence of a third from the riff, which would determine whether the riff is D pentatonic minor or D mixolydian, it's these guitar chords, clearly major, that make us hear the riff as mixolydian. The riff was famously appropriated in the Jam's 'Start', and a similar one occurs in Jeff Beck's 'Rock My Plimsole', though there it has an additional note, the flattened fifth inserted between IV and V, and is taken at a slower speed. Variations on this mixolydian pattern, with the octave leap and no open strings, lend themselves to 12-bar blues because they are so easily transposed.

Artist	The Beatles
Title	Paperback Writer
Writer	Lennon/McCartney
Released	single: (UK) Parlophone; (US) Capitol, 1966

'Paperback Writer' features one of the Beatles' heaviest intros, thanks to the opening riff, and signalled a significant change in their music, away from the beat-pop of the early hits. The song itself is little more than a G-C change supporting a clever lyric. The riff is on the chord of G7, using notes I-IV-V-VIII-V-*b*VII (G-C-D-G-D-F), with several hammer-ons. After the complex vocal harmony which starts the song, the riff kicks in with maximum dynamic contrast, even without bass. Its power is evident despite the eccentric 1960s stereo mix that squashes it over to the left of the stereo image. The riff is comparable to the earlier 'I Feel Fine', though that had a noticeably cleaner guitar tone. As with 'Taxman', the rhythm guitar chords colour the riff as mixolydian, not pentatonic, despite the lack of a third in the riff.

Artist	Rolling Stones
Title	'Jumpin' Jack Flash'
Writer	Richards/Jagger
Released	single: (UK) Decca, 1968; (US) London, 1968

Here the Stones start to develop their mature riff style, compared to the early hits. This riff sounds as though it might be in fourths, but I don't think it is. It

> "the guitar doesn't double the riff – as it would with such a riff in later heavy rock"

starts with an emphatically struck B major chord and then a passage in single notes using IV-V-*b*VII of the scale (here E-F#-A) played three times. The effect of the riff lies in the harmonic 'drag' caused by the thrice-repeated emphasis on the flattened seventh, which is like a sulky child who has to be dragged back to the tonic B major chord and doesn't want to come. Jagger's drawling vocal only strengthens the impression. The remainder of the song uses E, D, A and B – in B major this is chords I, *b*III, IV and *b*VII. So the mixolydian influence is felt at the level of the chords as well.

Artist	**Deep Purple**
Title	**'Speed King'**
Writer	**Blackmore/Gillan/Glover/Lord/Paice**
Released	**album: *Deep Purple In Rock*, Harvest (UK), Warners (US), 1970**

The verse is built on a F, G, C, B*b* chord sequence (*b*VII, I, IV, III) but the interesting bit comes on the chorus where there's a riff using the notes C-B*b*, alternating several times, then dropping from the C down to the E (not E*b*, the blues third) which clearly implies the major scale, just as B*b* implies the mixolydian. As the riff climbs up we get E-F-F#-G – a flattened fifth F# inserted as a chromatic passing note. The drop to the E from C (a sixth) makes the E sound lower than it actually is. This is a well-known trick among bass players which guitarists have not taken as much advantage of as perhaps they might in constructing riffs. Hendrix does the same drop in 'Hey Joe' towards the end of the song when he brings in the single-note run over the C, G, D, A, E chord sequence. For a really funky riff, try chaining together several of these sixth drops in a rising phrase, and be mindful of where you put the accents.

Artist	**Queen**
Title	**'Now I'm Here'**
Writer	**May**
Released	**album: *Sheer Heart Attack*, EMI (UK), Elektra (US), 1974 single (UK): EMI, 1975**

Inspired by May's first experience of touring the US, 'Now I'm Here' remains one of the best hard rock tracks Queen ever recorded, and it paid tribute to Chuck Berry with its "go, go little Queenie" reference on the coda. It starts with damped fifths by May (possibly three guitars, left, centre and right) and then a descending sequence from D to C to B similar to that in Cream's 'Badge'. After Mercury's echoed vocal phrases, it erupts on a Who-like Asus4 A Bsus4 B roar ("just a new man") and then crashes into a 'Black-Dog'-like convoluted four-bar riff. This riff is unusual because of its length – it actually takes four bars to play it, as opposed to the standard practice of dividing the four bars into two answering phrases, or smaller single-bar units. May takes the notes from E mixolydian but adds G and B*b* as passing notes, giving a blues feel. In addition, some of the riff's notes are harmonised as fifths, giving it a chunky feel. When the riff appears at the coda it's cleverly altered to lead into the mixolydian B, E, A chord changes.

　　For a hard rock song 'Now I'm Here' has plenty of musical ideas to match its big arrangement. The song makes much use of transposition – taking phrases and moving them up in pitch. The verse daisy-chains a sequence of V-I cadences: a chord sequence of G, C, A, D, B, E, C#, F#, for example, on the "whatever came of you and me" part.

15. AEOLIAN MODE / NATURAL MINOR RIFFS

The most common minor scale for soloing in popular music is the natural minor or aeolian mode. In A minor this would be A-B-C-D-E-F-G:

Notice there are no sharps or flats needed to get the pattern of intervals, which is 2-1-2-2-1-2-2 if you start on A. The aeolian mode differs from the A pentatonic minor in adding two notes: B and F. These notes can be very expressive, and bring a new dimension to any aeolian-based riff. It's the inclusion of these notes that reveals whether a riff is made from the aeolian mode or merely the pentatonic minor.

There is another type of minor scale that can be used for an exotic riff: the harmonic minor. This involves one note change from the natural minor – the seventh note is raised a semitone to G#, which creates a large one-and-a-half tone jump between notes six and seven (F-G#), giving the scale an unusual flavour:

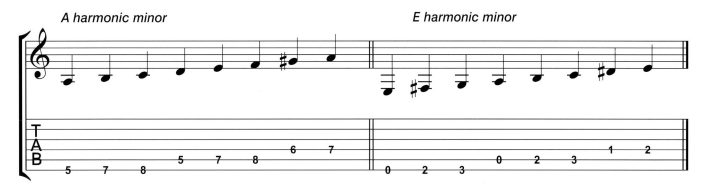

The harmonic minor can be heard in the riffs of Queen's 'Death On Two Legs' (and listen for the tritone on the 'false' intro) and 'Flick Of The Wrist' (the notes B, C, D#, E and F# taken from the E harmonic minor scale of E-F#-G-A-B-C-D#-E), and Robert Plant's 'Wreckless Love', which takes E-F-G#-A (the last four notes of an A harmonic minor) and plays them over an A5-G5 tone riff. UK band Muse end up with a 'classical' feel to some of their songs because of guitarist Matthew Bellamy's fondness for the harmonic minor, with E harmonic minor on 'Sunburn' and 'New Born', F# harmonic minor in 'Muscle Museum' (an F, or strictly-speaking E#, clearly heard at 1.54-2.00), and D harmonic minor in the solo on 'Micro Cuts' (2.42-3.06) and in 'Darkshines'. The chord sequences often imply the harmonic minor by having the major chord V in the minor key. 'Feeling Good', for example, is Gm, Gm/F, Eb, Dsus4, D – implying G harmonic minor.

COMPARING SCALES

Minor scales:

1	2	3	4	5	6	7
E pentatonic minor						
E		G	A	B		D
E natural minor						
E	F#	G	A	B	C	D
E harmonic minor						
E	F#	G	A	B	C	D#

RIFF GALLERY:
natural minor/aeolian riffs

Artist	**Paul Kantner, Grace Slick, David Freiburg**
Title	**'Flowers In The Night'**
Writer	**Kantner/Slick**
Released	album: ***Baron Von Tollbooth & The Chrome Nun*, Grunt/RCA, 1973**

In the 1970s the two leading lights of Jefferson Airplane, Paul Kantner and Grace Slick, made several spin-off albums; this was the second. It's a fine set of melodic songs with many of the Airplane trademarks and a dense production that ensures hours of listening pleasure as you discover new instrumental parts. This album dates from an era when musicians jammed lead guitar all the way through a track if they wished.

Drums kick off 'Flowers In The Night', and then, on the left, in comes a wonderful guitar riff that takes four bars to unfold its three phrases. The first phrase is two bars long, starts on the bottom E and uses the E blues scale but ends with G-F#-G. The second phrase is a rapid D major arpeggio (using the notes D, F# and A). The third is a descending phrase starting on the top string and ending with a bluesy A-B slide on the third string. The complete riff spans just over two octaves (over the chords Em, G, D and Em), has a superb upward motion, is played through much of the verse, and does slightly unexpected things *en route*. The basic scale is E natural minor/E aeolian (E-F#-G-A-B-C-D).

Artist	**Wishbone Ash**
Title	**'The King Will Come'**
Writer	**M Turner/D Turner/Powell/Upton**
Released	album: ***Argus*, (UK) MCA, 1972; (US) Decca, 1972**

Wishbone Ash were a staple of the UK rock circuit in the early 1970s, enjoying reasonable album sales while never quite moving into the same league as the big-hitters. For a rock band their albums have a very English, almost polite quality, which is a weakness for those who like their rock'n'roll 'red in tooth and claw', yet was part of their particular charm. But well before Thin Lizzy and Queen, Wishbone pioneered the harmony lead guitar approach, where improvisational solos would alternate with carefully arranged stretches of melodic playing.

First heard at 1.04, after the slow crescendo of the intro, the double-tracked riff of 'The King Will Come' is intriguing because it leaps an octave plus a minor sixth from a D on the fifth fret of the A-string to a clipped Bb on the sixth fret of the top E. The underlying scale is D natural minor (D-E-F-G-A-Bb-C). Listen also for the expressive vibrato on the low D each time. After the verse's end there is another riff on the same scale answered by high fourths, then a descending C-G/B arpeggio. During the first guitar solo you can hear the rhythm guitar and bass play a chordal version of the first riff. The track is full of nice guitar ideas – such as the almost Renbourn-like snap'n'roll lick from 4.25.

Two other tracks on *Argus* are worth attention from the riff point-of-view: first, the single 'Blowin' Free' with its top-string triads over a D pedal note; and 'Throw Down The Sword', with its riff harmonised in sixths.

Artist	**The Police**
Title	**'Walking On The Moon'**
Writer	**Sting**
Released	album: ***Reggatta De Blanc***, **A&M, 1979**
	single (UK): A&M, 1979

And now, a natural minor riff played on bass. Few chart records have ever used space so imaginatively in an arrangement as 'Walking On The Moon'. Alone in the reverb, with Copeland's rattling percussion hitting all kinds of accents unknown to rock'n'roll, Sting's bass plays the simplest of two-bar riffs, taking notes from D natural minor (C-C-D, F-E-C). In-between the two phrases of the riff, the guitar sends a Dm7add11 chord floating into the distance (its sustain enhanced by a quick echo and chorus). This soundscape was the perfect aural evocation of a metaphor: white-suited men slowly bouncing over moondust, weightless against black; a young man intoxicated by love, walking back from his girlfriend's house having presumably missed the last bus.

It just goes to prove that a riff doesn't have to be chained to the usual rock'n'roll themes.

16. THE DORIAN RIFF

The dorian mode can also be thought of as a minor mode. The A dorian scale is A-B-C-D-E-F#-G . The only difference between it and A natural minor is that the sixth note is sharpened. This gives the dorian a more 'angular', tense quality:

The sharpened sixth is not quite as 'depressed' as the sixth found on the natural minor scale. The analogy I like to use is that the aeolian mode represents a group of emotions like regret, sadness and melancholy which are passive and introverted, whereas the dorian makes them more active and extrovert. It's worth noticing that if you play the dorian mode in fifths (which might be likely in a rock riff) a C# will be introduced above the F#, the sixth of the scale:

This C# will temporarily undermine the sense of A dorian as a minor mode in which the third note should be C. Conversely, if you harmonise the aeolian mode in fifths, a dorian note will appear as a fifth above the second note of the scale. A aeolian is A-B-C-D-E-F-G. A fifth on B needs F#. A riff with this effect can be heard in Guns N' Roses' 'The Garden', where fifths are played on C#, E, D# and B.

The main exponent of the dorian mode in rock has probably been Carlos Santana, as a track like 'Oye Como Va' shows. Jimmy Page's guitar solo on the live version of Led Zep's 'No Quarter' also has a strong dorian flavour (as does his live solo on the *BBC Sessions* 'Immigrant Song'). The riff in Wings' James Bond song 'Live And Let Die' (later covered by Guns N' Roses) is constructed from a G dorian scale, in an a1, a2 form. Black Sabbath's 'Sleeping Village' starts with one of those acoustic arpeggio minor add9 chords that Metallica are fond of, before a main riff on A pentatonic major comes in, followed by a dorian A riff coming down A-G-F#-D-E (reminiscent of a phrase in *The Prisoner* TV series). There's a hint of the dorian in the Sabs' 'Looking For Today'. The Smashing Pumpkins' 'Quiet' has a dorian flavour, with the E dorian scale (E-F#-G-A-B-C#-D) harmonised in fifths, though the G# in C#5 often cancels out the minor third (E-G) of the dorian scale proper. Bon Jovi's 'Homeward Bound Train' is E dorian.

**RIFF GALLERY:
dorian mode riffs**

Artist	Thin Lizzy
Title	**'Don't Believe A Word'**
Writer	**Lynott**
Released	**album: *Johnny The Fox*, (UK) Vertigo, (US) Mercury, 1976 single (UK): Vertigo, 1976**

'Don't Believe A Word' opens with a dorian riff in A, with the lower guitar moving down from A to G to F# while the upper moves A-G-A. The upper guitar then comes down in thirds with the lower, so the riff develops as it repeats. Interestingly, the rest of the song features D minor chords which contain F natural, so it isn't consistently dorian. As a general point modes tend not to occur in rock in a 'pure' form where tracks stay absolutely within mode, both melodically and chord-wise. It's more usual to have the modes acting as a flavour. Brian Robertson's lead guitar solo in 'Don't Believe A Word' is mostly A pentatonic minor but it does include one striking chromatic phrase where an F# can be heard.

If you write an A pentatonic minor riff, try sharpening the Fs and see if you prefer the sound. If you are writing a chord riff then the dorian offers some interesting possibilities. Chord IV in A natural minor would be D minor, but in the dorian mode you could make it D major or D7 or D9.

Artist	Pink Floyd
Title	**'Shine On You Crazy Diamond'**
Writer	**Gilmour/Waters/Wright**
Released	**album: *Wish You Were Here*, (UK) Harvest, (US) Columbia, 1975**

The guitar phrase in 'Shine On You Crazy Diamond' isn't really a riff in the way that 'Don't Believe A Word' is a riff. It doesn't have the rhythmic quality, for example, which is typical of riffs. But that said, it is so well-known, and such a perfect expression of the angular dorian mode, I had to include it. It consists of a four-note arpeggio, B♭-F-G-E – which implies a Gm7 chord. If the scale were G natural minor the sixth note would be E♭. G dorian has E. Dave Gilmour's stroke of inspiration was to voice this riff in such a way that he uses two of the guitar's open strings so the notes can ring against each other (with the help of echo). In a different key, it wouldn't have been as effective. And sure enough, when the rest of the band come in they do so on a C chord, not C minor as would be the case in G Aeolian – the dorian chord IV is always major.

Artist	**The Who**
Title	**'5.15'**
Writer	**Townshend**
Released	**single: (UK) Track, (US) MCA, 1973**
	album: _Quadrophenia_, Track/MCA, 1973

Today's puzzle: when is a dorian riff not a dorian riff? This riff in this song (the tale of Jimmy The Mod's train ride to Brighton) poses a good illustration of how interpreting the scale a riff draws on is not always straightforward. '5.15' has a superb single-note riff that comes crashing in after the piano introduction and the line "why should I care?". The first phrase has G-B♭-C; the second has a descending run of G-F-E-C-D. Put these together and we would appear to have G dorian (G-A-B♭-C-D-E-F), from which only the A is missing. However, the crucial determinant that influences how we hear this is the crashing G chords in the backing and the clear signalling of G major when the melody starts. The riff is not heard as G dorian because it is not supported by an unambiguous G minor. Instead, we hear the riff as G mixolydian with a blues flattened third (B♭). The lesson is that in order for a modal riff to be heard as such it must be supported by a harmony that will not undermine it.

Artist	**Def Leppard**
Title	**'Pour Some Sugar On Me'**
Writer	**Clark/Collen/Elliott/Lange/Savage**
Released	**album: _Hysteria_, (UK) Bludgeon Riffola/Vertigo, (US) Mercury, 1987**
	single: (UK) Vertigo, 1987; (US) Mercury, 1988

After the solo vocal intro, the first riff comes in on a C# dorian idea, over four bars, structured a1, a2, a1, a3. The a1 phrase only uses C#, B and G#, but the a2 steps sideways onto A# -– the raised sixth of the dorian scale. Notice that these notes also belong to the C# mixolydian, but the flattened third in the vocal melody pushes the song toward the minor at this point. Halfway through the verse, at 0.33, a second riff enters, which is C# and A#, this time with a definite major feel (compare with the 'Radancer' riff). This second riff supports the vocal for the rest of the verse. The chorus itself is a I-IV-V riff in E. This E chord sounds lower than it actually is because of the use of C# as the tonal centre for the verse. (Def Leppard are playing at concert pitch here, unlike many rock bands who regularly detune a semitone – see Section Four for more on tuning.)

Artist	Def Leppard
Title	'Gods Of War'
Writer	Clark/Collen/Elliott/Lange/Savage
Released	album: *Hysteria*, (UK) Bludgeon Riffola/Vertigo, (US) Mercury, 1987

Like several tracks on the *Hysteria* album, 'Gods Of War' makes clever use of C# as a tonal centre. C# has never been a popular key for guitarists (all the standard chords in C# major are barre chords, so there are no easy 'open' chords) but it does have the effect of emphasising the resonance of chords like E (a blues flattened third) and A (a bVI) and making them sound meatier than usual. This C# is all the more striking because the sound effects-heavy intro implies a D.

'Gods Of War' has no less than three riffs of interest. The first is an angular ascending pattern that uses an octave leap from C#, followed by a leap from G# to F# a seventh higher. It takes three forms: a1 (ends on a B), a2 (ends on E), a3 (ends on A), with a4 as a different group of notes to finish. When this riff is partially played at the 4.00 mark there is a great touch when the last note of a1 is subject to a bit of tremolo arm 'gargling' as it feeds back.

Riff two is an E major riff with a repeated hammer-on/pull-off onto the open B-string (which is almost folky). On the second and fourth phrases it ends on a D instead of D#, implying a blues E. The third riff comes at the end, under the voices of Thatcher and Reagan. A distant relative of the coda riff on the Beatles' 'I Want You (She's So Heavy)', it consists of a sequence of arpeggios starting on A minor. Interest is added by the fact that several of the chords are inversions and oddly accented. The riff is actually three bars of 4/4, though you could be forgiven for thinking it was in a strange time signature.

Artist	Living Colour
Title	'Cult Of Personality'
Writer	Reid/Glover/Calhoun/Skillings
Released	album: *Vivid*, Epic, 1988 single: Epic, 1988 & 1989

There was always more musical intelligence in Living Colour than most comparable bands from the 1980s – they had a way of throwing in the odd accent or beat here and there to make you sit up and take notice. *Vivid* is an effective splicing of heavy rock and funk, an approach that requires much technique, and shows there's nothing like a touch of soul to make hard rock groove a little.

'Cult Of Personality' starts with a fine G Dorian riff from guitarist Vernon Reid, which serves as the verse with answering fifths on either Bb-F or Bb-C, and a very jazzy overlaid chord every now and again. The riff is subject to an excellent extension when it's turned into a longer scale figure. The song's bridge also features similar inversions (as found in the album's other brilliant riff song, 'Desperate People'). Listen also for the Chuck Berry thirds in the solo as the track nears the four-minute mark.

17. THE PHRYGIAN RIFF

The other mode which has an affinity with the natural minor is the phrygian, which in A is A-Bb-C-D-E-F-G. Notice that notes 1-3-5 make an A minor chord, just as is the case with the dorian's 1-3-5.

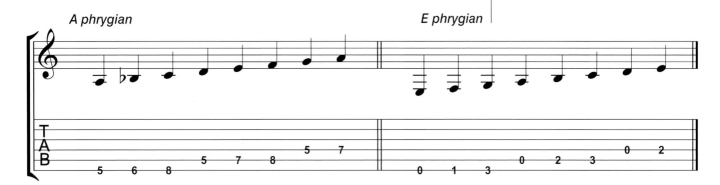

A phrygian   *E phrygian*

Think of the Phrygian as the natural minor with a flattened second. It has a distinctive Spanish sound, and is heard in much flamenco music. Of all possible pitches, the phrygian is best suited to E on the guitar (E-F-G-A-B-C-D) because this enables the player to make full use of the open strings. The open strings and first position note lay-out give the guitar a natural leaning toward E phrygian. Judas Priest's 'Metal Meltdown', Linkin Park's 'A Place For My Head' and 'Papercut', and Limp Bizkit's 'Stalemate' all suggest this mode.

Artist	**Siouxsie & The Banshees**
Title	**'Paradise Place'**
Writer	**Siouxsie & The Banshees**
Released	**albums: *Kaleidoscope*, Wonderland/Polydor, 1980 & *Nocturne*, Polydor/Geffen (US), 1983**

**RIFF GALLERY:
phrygian mode riffs**

As a rock band who never thought of themselves as such, Siouxsie & The Banshees predictably came up with riffs that were unorthodox. No pentatonics for them. The little-known 'Paradise Place', from *Kaleidoscope* and the live double *Nocturne*, achieved a far more intense performance on-stage. 'Paradise Place' is in the style of so-called 'raga-rock' (see the entry for REM's 'Time After Time' under 'drone-note riffs' in Section Three) but with a hard edge given to it by the Banshees – there's nothing dreamy or laid-back about this. For this track on-stage Siouxsie would use a Vox Teardrop guitar in an open tuning to augment Robert Smith (playing John McGeoch's original guitar part). The riff makes powerful use of a top E-string drone with a single melody line moving from E to D to E to F. This could imply the E phrygian mode (E-F-G-A-B-C-D). Underneath it, the bass guitar moves from E to C to A and down to E.

Another Banshees track, 'Bring Me The Head Of The Preacher Man', (from *Hyaena*) also has a stunning flamenco-type E phrygian riff which gets faster and faster as the song goes on. The implied chords are E minor and F (the crucial change for the phrygian), and further on in the song there is a section moving from B minor to C (implying a B phrygian).

Artist	**Deep Purple**
Title	**'Perfect Strangers'**
Writer	**Blackmore/Gillan/Glover**
Released	**single: (UK) Polydor, 1985; (US) Mercury, 1985 album: *Perfect Strangers*, Polydor/Mercury, 1984**

It's not often that, 16 years into a career, a rock band come up with a track worthy to sit beside the best material of their first five years, but that's what Deep

Purple managed with 'Perfect Strangers'. Zep's 'Kashmir' had created a sub-genre of epic, slow tempo, grandiloquent songs with odd-metre and/or odd-scale riffs, and a hint of Eastern promise. 'Perfect Strangers' is one of the best. After an intro of dirty Hammond organ, riff 1 enters with the rhythm section: a tone-shift riff C5-D5, F5-G5, with long gaps between them, which continues through much of the verse. When the music moves onto an A chord, with the notes A-G-E played individually, Blackmore adds some of his characteristic fourths.

The chorus moves through some conventional full chords (F, C, Dm, G, Dm, C), ending with a fine change from G to Gm. At this point the song plunges onto riff 2. This is based on the A phrygian scale (A-B*b*-C-D-E-F-G). When this riff re-appears after the second chorus, for the coda, it is transposed onto E phrygian. By doing it this way round, Purple maximise the power of the last riff because it's using the lowest notes on both guitar and bass. At various points an open E-string punctuates the scale, which is played roughly an octave higher. At the same time 5/4 bars appear, and the riff itself is lengthened with an extra bar of 4/4. This asymmetry, combined with the Bonham-esque drumming, gives a powerful effect.

18. THE LYDIAN RIFF

The two remaining modes are far less frequently encountered. The lydian mode is like the mixolydian in only being one note different from the major scale. A lydian in A is A-B-C#-D#-E-F#-G# – basically a major scale with a sharpened fourth:

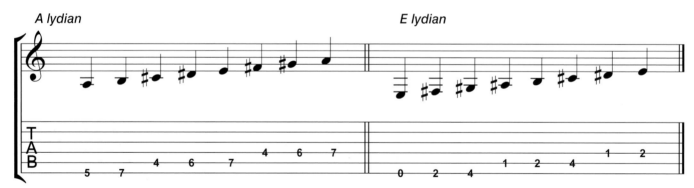

The lydian mode was popular in speed metal and similar late-1980s guitar styles. It has an unsettling effect because of the presence of the raised fourth – our old friend the tritone in a different guise as an augmented fourth rather than a flattened fifth. The lydian mode will therefore lend itself to generating tritone riffs, but with major chords supporting them.

By subtly introducing the lydian note into the harmony we can give ourselves an opportunity of using the lydian mode in a more melodic way. Remember you do not have to keep the whole of the song in the mode. A more flexible method for writing riffs on the lydian mode is to keep the song in a straight major key and use the mode on the riff.

Artist	**Led Zeppelin**
Title	**'Dancing Days'**
Writer	**Page/Plant**
Released	**album: _Houses Of The Holy_, Atlantic, 1973**

'Dancing Days' is an awesome deployment of the erotic possibilities of the tritone (G-C#), here derived from a G lydian (G-A-B-C#-D-E-F#). In the 1980s and 1990s, heavy rock bands made much use of this in the bass register of the guitar. 'Dancing Days' opens with this single-bar riff (four bars in total) blazing in the _middle_ register. Page accentuates the riff by bending the C# up to D twice and then coming off onto B. Underneath, the accompaniment is playing a G-B_b_ (blues _b_III) idea in-between the upper bend to add to the tension. Unusually, the variation on the basic one-bar riff comes each third time in the form of overlaid, strident sixths on a separate guitar track.

Once the song enters the verse, Page innovates further by taking a standard-issue Keef/Stones rhythm riff and moving it from its initial C chord up a semitone to C#. C# is a chord that is foreign to G major. He adds another tritone idea over this C-C# change by altering the notes that are held – on the C chord the notes F and A are added and taken away. Over the C# the upper note is sharpened, so we hear G instead of F# – G is a tritone above C#.

There's also an arrangement detail that's worth noting in the coda, where the main riff is pushed up an octave.

---

19. THE LOCRIAN MODE

The locrian mode is the 'odd man out' of the modes. This is because it's neither major nor minor but diminished. The A locrian is A-B_b_-C-D-E_b_-F-G – like the natural minor with a flattened second _and_ fifth.

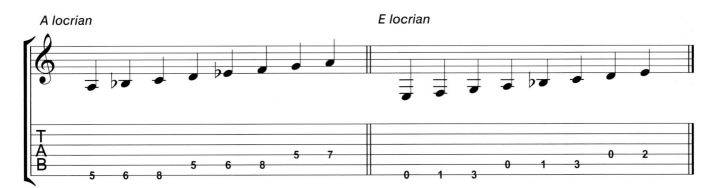

Of all the scales we have looked at, this is the first where there is not a perfect fifth between the first and the fifth. All the other modes on A have E as their fifth note. This makes the locrian mode unsettling. Its chord I is a diminished triad, and the locrian is structured around a tritone between first and fifth, so it's well-suited to expressing negative emotions such as anger and alienation. As I mentioned in the introduction, this mode has become more significant in the last few years, cropping up as a trademark in the music of bands like Linkin Park and Limp Bizkit. Its use indicates a rejection of the harmony on which rock has been traditionally based. Twenty-first-century rock has come a long way from the blues and pentatonics.

In practical terms it should be said that few rock songs that use modes such as the phrygian, lydian or locrian actually maintain a harmony rigorously fixed on them. What usually happens is that the scale is harmonised in fiths and the riffs are then played from those fifths. This is certainly the simplest approach. A good example would be tracks like 'Disasterpiece' by Slipknot, where the demonic effect is heightened by extreme detuning of the guitar. Their track 'Everything Ends' uses an A locrian scale with the fourth note sometimes flattened. The 1-b2 movement is everywhere in their music. The same effects can be heard in Korn's 'It's On' and 'Dead Bodies Everywhere', and in Sepultura's 'Roots Bloody Roots', which may well be on a seven-string guitar because of the deep B and C fifths that feature in the riff.

20. CHROMATIC SCALE RIFFS

A chromatic scale proper would consist of all 12 semitones. This is not used for riffs – but adding a few off-scale notes to a riff can give it a chromatic quality. The Riff Gallery for this section groups together famous songs which have riffs written in this way. Although they may be based on one of the scales or modes described previously, they include notes which are not on that scale or mode. Chromatic riffs tend to be characterised by step-wise movement. They lend themselves to creating longer riffs at faster tempos than pentatonics because you are not moving so soon across the strings to get the next note. They also impart a jazzy quality to the riff, or otherwise blur the tonality.

Check out Free's 'Over The Green Hills' for a speeded-up chromatic descending riff on E. Deep Purple 'Space Truckin'' has a chromatic riff starting on A, going up to E-Eb-D-C-B-Bb, and in Pink Floyd's 'Money', B-D-Db-C is the four-note riff leading to the guitar solo. Metallica's 'The Thing That Should Not Be' has chromatic touches, as does The Stooges' 'Not Right' (C5-B5-Bb5-A5), Stone Temple Pilots' 'Heaven And Hot Rods', Soundgarden's 'The Day I Tried To Live', Pearl Jam's 'Spin The Black Circle', Pantera's 'Mouth For War', and the chorus of T.Rex's 'Jeepster' (C-B-Bb-A). Extreme's 'Colour Me Blind' has a first riff with distinctive step-wise chromatic movement and a few leaps accentuated by squealing harmonics. The same band's 'Peacemaker Die' and 'Rest In Peace' show an approach to riff-writing where the guitar is almost playing lead phrases. Rory Gallagher's 'Blister On The Moon' also features a riff in which an E chord introduces a lead phrase. Chromatic riffs at quicker tempos have this tendency. Stability and focus is created by a steady drumbeat and the guitar clearly stating the root note of the basic chord.

**RIFF GALLERY:
chromatic effects in riffs**

Artist	The Beatles
Title	'Lady Madonna'
Writer	Lennon/McCartney
Released	single: Parlophone (UK), Capitol (US), 1968
	album: *The Beatles (White Album)*, Apple, 1968

'Lady Madonna' reprises the 1950s-derived 'Pretty Woman' riff. The first phrase is A-C-C# over an A chord, then D-F#-A over a D chord. This happens twice. The third time the D chord has D-D-E-E before the harmony changes to F and G chords with the riff using those root notes to ascend finally to the A an octave above the A where it started. No one scale will cover all these variations. The closest is A mixolydian with a blues flattened third added, which just leaves the F (bVI) as the additional note.

The riff is first heard, in a slightly different form, in the left hand of the piano part, and then in the bass on the opposite side of the stereo image. At 0.44 two guitars start playing it, followed about ten seconds later by a sax. In the fullest statement, with all these instruments, the riff achieves an exhilarating stomp. One significant musical factor in its success is the fact that there is a phrase pitched against it which comes downward – either the right hand of the piano or the actual vocal melody – an example of contrary motion applied to a riff

Artist	**King Crimson**
Title	**'21st Century Schizoid Man'**
Writer	**Fripp/McDonald/Lake/Giles/Sinfield**
Released	**single: (UK) Island, (US) Atlantic, 1969**
	album: *In The Court Of The Crimson King*,
	Island/Atlantic, 1969

King Crimson were one of the quintessential progressive outfits, with a leaning towards jazz-rock improvisation, apparent in '21st Century Schizoid Man'. In Robert Fripp they had a strong-willed, intellectual guitarist with a European style that contrasted with the prevalent blues-rock. This song made an impact on its first listeners because of the viciously distorted vocal and accompanying discordant guitar chord. The verse is prefaced by a riff in C pentatonic minor which comprises a single-note phrase and a drop onto F5-F#5 and G5. It's played in unison by guitars (along with a harmonised line to thicken it up), plus saxes and bass, to give an epic effect. Notice how on the third time the fifth chords are replaced by higher single notes for F, F# and G. This riff acts as a kind of vocal-less chorus between the verses. After the second verse the riff variation is repeated and gradually sped up. This leads to the introduction of riff 2, which takes the form of a phrase (a1), and its variation (a2), repeated. It's also in C minor, but uses chromatic semitone movement to go from C-E*b*-E-F and then from C downward, B-B*b*-G. With each repetition of the whole eight-bar figure the fourth phrase is changed while the first three phrases stay the same. Some of the final phrases are worth study as examples of how to link up with the start of the riff an octave above where it was first heard.

Artist	**Led Zeppelin**
Title	**'Dazed And Confused'**
Writer	**Page**
Released	**album: *Led Zeppelin*, Atlantic, 1969**

Page first used the riff on the Yardbirds version of this song (sometimes called 'I'm Confused'). This was Zep's first attempt at an extended song, complete with shadowy bridge section and misogynist lyrics which, post-1990s rap and metal, now look small beer. The memorable riff starts with a leap of a tenth from E up to G and then a descent G-F#-F-E, and then D-C#-C-B. Page brings out the gothic menace by doubling it with a higher lead guitar two octaves above and by incorporating various bent notes into the riff. The riff is used both as an instrumental link and for the verse. A second one-bar riff on B enters to break it up. This one's notes are B-E-F#-A-B – the I-IV-V-*b*VII idea encountered in 'Paperback Writer'. The 'Dazed' riff is made all the more effective because the notes do not simply ascend and descend. As the band made 'Dazed And Confused' one of the cornerpieces of their set, the tempo gradually dropped to a funereal pace quite different from the brisk walk of the original studio cut.

"the riff is made all the more effective because the notes do not simply ascend and descend"

Artist	**Jimi Hendrix**	
Title	**'Love Or Confusion'**	
Writer	**Hendrix**	
Released	**album: _Are You Experienced_, Track/Reprise, 1967**	

This example of a chromatic riff comes just as the verse is reaching the hook-line. You can hear it start at 0.34 on the bass guitar, with the notes G-B♭-A-A♭, four times, and twice more with the guitar and a more urgent rhythm. As it occurs here it is more of a fill than a riff. Still, it gives the idea of what could be done.

Hendrix's innovation was not just in guitar pyrotechnics, figurative or real. Much of this song is built on a G-F change, which Hendrix makes G5-Fsus2 in order to achieve, coupled with the bassline, a more subtle harmonic colour. Also listen out for the fuzz guitar that holds G through much of the verse, the tremolo scoop into verse two and into the key change bridge, the octaves under the solo and the majestic entrance to the last verse.

Artist	**Led Zeppelin**	
Title	**'Black Dog'**	
Writer	**Page/Plant/Jones**	
Released	**album: _Untitled (Four Symbols)_, Atlantic, 1971**	
	single (US): Atlantic, 1971	

'Black Dog' has three riffs. The first is a linear riff based on the A pentatonic minor scale but including a chromatic G# and a hint of a C# on a bend. The chromatic quality grows when the riff is transposed down a fourth and a variation is created which emphasises the seventh (D#) on the E pentatonic minor. Although it sounds as though the music is now in a hideously complicated time signature, it is only a matter of shifted accents. This riff was the responsibility of John Paul Jones (see the interview with JPJ in Section Five).

Riff two is based on an A5-C5 change with a contrasting A pentatonic major run. Riff three is a powerful tone-shift A5-G riff with accented G and D chords. This last riff is used for the guitar solo. The arrangement of 'Black Dog', alternating solo voice with band passages, was influenced by Fleetwood Mac's 'Oh Well'. Compare it also with Jethro Tull's 'A New Day Yesterday' where a similar riff idea to the first variation in 'Black Dog' is put to very different effect.

Artist	**Queen**	
Title	**'Stone Cold Crazy'**	
Writer	**May/Mercury/Taylor/Deacon**	
Released	**album: _Sheer Heart Attack_, EMI/Elektra, 1974**	

Coming in on an air-raid siren of feedback, 'Stone Cold Crazy' qualifies as a chromatic riff for several reasons. Although the main element to the riff is a G5-B♭5 change, which takes two bars and sounds like G pentatonic minor, bars 3-4 bring in a semitone move which worms its way upward to D via a B, C and D♭. The riff is played four times, with an additional guitar overdubbed halfway through to give some notes an octave doubling. The fourth-time riff ends with a different phrase that heads downward, G-F-D-B♭. This gives the riff the structure a1 + a2 (three times), a1 + a3.

The verse is a solo vocal with only percussion accompaniment. The riff's second appearance is curtailed with another chromatic G-A-A#-B phrase which leads to a guitar solo over a B minor chord (0.51), and then a return to the first riff. At 1.20 a second solo is introduced with another chromatic chord change from B*b* to B minor. The two tonal centres of G minor and B minor are quite distant from each other, which accounts for the song's strange, dislocated feel – an exotic world of riffery wrapped up in just over two minutes.

Artist	**The Cult**
Title	**'Automatic Blues'**
Writer	**Astbury/Duffy**
Released	**single: Beggars Banquet (UK), Sire (US), 1989**
	album: *Sonic Temple*, Beggars Banquet/Sire, 1989

A neat way of creating the feel of a chromatic riff from a pentatonic one is to put a passing note between the blues flattened third and the fourth of the scale. This note is the major third of the scale. The effect is reminiscent of scales used in bebop jazz, where a blues third is added to a major scale (E-F#-G-G#-A-B-C#-D#-E) or a pentatonic major (E-F#-G-G#-B-C#-E). The riff in 'Automatic Blues' consists of the notes E-G-G#-A-G-E. The form is a1, a2, a3, a1, with each riff ending on a different higher note. Fun as the riff is, what lifts it out of the ordinary is the timing and the arrangement. The song is an excellent example of the time-honoured technique of alternating vocal and riff. This leaves the singer the chance to play around with the point where the vocals end, knowing the riff is going to enter on a certain off-beat. It's cleverly done here. Then, under the guitar solo, a second riff uses the notes D-C#-A-G-E.

Artist	**Radiohead**
Title	**'Paranoid Android'**
Writer	**Yorke/Greenwood/Selway/O'Brien/Greenwood**
Released	**album: *OK Computer*, Parlophone/Capitol, 1997**
	single (UK): Parlophone, 1997

Radiohead are not exactly a band associated with riffs. This makes the glimpse of riff heaven provided by 'Paranoid Android' all the more startling. As an overall song it not only has great guitar playing, it manages to pull off just about every other trick in the way of melody, dynamics, tempo, key and time-signature changes. There's plenty to enjoy here from a guitar and writing viewpoint.

The song uses several keys, including Gm, Dm and Am, shifting between them in an ambiguous way. The opening acoustic sequence cries out that it must be in some weird tuning, especially when you discover that the opening chord change is from a form of Cm to Gm – but it isn't. The chords move from this Gm to a first inversion Dmadd9 and then E7. The music sounds like it's going into Am, but this only happens after the second verse.

The next section involves a skeletal heavy riff plucked from the depths of heavy metal hell and played acoustically. Most rock bands would have made this riff a straight pentatonic one, but Radiohead introduce an A*b* note, implying a chromatic Am-A*b* chord change, followed by C, A*b*6, B*b* chord sequence. When the heavy guitars come in, the riff's power is unleashed – but notice they don't overplay the headbanging, only repeating that heavy riff a handful of times. After the solo, the music enters its hymn-like third section: it starts on a Cm chord, changes key to Dm via an A7, and then finds its way to E7 and A before repeating. Notice the sense of dislocation when the music goes from A back to C minor. I guarantee that in 40 years of hit singles this is the only song to use this change.

The riff returns toward the end of the section, to introduce the second guitar break. Its power is all the stronger for the contrasting quiet of the middle section, making 'Paranoid Android' an object lesson in dynamics.

"its power is all the stronger for the contrasting quiet of the middle section"

Chord-based RIFFS

Riffs can sometimes take the form of chords – groups of three or more notes that make up harmonies in music. This section examines different kinds of chord-based riff, and the various ways a riff can generate harmony.

21. PEDAL-NOTE RIFFS

So far we have looked at intervals and scales as sources for writing riffs. Our third group of possibilities comes from more obviously harmonic and chord-based ideas. We've already discussed pairs of notes in riffs, but one other special way of getting a riff from a pair of notes is to exploit one of the guitar's natural resources: the open string.

A 'pedal' note is one that remains the same, usually low-down in the arrangement, while other notes or chords change above it. On the guitar the favourite pedal note strings are the open E, A and D-strings. For riffs, pick any of the lower three strings and move a scale or even a sequence of intervals like thirds on the string(s) above it.

Thirds over an A pedal Here are thirds using the A mixolydian mode over an A string:

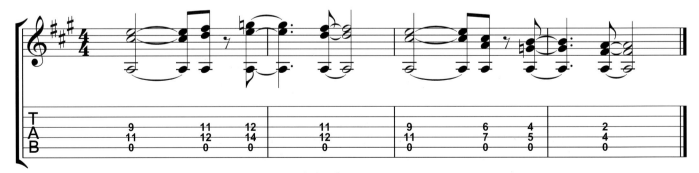

Ozzy Osbourne's 'Shot In The Dark' chorus and intro moves chords over a fifth string pedal, as does the main riff of Led Zep's 'Ten Years Gone'. The bridge section of Van Halen's 'Jamie's Cryin'' puts thirds over a fifth-string pedal. The

Who's 'I Can See For Miles' has an E pedal over which chords change (and could be compared with the Stooges' 'Real Cool Time'), and the intro of 'Pinball Wizard' features chord changes over an F# pedal. The Cult's 'Sweet Soul Sister' puts an A blues scale over an A pedal note, and 'She Sells Sanctuary' uses a D pedal. The Stooges' 'I Wanna Be Your Dog' puts G5-F#5-E5 over an open E string (these fifths imply the E natural minor scale). The Queens Of The Stone Age's 'Better Living Through Chemistry' opens with an ambiguous scale played over an F pedal – this scale implies both F major and F minor. Smashing Pumpkins 'Cherub Rock' puts octaves over a pedal E, the octaves drawing on the E mixolydian scale. Faith No More's 'From Out Of Nowhere' puts a C5-E♭5-F5 riff over a C pedal. Bon Jovi's 'Roulette' has fifths over an E pedal, and 'In And Out Of Love' has as its second (verse) riff triads over an A pedal.

On keyboards it's easy to write a song in which chords in the right hand change over a static bass note. This songwriting technique creates a sense of drama. On the guitar you can only easily do this over E, A, or D. A fretted pedal note like C or G will fix your fretting hand in one place, so any riff will have to use notes that are reachable from that position. A well-known riff-writing technique involves getting the bass player to play a pedal note while you play a riff of single-notes or intervals like fourths and fifths over the top. This features heavily on ZZ Top records.

Artist	**Fleetwood Mac**
Title	**'The Green Manalishi (With The Two-Prong Crown)'**
Writer	**Green**
Released	**single: Reprise, 1970**

For a brief time in 1969-70 Peter Green's Fleetwood Mac became something more than a competent English blues band. They created a musical world of their own – part blues, part late psychedelia, part pop – which provided the best context imaginable for Green's poetic guitar skills. Green may have been a fine blues player – perhaps the subtlest of the English guitar heroes – but his finest guitar work happened in contexts other than a 12-bar. The shuddering nightmare of 'The Green Manalishi' is a case in point.

It has two notable riffs: the first comes after the first line of lyric and consists of I, ♭III, IV chords. The coda riff is based on thirds moving down the fifth and fourth strings over an E pedal. The implied chords are Em to C but the pedal stays in place on the guitars, although the bass moves to a C. Over this the guitars are stacked up in an impressive piece of arranging, with its spooky lead guitar in the background, like a lost stanza of Nostradamus.

Artist	**REM**
Title	**'Green Grow The Rushes'**
Writer	**Berry/Buck/Mills/Stipe**
Released	**album: *Fables Of The Reconstruction*, IRS, 1985**

Here is a classic example of a riff based on a tonic pedal. The song is in D, and Buck selects the open D-string as a drone. He then plays three one-bar rhythmically similar phrases coming down the third string from the 14th fret A. The scale he uses is D mixolydian – D major with a lowered seventh (D-E-F#-G-A-B-C). This mode is favoured for its dreamy quality when used in this manner. Playing a D pedal on the guitar has a lighter feel than an A or E pedal. Two other pedal-note REM songs are '7 Chinese Brothers' (over D) and 'Be Mine' (over E and A).

Artist	The Sensational Alex Harvey Band
Title	'The Faith Healer'
Writer	A Harvey/H McKenna
Released	album: *Next*, Phonogram/Vertigo, 1973
	single (UK): Phonogram/Vertigo, 1974

At a time when the UK music scene was divided between chart pop and glam-rock on one hand and prog-rock on the other, the Alex Harvey Band carved out a niche for themselves that wasn't in either camp. Too hard and idiosyncratic for the charts, but keeping clear of pretension, they became a popular live and recording act – threatening and funny by turns.

'Faith Healer' is a colourful arrangement, with exotic percussion, distinct from much of the rock of its, or any other, era. The first riff is a sequence of fourths derived from D pentatonic minor and played over the throbbing D pedal which has already been going for 47 seconds before the riff enters and then drops out again, re-entering at 1.13. The guitar does not carry the pedal, though a second guitar on the other side of the stereo image enters eventually with a D5 that supports it. The riff fits between the vocal lines. At 3.06 a second riff comes in, also based on D pentatonic minor, in single notes, with an emphasised tone-shift element. Listen out for the exotic B♭-A-G-E♭ phrase over a G pedal which is repeated during the song's coda.

---

22. DRONE-NOTE RIFFS

We can define a 'drone' note as one which is either in the middle of what you're playing or above it. Have a look at this example:

Fifths with a G drone note

In first position we have an Fsus2, at the third fret we have a G5 with the G doubled, at fret six we have a B♭6/Gm7, and at fret eight the same shape creates a C5 with the G doubled again. The open G acts as a drone. Obviously, how you play the riff and how long you allow the G to ring will have an effect on how the riff will sound.

That example was based on the interval of a fifth combined with an open string. You can also use scales, as you did over pedal notes. Play the right scale for the key or the progression up and down one string (instead of across the fretboard) and hit an open string above it. The result is a bigger sound, and one that not only might make a riff but will reinforce the harmony. This is a significant factor if you are playing in a power-trio, and is a good technique for lead guitar, as the Edge demonstrates on the guitar solo from 'Sunday Bloody Sunday'.

The simplest application is to treat the open string as the root note of a major or minor chord. So if you want a high riff over an E chord (major or minor) in the overall harmony, the top open E is available as a drone. The open B will work for B major or B minor, and the open G-string for G major or minor. The fretting hand then chooses the riff notes from the right scale up and down an adjacent string. Since the top three strings make an E minor chord and the second, third and fourth make an open G, if you are playing in either of these keys you could have *two* drone notes vibrating, rather than one.

The open strings can also function as the third or fifth of the chord. E is the third of C major (C-E-G) and C#minor (C#-E-G#), B is the third of G major and G# minor, and G is the third of Eb major and E minor. E is the fifth of A major/minor, B is the fifth of E major/minor, and G is the fifth of C major/minor. You can treat E, B or G as the sixth or seventh of a chord for even stranger effects. If you compose a riff using the open string as something other than a root note for the given chord, remember this may not work if the bars given to the riff involve a chord change or changes. Songs like REM's 'Time After Time' and the Velvet Underground's 'Venus In Furs' give an idea of the possible texture achievable with drone notes.

RIFF GALLERY: drone-note riffs

Artist	Led Zeppelin
Title	'When The Levee Breaks'
Writer	Page/Plant/Jones/Bonham/Minnie
Released	album: *Untitled (Four Symbols)*, Atlantic, 1971

The main riff of 'Levee' is based on a blues flattened third idea combined with fifths. What brings it alive is the open tuning on an electric 12-string (possibly EACFAC), which gives the riff a droning quality that fits the overall hypnotic effect. For quite a lot of the track the top two strings are sounding. There is a secondary riff which comes just before the verse starts, with heavily accented fifths using the flattened seventh and the flattened third – a quintessential, dynamic Zep moment.

In lesser hands these simple musical elements would probably have been nowhere near as engaging. But the band make it work through skillful arrangement, not masses of overdubs – in fact, by not adding other ideas the intensity never drops. The result is Zep's greatest take on the blues. You only have to compare it with Memphis Minnie's 1929 song of the same title to realise the breadth of the band's imagination and power – particularly Bonham's amazing, much-sampled drum part and the production skills of Jimmy Page and Glyn Johns. Interestingly, the magic of 'When The Levee Breaks' was not repeatable on-stage – the song never became a fixture of their live act.

Artist	REM
Title	'Time After Time (annElise)'
Writer	Berry/Buck/Mills/Stipe
Released	album: *Reckoning*, IRS, 1984

In a very different vein to Led Zeppelin, this track from REM's second album shows how the use of drone notes gave rise to the term 'raga-rock' – a term coined to describe tracks that imitate the droning strings of an Indian sitar. This style originated in the 1960s with bands like the Velvet Underground. The Indian effect is emphasised here by the opening percussion (congas) and the rapid arpeggio rolls on the guitars that punctuate the first minute, on what sounds like a sus2 chord. The top E string is sounded throughout the verse in

16ths, sometimes panned back and forth. Notice how, when the song hits the two-minute mark, the drone note temporarily disappears into the background. This song is a good example of the hypnotic effect of a drone note – being static, it suggests the music is merely looping around.

23. ARPEGGIO RIFFS

There's one last approach to mention before we reach riffs made from full chords. If the notes of a chord are played one after the other in a rising or falling pattern you have what is known as an *arpeggio*. If an arpeggio is brief enough, catchy enough, and with enough rhythmic emphasis, then it can qualify as a riff. Arpeggios imply a chord (handy in a power-trio) but can have more clarity because the notes are offered to the listener one at a time. The favoured arpeggios on the guitar are those that either start with an open string, or feature one or more open strings, which makes fingering easier. Arpeggio riffs also tend to have more impact when played on the lower strings – this gives them more force and body, compared to generally more decorative higher arpeggios

Here's an example of an arpeggio that might be considered a riff:

Arpeggio riff

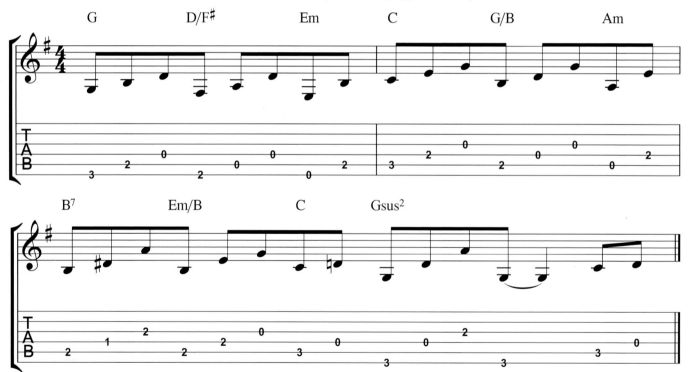

An arpeggio can be made from any chord, and it doesn't have to be a straight major or minor. The dominant 7 and 9 chords, for example, have been very popular in rock. But keep in mind that the more notes there are in the chord the longer it will take to play your way through the arpeggiated riff.

Arpeggio riffs are effective either with the bass doubling an octave lower, or harmonised. Another arrangement idea is to have the bass only play the root notes of the arpeggio and accent them, thus emphasising the chord changes. This is how the arpeggio riff in the middle of Cream's 'Badge' works. They often occur on intros, as with Paul Weller's 'Sunflower' where the notes on the third string descend D-C#-C-B while the top two strings remain on E and B; in Type O Negative's 'My

Girlfriend's Girlfriend'; on the intro and verse of The Strokes' 'Is This It'; on the intro of the Stone Roses' 'Made Of Stone'; and on Radiohead's 'My Iron Lung'. The Doors' famous 'Light My Fire' has a long bridge/solo section carried by an A minor/B minor arpeggio bass riff. Guns N' Roses' 'Sweet Child O' Mine' has an intro with one of the most famous guitar arpeggios of all time – this figure, played high at the 12th fret, spans in total an octave and a fourth, starts with an octave leap (D-D), and takes the form a1, a2, a3, a1, in which the bass notes cycles through D-E-G and then D again. Living Colour's 'I Want To Know' uses an arpeggio riff to link the chorus to the verse.

Rainbow's 'Jealous Lover' has a fine arpeggio riff on F# – it climbs up first, then comes down onto the bottom E, before re-ascending. It's another good example of a riff exploiting the possibilities of F# as a key centre. During the verse Blackmore uses the same dramatic arpeggiated power chords (root-fifth-octave) that he used in 'Smoke On The Water'. The Byrds' 'Turn! Turn! Turn!' is an example of an arpeggio riff that depends on three separate instrumental parts. The arpeggios occur on an electric 12-string, in a finger-picking style, but the descending fifths in the bass, and the accentuated Bm A chord change at the end of each two-bar phrase, are essential to the effect. The Soundgarden track 'Black Hole Sun' also depends on arpeggios.

Artist	**U2**
Title	**'Sunday Bloody Sunday'**
Writer	**Bono/Edge/Mullen/Clayton**
Released	**album: *War*, Island, 1983**

As we saw in Section One, thanks to The Edge's smart use of an echo unit, simple phrases could now sound interesting, and by playing against the echo pattern new rhythms and harmonies could be generated. 'Sunday Bloody Sunday' takes a standard rock progression of VI-I-IV in a major key (here D) and plays arpeggios over those chords (B-D-F#, A-D-F#, G-D-E) so that the chords B minor, D and G6 are implied. Allied with the martial drum rhythm and Bono's impassioned anti-violence lyric, the effect is powerful, as can be heard on both the *War* album and the live *Under A Blood Red Sky*. The riff takes a second form at the start of the verse where Edge plays the progression as chords. The later U2 song, 'A Sort Of Homecoming', revisits those arpeggios to present them in a more lyrical way.

Artist	**Roy Orbison**
Title	**'Oh Pretty Woman'**
Writer	**Orbison/Dees**
Released	**single: (US) Monument; (UK) London, 1964**

Coupled with the driving four-to-the-bar drums, this was one of the most famous early uses of a guitar riff in a song. In 'Pretty Woman' the riff is pulled in to stoke anticipation: when we hear it for the first time it consists only of five notes, ending on an unresolved D – the flattened seventh of an E7 chord (the song is in A major). This is played twice on an acoustic 12-string. Only then do we hear the riff in its full form, extended to eight notes and reaching as far as F# before its down-turn. These notes – E-G#-B-D-F# – constitute a dominant ninth arpeggio. In this second form, halfway between a scale and an arpeggio, it's played four times, with added instruments such as electric guitar and bass, to lead into the verse. After the second verse it is slightly shortened as the song moves into the bridge. At the conclusion expectation is generated by the riff's shortened form twice, followed by no less than nine repetitions of the riff's second form. This ties in with the lyric's discovery that the woman he thought was *not* interested turns out to *be* interested after all. The creative tip here is to write a riff, then make a shortened version in order to delay the full thing.

Artist	**The Beatles**
Title	**'Day Tripper'**
Writer	**Lennon/McCartney**
Released	**single: Parlophone/Capitol, 1965**

The riff for 'Day Tripper' is a development of the riff from 'Pretty Woman'. The connection is all the more apparent because of the song's frequent one-chord crescendo technique. Like 'Pretty Woman' the notes imply an E dominant9 chord (E-G#-B-D-F#) with the inclusion of a G (blues bIII) as an additional second note. The interesting bit is the last few notes, which jump around unpredictably, in contrast to a riff that simply goes straight up and then down. During the verse the riff is transposed onto A. Notice that the riff is doubled by bass guitar on the intro. 'Day Tripper' was recorded a few days after 'Drive My Car', a track that featured a similar riff.

Artist	**Van Halen**
Title	**'Ain't Talkin' 'Bout Love'**
Writer	**E Van Halen/A Van Halen/Anthony/Roth**
Released	**album: *Van Halen*, Warners, 1978**
	single (US): Warners, 1978

This famous arpeggio riff (based on A minor, G and C) cranks in on the left, and you can hear the notes racketing about in the reverb on the right. Van Halen's legendary 'brown sound' guitar tone is a mixture of echo/distortion and phasing on a customised Strat with a Gibson humbucker pickup at the bridge through a Marshall Super Lead 100-watt amp. Few bands or producers would have resisted doubling the guitar riff on the right, but it sounds amazingly full as it is. The riff is heard four times before mutating into a more chordal form where the Am-G5 are fully played with a descending C-B in single notes. Eddie interjects lead fills toward the end of each second bar in the riff's second form. A third variation is used for the verse. This riff virtually carries the whole song, since the only other chords come in on the coda. At 1.52 the riff is heard very quietly and with a cleaner tone. Van Halen's guitar provides the track almost with a second 'voice'.

Artist	**Bryan Adams**
Title	**'Run To You'**
Writer	**Adams/Vallance**
Released	**single: A&M, 1984**
	album: *Reckless*, A&M, 1985

The songs of Canadian-rocker Bryan Adams tend not to be built around riffs in a hard rock way, but 'Run To You' was an exception. The riff is unusual because it uses thirds on the bass strings – generally, the lower the pitch of thirds, the muddier they sound. Adams plays here with a capo at the second fret so the actual pitch starts on F#m, but for ease of reference I will describe the riff as if it were in E minor.

The first bar uses E-B-D which ascends to a G-B-D triad and then A-C#-D. The D-string has remained open throughout. The chords implied are Em7, G and A. On the A the fretted C# and open D clash against each other, lending piquancy to the riff. The guitar tone is necessarily free of distortion for this riff, with some chorus and delay. Urgency is imparted by the quarter-note sidestick from the drummer. Notice that this riff is carried on through much of the verse.

Artist	**The Seahorses**
Title	**'Love Is The Law'**
Writer	**Squire**
Released	**single (UK): Geffen, 1997**
	album: *Do It Yourself*, Geffen, 1997

Ex-Stone Roses guitarist John Squire has turned out to be the great lost talent of British Guitar Herodom, but this single from his short-lived Seahorses period did contribute to the ranks of memorable 1990s guitar riffs. The riff (which you need to use a capo to play) is an arpeggio-type figure on an open A chord – the sustained A string helps support the higher notes. It's a distant relative of the Smiths' 'What Difference Does It Make', though the string-bend in the last bar of each riff is definitely not from Johnny Marr. For considerable stretches of the song the riff isn't made much use of, though it is heard with a different guitar in the centre of the mix at 3.10, now transposed down from A to E. For another John Squire arpeggio riff try 'Waterfall' on the Roses' debut album.

24. THE MAJOR CHORD RIFF

As I pointed out in the introduction, just as there's a fine line between arpeggios and scales, there is also a fine line between ''riffs made of chords' and chord progressions. For example, is the Spin Doctors' 'Two Princes' a four-chord riff or a progression? I think we can usefully talk about chord changes taking on the function of a riff when the changes are sufficiently short, repeated often, and are rhythmic enough. But I'm not claiming these definitions are rigid.

Chord riffs have the obvious attraction that they create a full sound. It's possible to create a riff from the rhythmic way in which a single chord is played, as happens on many James Brown tracks like 'Sex Machine', where the guitar basically plays a ninth, or the Red Hot Chili Peppers' 'Get Up And Jump', 'Backwoods', and 'Behind The Sun', or Stone Temple Pilots' 'No Way Out'.

Another way of generating riffs is to take a chord and move it a semitone step back or forth, or to lift a finger or two fingers off the chord to alter notes within it, as Peter Buck did in REM's 'Departure'. Since a major key has three major chords in it – namely I, IV and V (E, A, B in E major) – these are the three most likely to be used for a riff – or at least that would be the case were it not for rock's blues flattened seventh and corresponding liking for the mixolydian mode and its harmony. There are probably two or three mixolydian I-*b*VII-IV riffs for every major key I-IV-V. It is possible to make up other chord riffs by turning chords II, III and VI into major chords and combining one of them with the main three (more than that and you may undermine the key).

Bachman Turner Overdrive's 'You Ain't Seen Nothing Yet' and Arrow's 'New York Groove' are I-V-IV riff songs. Sheryl Crow's 'Soak Up The Sun' starts as a I-V-IV riff. Pulp's 'This Is Hardcore' is not what would be described as a riff song, but listen to the opening, where a Gmaj7 on brass sounds several times over a heavy, slow drumbeat – that has the focus and power of a riff.

> "there's a fine line between 'riffs made of chords' and chord progressions"

RIFF GALLERY:
major chord riffs

Artist	The Troggs
Title	'Wild Thing'
Writer	'Taylor'
Released	single: Fontana, 1966
	album: (UK) *From Nowhere...*; (US) *Wild Thing*,
	Fontana, 1966

Perhaps the definitive use of a I-IV-V-IV chord riff, 'Wild Thing' is now known to more people through Jimi Hendrix's version (as on the Monterey 1967 set). It has always appealed to young players because the chords (A, D and E) are easy to play and to change. The riff is also effective because these chords use the three lowest open strings for their root notes.

Its effectiveness was enhanced by the stomping drum rhythm, and an eccentric arrangement in which the verse leaves the vocal almost unsupported. The only change in the verse is to lift the A chord on and off. Instead of a guitar break we get a recorder break, not exactly in tune, to add a bizarre element of rustic delinquency. It was like rock'n'roll played by the local village idiots. But sometimes dumb is the new clever.

From the same innocent era, the verse of the Monkees 'A Little Bit Me, A Little Bit You' has the same chords, but I leave it to you to decide whether that is a riff or a progression. Likewise, Wayne Fontana & The Mindbenders' 'Game Of Love' (1965), where the verse is I-IV-V-IV, but more a progression than a riff.

Artist	Nirvana
Title	'Smells Like Teen Spirit'
Writer	Cobain/Nirvana
Released	album: *Nevermind*, Geffen, 1991
	single: Geffen, 1991

One of the most famous chord-riff sequences ever, 'Teen Spirit' is also memorable for its clever arrangement, with powerful dynamics, of which Nirvana had an intuitive grasp. The verses are sinister and quiet, the choruses raucous. The verse is the same chord sequence as the chorus but on the verse only the bass is playing the root notes in eighths, so the chords are implied, not stated. 'Teen Spirit' is like the key-striding sequence F-B♭-G-C, but Cobain's twist of genius was to dislocate this sequence by forcing the second two chords a minor third away from the first two: F-B♭-A♭-D♭. There's a further fragment of dislocated harmony at the end of the chorus: F-G♭-B♭-A♭.

Artist	The Who
Title	'Baba O'Reily'
Writer	Townshend
Released	album: *Who's Next*, Track/Decca, 1971

Few bands have put the rock guitar riff to such sublime use as The Who did on the classic *Who's Next*, which fuses the energy and drama of rock with significant lyric themes. The album was also innovative in its use of synths, and The Who never enjoyed a better production.

As a rock guitarist Pete Townshend was always in a different area of the ballpark to everyone else. As he readily admitted himself, he was never a quick or fluent lead player: his gift was rhythm and punctuating a song with gargantuan chords. 'Baba O'Reily' is a fine instance of a titanic Who riff. The key, F major, is unusual on the guitar, and the entry of the guitar riff is delayed. The sequencer synth starts with an arpeggio based on F major; then piano enters on the I-V-IV chords, and then drums enter. These instruments carry the song through the first verse, which is where Townshend finally enters on guitar with the F-C-B*b* chord riff. There is a fabulous live version of this on the soundtrack of the film *The Kids Are Alright* – the last time they played it with Keith Moon.

Artist	**David Bowie**
Title	**'Queen Bitch'**
Writer	**Bowie**
Released	**album: *Hunky Dory*, RCA, 1971**

Hunky Dory was Bowie's transitional album from the singer-songwriter mode of his earlier music toward the more commercial rock of *Ziggy Stardust* and *Aladdin Sane*. 'Queen Bitch' opens with a strummed acoustic 12-string moving C-G-F (I-V-IV). One might be unsure as to whether this constitutes a riff, but when Mick Ronson's electric guitar blasts in, first on the right and then also on the left, there's no doubt. It's an exhilarating moment.

Since the tempo makes the changes fast, many guitarists who want to play 'Queen Bitch' have a problem moving their fingers that quickly. The solution is not to fully barre the F and the G but play them with a partial first finger barre on the top two strings only and a thumb on the bottom string (with full barres the thumb frequently has to change position on the back of the neck, which takes marginally more time). Also the third finger never leaves the fifth string, so it becomes a guide holding everything together.

Insofar as the riff has a variation it's the fact that the second C-G-F has the C just before the bar-line in a typical rock 'anticipation'. Throughout the verse the riff comes in at the end of each lyric line, a neat way of dovetailing a riff into a verse without drawing attention away from the words.

25. THE MIXOLYDIAN CHORD RIFF

Of all the modes outside of the major scale, the mixolydian is the one that deserves a section to itself because of the number of rock songs that have riffs drawn from its harmony. Remember that the only difference between a major scale and the mixolydian mode is the flattened seventh note. E major is E-F#-G#-A-B-C#-D#, while E mixolydian is E-F#-G#-A-B-C#-D – this D natural makes available two different chords to what would be expected in E major: chord VII becomes D instead of D diminished, and chord V becomes B minor instead of B. The latter is unusual because turning chord V of any major key into its equivalent minor undermines the key. These two chords lead to the two basic mixolydian chord riffs: I-*b*VII-IV (in A this is A-G-D), and I-IV-Vm (A-D-E minor).

Black Rebel Motorcycle Club's 'Love Burns' ends with an acoustic coda using an E-D-A mixolydian riff in 5/4. The first riff of AC/DC's 'Back In Black' is based on an E-D-A sequence, an E pentatonic minor run like the riff of 'Shakin' All Over', the E-D-A sequence again, and then a clever 'tripping-over' chromatic phrase where the accents are shifted away from the normal rock beat.

One of the AC/DC trademarks is that the A chord has C# on the bass guitar the first time, turning it into a first inversion. Many of their songs take familiar rock pentatonic chord riffs and put a harmonic twist on them by using either inversions or pedal notes in the bass. The idea can be extended with the addition of the flattened third blues chord, as in Lenny Kravitz's 'Fly Away', which uses A, C, G and

D (I, *b*III, *b*VII and IV).

A variation on the I-*b*VII-IV would be I-V-*b*VII-IV, heard (as E5-B5-D5-A5) on the Offspring's 'She's Got Issues', and *b*VII-IV-I-IV-I on U2's 'Desire' (also in E). For the intro and chorus of 'Living After Midnight', Judas Priest put this in an E-D-A-B sequence (I-*b*VII-IV-V).

RIFF GALLERY:
mixolydian chord riffs

Artist	**The Kingsmen**	
Title	**'Louie Louie'**	
Writer	**R Berry**	
Released	**single: (US) Jerden/Wand, 1963; (UK) Pye, 1964**	

This was a ground-breaking record because of its sheer primitive quality. Some people have called it the first garage rock record. In the early 1960s it was a staple of bar bands and by the end of the decade had racked up something like 300 cover versions.

This riff belongs in the mixolydian camp because it uses the minor form of chord V, which is one of the chords that mixolydian harmony offers. The song is in A and the chords are A D and E minor – this is the mixolydian version of the I-IV-V major key riff. This single riff, lasting two bars, carries the entire song, with only the occasional change of accent to add variety.

Eric Clapton's 'She's Waiting' is a song that uses a similar mixolydian riff with the minor chord V.

Artist	**Rolling Stones**	
Title	**'Not Fade Away '**	
Writer	**Petty/Hardin**	
Released	**single: (UK) Decca, 1964; (US) London, 1964**	

The Stones' third single, originally recorded by Buddy Holly, 'Not Fade Away' had a chord riff that popularised a rhythm known as the Bo Diddley beat, named after the 1950s US rocker with the box-shaped guitars and sheriff's hat. The main chord change is E to A, with the A chord only struck for a moment. During the verse this change is transposed to A to D. The three chords suggest a typical blues-derived E mixolydian harmony.

It's a good example of how the guitar's three most popular chords can be used when E, rather than A, is taken as the key chord. (For A-D-E when A is the key chord, see 'Wild Thing'). The other possibility – with D as chord I, E as a major form of the normally minor chord II and A as chord V – isn't so common. On the Stones' cut exotic percussion like maracas also helps things along.

Another Stones song based on the E-D-A change is 'The Last Time': here, over the strummed acoustic chords, the electric part borrows a classic blues lick, as heard on Howlin' Wolf's 'Smokestack Lightning' – it consists of a slide on the third string from A to B (frets 2-4) implying an E7 chord. During the second half of the riff a C# is thrown in when the underlying chord is A. Notice that this riff is not transposed onto either A or D during the chorus. 'The Last Time' can be thought of as a distant relative of Bowie's 'Rebel Rebel'.

Artist	The Who
Title	'I Can't Explain'
Writer	Townshend
Released	single: (UK) Brunswick, (US) Decca, 1965

The Who's debut single began a career of memorable riff-making. With Townshend's orientation to rhythm guitar it's no surprise that many of the Who's best riffs are chordal. 'I Can't Explain' uses a I-*b*VII-IV-I sequence. The I-*b*VII-IV mixolydian riff is in fact the definitive Who chord change, occurring again and again in their songs. In this instance it is in E major, moving E-D-A and back to E. The variation is I-*b*VII-V-I (E-D-B-E) in the middle and at the end of a verse. The guitar sound is very distinctive, with an organ-like tone because of the electric 12-string. Rumour has it that Jimmy Page played on the session, supporting the riff by playing fifths underneath the 12-string chords. The late John Entwistle once told Roy Carr that it was written as an answer to The Kinks' 'You Really Got Me', though lurking behind both records is 'Louie Louie'. Notice the strong contrast created by the bridge section ("Can't explain/I think it's love") which is a pop I-VI-IV-V (E-C#m-A-B) progression in E major, and not mixolydian. A *b*VII-IV-I riff occurs in another Shel Talmy production, The Creation's 'Making Time' (1966), which sounds very Who-like.

Artist	Them
Title	'Gloria'
Writer	Berns
Released	single: (UK) B-side of 'Please Don't Go', Decca, 1964; (US) Parrot, 1965/66 album: *Them*, Decca/Parrot, 1965

'Gloria' is famous not only for the spelling-out-letters lyric (always a great ruse to see if the singer can find a way of fitting the word in the available space), but also for its single-minded chord riff. Like 'Louie Louie', almost the entire song is carried on the E-D-A change (I-*b*VII-IV), bashed out with garage-band fervour. This is the same as the verse of 'I Can't Explain' but with a different rhythm. The exception is the guitar break where the chords are played E-D-A-D on triads around the 12th fret. The concentration on a single riff throughout an entire song marks a development in the rockier side of earlier 1960s pop music.

Artist	The Who
Title	'Won't Get Fooled Again'
Writer	Townshend
Released	single: (UK) Track, (US) Decca, 1971 album: *Who's Next*, Track/Decca, 1971

'Won't Get Fooled Again' is the Who's definitive expression of the I-*b*VII-IV riff by Townshend, this time in A, using A, G and D – A being one of the most resonant guitar keys in which this riff might be played. All the band's musical powers are captured on the recording: Entwistle's fluid bass, Moon's surging, unpredictable drums, Daltrey's bark'n'scream vocal, and Townshend's windmill guitar-playing, for which the term 'power-chord' must surely have been invented.

Townshend was drawn to this chord combination again and again. It crops up in a host of Who songs, including '5.15' (verse, G-F-C), 'The Seeker' (intro and chorus), 'Round And Round' (link), 'Naked Eye' (verse) etc. In the bridge of 'Won't Get Fooled Again' it is transposed up to B-A-E (for the "I know that the

"the concentration on a single riff throughout an entire song marks a development in the rockier side of 1960s pop music"

hypnotised never lie"). Compare that with the Bm-A-E change in the loud bridge section of 'Behind Blue Eyes', which is the other type of mixolydian riff. A song like 'Drowned' is a variation, going I-IV-*b*VII-IV.

Artist	**Led Zeppelin**
Title	**'Communication Breakdown'**
Writer	**Page/Jones/Bonham**
Released	**album: *Led Zeppelin*, Atlantic, 1969**

Nothing could be further from the turgid clichés of so-called Zeppelin-inspired metal than this, a taut 2.26 that seems closer to the garage rock of a band like the MC5, but played with rampaging energy and impeccable musicianship. It's a sonic blitz punctuated by a mad Page solo that careers off the splash of white noise from Bonham's cymbals. The riff is two bars of the I-bVII-IV change, this time going E-D-A-D. A fast string of eighths on the bottom E is dramatically interrupted by the D and A chords played around the fifth fret, probably on a Telecaster. Zep returned to this riff on 'In The Evening', also in E.

Artist	**Cream**
Title	**'Tales Of Brave Ulysses'**
Writer	**Sharp/Clapton**
Released	**album: *Disraeli Gears*, Reaction (UK), Atco (US), 1967**

Here's an example of a mixolydian riff with extra harmonic development. From the same album that featured 'Sunshine Of Your Love', comes Cream's evocation of the Homeric legend of Ulysses. Used almost throughout the whole song, this riff consists of the chords D-Cadd9-G/B-B*b* (or Gm/Bb). It's built on a descending bassline using the progression D-C-B-B*b*. The first three chords are the I-*b*VII-IV riff. These chord shapes have been used in quite a few guitar-based songs because they are easy to play, though not necessarily as riffs (eg The Beatles' 'Dear Prudence'). Cream liked the progression sufficiently to write another song with a variation on it, 'White Room', where Jack Bruce pulls off a clever bass trick by putting an F under the Cadd9 chord every other time. In both songs additional sonic colour is added by Clapton's wah-wah pedal. There is a ferocious live version of 'Tales' on one of the Cream live albums.

Part of this descending riff idea occurs in Blind Faith's 'Can't Find My Way Home', the Stone Roses' 'Tears', Dokken's 'Little Girl', and Neil Young's 'Needle And The Damage Done'. It also occurs as A5-G-D/F#-F on the intro of the White Stripes' 'Dead Leaves And The Dirty Ground'. The D-C-G/B mixolydian chord progression features on many rock songs, including 'Feel Like Making Love' and Radiohead's 'The Bends'. A variation starting on D minor is the arpeggio riff to Siouxsie & The Banshees' 'Spellbound'.

Artist	**Thin Lizzy**
Title	**'The Rocker'**
Writer	**Lynott/Bell/Downey**
Released	**album: *Vagabonds Of The Western World*, Decca/ London, 1973** **single (UK): Decca, 1973**

For sheer dumbness, the macho lyric of 'The Rocker' takes some beating – but what a guitar riff. The song is based in A and the mixolydian *b*VII chord (G) is heard throughout. Original Lizzy guitarist Eric Bell plays block chord shapes at the fifth and third frets (A, G, C are all heard, possibly D) but doesn't hit all the strings, and adds hammer-ons within the A chord. It was played on a Strat, but that alone doesn't account for the beautiful liquid tone. The riff serves as the chorus, where its effect partly depends on what the bass is doing – an A minor line using the notes A, B, C and G. Putting a minor scale-based bassline under a major chord is a good way to make tension in a progression or riff. Midway through the song (1.56) the riff appears as a link with heavy phasing.

The creative lesson of 'The Rocker' is to use block chord shapes for a riff but only play a few notes within them. To hear how fine the studio version is, compare it with the one on Lizzy's famous but over-rated live album *Live And Dangerous* (1978).

26. THE MINOR CHORD RIFF

It's rare in rock to find a riff entirely made of minor chords. The very fact that rock uses so many fifths instead of full chords demonstrates its unease about the overt emotion of the minor chord. So for this category we'll allow chord-based riffs that include a prominent minor chord.

The commonest riff led by a minor chord is either I-VII-VI from the natural minor scale (A minor-G-F in A minor), or with a major or minor chord V (E or E minor in A minor) tacked on the end. The former is the progression that (allowing for different guitar voicings) drives Blue Oyster Cult's 'Don't Fear The Reaper', Patti Smith's 'Because The Night', 'Layla', 'Sultans Of Swing', Bowie's 'Panic In Detroit', and the solo and final verse of 'Stairway To Heaven', among many others. Another popular chord riff with a minor chord is I-V-VI-IV (G-D-Em-C) as heard on Rainbow's 'Since You've Been Gone', and I-IV-VI-V (G-C-Em-D), the chorus of Boston's 'More Than A Feeling'. The White Stripes' 'I Think I Smell A Rat' almost manages to sustain a whole song on a rhythmic use of an A minor chord (and listen for the A and E natural minor lead phrases). The Queens Of The Stone Age's 'Auto Pilot' makes a riff out of a Bm-D-A/C# progression which runs through the intro and much of the verses. Deep Purple's 'Demon's Eye' features a minor arpeggio on G minor.

Artist	**The Beatles**	
Title	**'Come Together'**	
Writer	**Lennon/McCartney**	
Released	**album: *Abbey Road*, Apple, 1969**	

**RIFF GALLERY:
minor chord riffs**

This spooky riff from the twilight of the Beatles' career is a blend of bass and guitar parts. The basic chord is Dm7; the bass guitar plays a D minor arpeggio that jumps D-G-A through the next octave to a high F and then slides back down from the fifth, A. The guitar overlays a Dm7 figure (D-G-A-C) so the C coincides with the bass's F. (The guitar riff is like a slowed-down version of the 'Paperback Writer' one.) The combined effect of these parts as a riff in 'Come Together' gives the song unusual texture.

Artist	Focus
Title	'Hocus Pocus'
Writer	Akkerman/Leer
Released	album: *Moving Waves*, (UK) Blue Horizon, (US) Sire, 1971 single: (UK) Polydor, 1972; (US) Sire, 1972/73

In the heyday of 1970s rock guitar, Jan Akkerman stood out. Like many fusionists, he sometimes played too many notes, and could be rather cool and cerebral. But there is much to admire about the best of his recorded work with Focus in the 1970s. Here was a rock guitarist who didn't play obvious blues licks, was phenomenally fast (few people had seen anything like it at the time), and had a funky sense of rhythm.

The highly inventive 'Hocus Pocus' riff is based on A minor, though it uses both minor and major chords. It comprises two four-bar phrases, each with slightly different endings. These are then repeated (giving 16 bars altogether) and an extra phrase is fitted on the end, consisting of Am-C-D, D-F-G, E7#9. The initial riff is a clear tone-shift from G to A over an open A-string, and subject to considerable multi-tracking which doubles the riff at higher pitches. This was a send-up of heavy rock – part of the musical joke is that a heavy rock band would never write a riff that used these chords, and so many of them. As for the three lead breaks in 'Hocus Pocus', well, they're something else…

Artist	The Police
Title	'Driven To Tears'
Writer	Sting
Released	album: *Zenyatta Mondatta*, A&M, 1980

Songs like 'Roxanne' might have been entertaining enough, but when The Police turned their considerable musical talents to more serious concerns they simply went up a gear. 'Driven To Tears' demonstrates that protest songs can be musically inventive as they make their lyrical point (in this case about poverty and the media). Cast in A minor, the main riff is a four-note phrase using the notes A, E and G over an Am7 backing. During the verse this is transposed up a tone to fit over Bm7. The chorus uses Dm7 and Em7 chords, with the occasional additional note. The song's urgency comes from the rhythm section – Sting's eighth-note bassline through the verse and Copeland's ever-inventive drumming. After the second chorus the riff is transposed down a minor third to F#, and then down a further tone to E for Summers' brilliant angular guitar solo.

Artist	Siouxsie & The Banshees
Title	'Candyman'
Writer	Siouxsie & The Banshees
Released	single (UK): Wonderland/Polydor, 1986 album: *Tinderbox*, Wonderland/Polydor (UK), Geffen (US), 1986

The Banshees had just acquired yet another guitarist, John Valentine Carruthers, when they made *Tinderbox*, one of their best albums. 'Candyman' was its fierce opener, a sordid tale of child abuse told in the band's usual melodramatic manner. Its placement here in the minor chord riff section is because of the highly inventive verse riff, pitched unusually on G minor with a sus4 arpeggio. As the bass descends on a four-note sequence, the rapidly picked guitar chord ascends two frets. Towards the end of the song the riff is transposed onto C minor in first position. The song also contains two other fast arpeggio passages, which make it well worth learning.

---

27. SUSPENDED CHORD RIFFS

There are two types of suspended chord: the suspended fourth and the suspended second. When it comes to riff-writing, both types are very useful, since they add drama to music. In both cases the third of the chord, the note that determines whether the chord is major or minor, is removed, leaving a bare fifth. But in a fifth there were only two notes left, whereas in a suspended chord there are three notes – the third is replaced by either the fourth or the second of the scale. Few riffs are made entirely of suspended chords – they almost always form part of a riff.

The suspended fourth

The notes of a C major chord are C-E-G; the notes of C minor are C-Eb-G. The only note that distinguishes them is the one in the middle, the third. In a suspended fourth that middle note rises to F. It sounds tense because it wants to fall back (resolve) either to E or Eb.

Resolving sus4

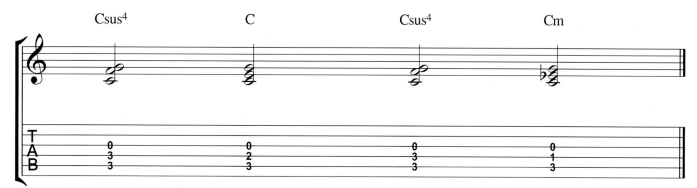

Suspended fourth chords are common in pop, rock and folk. They are often used in the build-up toward the transition from one section of a song to another. For a concentrated dose of suspended fourths try The Who's 'Pinball Wizard', Family's 'Burlesque', Springsteen's 'Two Hearts', the Stones' 'Rock And A Hard Place', and The Police's 'Spirits In The Material World'. The Manic Street Preachers' 'You Stole The Sun From My Heart' uses an arpeggio sus4maj7 (an unusual effect), and 'Tsunami' has a sus4 arpeggio, played high on what sounds like a Coral Sitar guitar to give an oriental sound. The verse of Def Leppard's 'Animal' uses a sus4 chord on C, and Simple Minds' 'Waterfront' is largely driven by a repeated 7sus4 chord.

The suspended second

The suspended second chord is not quite as dramatic as the suspended fourth. It can have an empty, spacey sound. Here the third of the chord *falls* to the second note of the scale. So C (C-E-G) becomes Csus2 (C-D-G) – see top of page 96.

It still sounds tense and unresolved because the second note wants to rise to E or Eb. Suspended seconds are common in pop, rock and folk, often combined with suspended fourths. The popularity of some of these chords is connected with how easy they are to play. The Asus2 and Dsus2 chords are popular because you only have to lift a finger off, and Esus4, Dsus4 and Asus4 only need a finger added. The

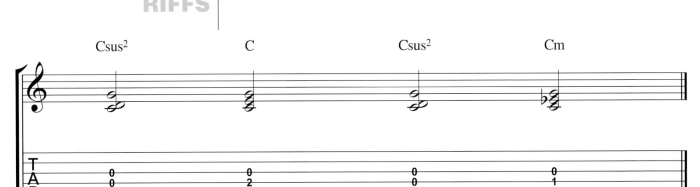

Resolving sus2

sound of a suspended second chord alters depending on how low or high the second is: the Csus2 has it low within the chord, the Dsus2 has it as the highest note.

The suspended second chord is closely related to the add9 chord, but the add9 has the third present. So while Csus2 is C-D-G, Cadd9 is C-E-G-D. There is also a form of add9 that doesn't have a third, which consists of two fifths put one on top of the other: C-G and G-D (or C-G-D). This could be termed a sus2 in a full voicing and '5add9' if there are only three notes, as spread out in the second and fourth

Variations on adding a second | chords here:

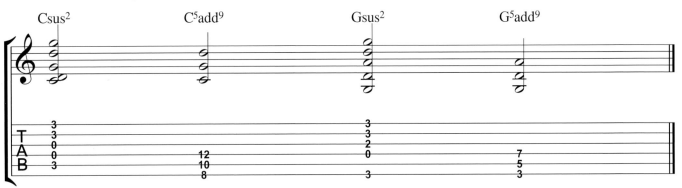

The last one (G5add9) is the chord figure Andy Summers used for the famous riff of the verse of The Police's 'Message In A Bottle'. This type of chord is also heard on the chorus of Linkin Park's 'Papercut', in E. I'm sure there's more music to be made in rock from this riff, it just needs a fresh angle. Incidentally, 'Message' features some prodigious harmonising of that musical idea.

The sus2, sus4 and add9 chords are inseparable from that style of rock known as 'jangle' – the folk-rock of bands like The Byrds, who based their music on the bright, ringing tone of the electric 12-string in songs like 'I'll Feel A Whole Lot Better' and 'All I Really Want To Do'. Elements of this sound can be heard in The Smiths, REM, in the Pretenders' 'Brass In Pocket', in the Bluetones' 'Slight Return', and many 'indie' bands of the 1990s, and in a 'high-octane' version in Springsteen's 'The Ties That Bind'. In this music riffs tend to be without distortion and constructed around effective chord changes with open strings and unusual voicings. Suspended chords are perfectly OK for heavy rock too: Smashing Pumpkins' 'Soma' has a haunting intro that shows what can be done with unusual chord voicings with plenty of open strings.

The suspended fourth and more

When the suspended fourth is combined with other notes on a chord, a classic rock riff idea is created. Barre your first finger across the top four strings at the second fret. This makes an A6 chord. We're going to ignore the top string and just work with strings two, three and four, which now form the major triad of A. As it's an A we can add the open fifth string to the chord. Now put your second finger on the third fret, second string. You're now playing A-E-A-D, which is A suspended fourth. Next step, use your third finger to hold down fret four on the fourth string. Now you're playing A-F#-A-D, which is either a second inversion D major or an Asus4/add 6, depending on musical context:

Sus4/6 rhythm

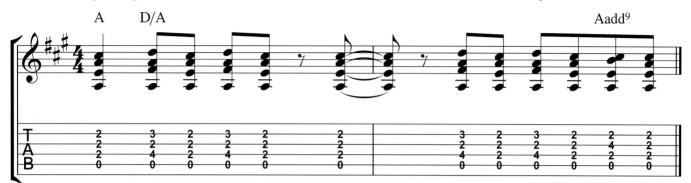

Hit the chord with the two fingers off (just holding the barre A chord), then put them both on, them take them off, etc etc. It's a sound you'll recognise from songs by the Stones such as 'Start Me Up', Free's 'All Right Now', Thin Lizzy's 'Rosalie', Be Bop Deluxe's 'Maid In Heaven', Bad Company's 'Can't Get Enough', David Bowie's 'John I'm Only Dancing', Sheryl Crow's 'If It Makes You Happy', ZZ Top's 'Jesus Just Left Chicago', Queen's 'Hammer To Fall', Springsteen's 'Crush On You', Manic Street Preachers' ''Slash And Burn', Elton John's 'Saturday Night's All Right For Fighting' and 'The Bitch Is Back', the Eagles' 'Life In The Fast Lane' (middle section), and Bowie's 'Jean Genie'. With the right amount of distortion in the chord you can get a pleasing, meaty sound from this figure. Then try the barre at the 14th fret and do the same figure for a very Brian May-sound (as on 'We Will Rock You').

Another related riff involves putting the third finger on the third string instead of the fourth, with the second finger doing its stuff on the second string.

Sus4/add 9 rhythm

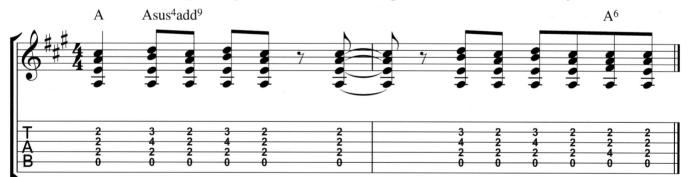

But what if we need to play this on a chord other than A? Well, forget about the fifth string, take the triad on strings four, three and two, and move it up to wherever you need it. Follow the note on the third string because that's the root.

For example, if you want to play this figure on D (see top of page 98) go to the seventh fret. Of course, with only three strings the sound is not as full as the example on A. If you can stretch with your little finger to the sixth string you'll find the right root note three frets ahead of wherever you are. So for D at the seventh fret, the little finger must hold down the D at fret ten on the bottom E-string. The little finger will also have to mute the fifth string .

This is an awkward shape to play at the best of times, let alone in full rock'n'roll mode duck-walking across a stage with a Fender Tele just above your knees or hoisted vertically on your chest. That's why Keith Richards is almost always in an open tuning when playing this riff. With the triad on the fourth, third, and second strings, strings one and five were redundant. But tune them both down a tone and,

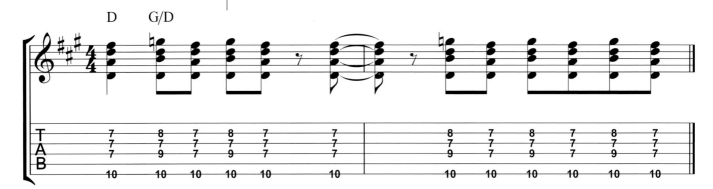

Adding the root note

hey presto... You can now barre across five strings, hit all of them, add the two notes and take them off, and get a fuller sound. (For more on this see 'Altered Tuning Riffs' in Section Four.) This should not be confused with the Doobie Brothers riff, which is a minor seventh chord shape in standard tuning with the second and third fingers going on and coming off. This minor7 idea was also used by Andy Summers on Police tracks like 'The Bed's Too Big Without You'.

RIFF GALLERY:
suspended chord riffs

Artist	**The Searchers**
Title	**'Needles And Pins'**
Writer	**Bono/Nitzsche**
Released	**single: (UK) Pye, (US) Kapp, 1964**
	album: (UK) *It's Fab! It's Gear! It's The Searchers*, Pye; (US) *Meet The Searchers*, Kapp, 1964

'Needles And Pins' (or 'Needles And *Pins-zer*', as they say) is an early British example of the 'jangle' guitar style. The opening riff is an A chord played on an electric 12-string: by lifting a finger off the second string an Asus2 chord is created; by putting it back and then putting the fourth finger on the third fret on the second string (playing a D) the Asus4 chord is produced. This type of suspended chord riff can also be heard on 'To Be Someone' (The Jam) 'Happy Xmas (War Is Over)', 'I Need You' (Beatles) and 'So Sad About Us' (The Who).

Artist	**The Beatles**
Title	**'Ticket To Ride'**
Writer	**Lennon/McCartney**
Released	**single: Parlophone (UK), Capitol (US), 1965**
	album: *Help!*, Parlophone/Capitol, 1965)

'Ticket To Ride' is the story of the coming of the electric 12-string to the forefront of pop music. Its chiming drone is heard on the opening bar, which is played on the top three strings, moving from A to Asus2. (Unusually, the lead guitar part was played by McCartney in this instance.) The droning sound of such a figure marks the advent of the psychedelic pop of the mid-1960s because of its static harmony, repetition, and emphasised higher frequencies. The 12-string dominates throughout bars 1-6 of the verse and then returns after the chorus. The guitar is balanced by bass and second guitar playing an A drone at different octaves. What is noticeable from the track as a whole is how much of it lacks full chords.

Lennon later (and slightly confusingly) called it one of the earliest heavy metal records, presumably because of its static riff and heavy drums.

Artist	**T.Rex**
Title	**'Cadillac'**
Writer	**Bolan**
Released	**single: B-side of 'Telegram Sam', EMI/Reprise, 1972** **album: re-issue of *The Slider*, Edsel, 1994**

Bolan's approach to electric guitar rhythm playing was shaped by the three years he spent in an acoustic duo – in the original Tyrannosaurus Rex he played guitar to the sound of bongos and congas. Unconsciously or otherwise, when he started writing riffs on electric, the bongo-influenced strumming patterns remained, as did the whole chords. For a rock guitarist, Bolan always made little use of fifths.

'Cadillac' is a two-bar riff made out of a D to Dsus4 change. The rhythm is syncopated in an almost Motown fashion. The only variation on the riff is as Bolan goes into the guitar breaks, where he takes out a couple of off-beat strikes of the D chord to make a little space. For contrast the verses end with a I-VI-IV-V sequence in C (C-Am-F-G) – just as happened in 'I Can't Explain'.

Artist	**David Bowie**
Title	**'The Jean Genie'**
Writer	**Bowie**
Released	**single: RCA, 1972** **album: *Aladdin Sane*, RCA, 1973**

By a strange coincidence, glamsters The Sweet released 'Blockbuster' at about the same time Bowie released 'Jean Genie', and both used the same Esus4 riff. The riff itself is the ultimate rock'n'roll chord of E major played with dirty distortion, the bottom E driving the beat and the sus4 making a fleeting decoration on the fourth beat. But listen carefully to the bass, which hits an A, and the second guitar which hits an A chord, on that fourth beat. Like 'Satisfaction', the sound of the riff is not self-contained but depends on the other instruments (in contrast to a riff like 'Rebel Rebel' which circles between D and E with open strings bleeding into one another, supported by the bass). Listen out for the sus4/6 chords on the chorus on B and A, and the high Dsus-D.

Artist	**The Beatles**
Title	**'I Feel Fine'**
Writer	**Lennon/McCartney**
Released	**single: Parlophone/Capitol, 1964**

"other adjacent strings within the chord are also hit and allowed to ring"

'I Feel Fine' is famous in the history of rock guitar for the blast of feedback with which it commences before moving onto a memorable riff with two components. The first few notes use the root note (with an octave leap), the flattened seventh and the fifth; the second piece is the 4-3-2-3 movement implying the momentary tension of a sus4 chord. All of this is generated on the guitar by holding a single barre chord and deftly picking the strings while lifting fingers on and off. The riff is played first on D up at the tenth fret, then on C and then at G (the key chord) at the third fret.

The riff is not doubled on the bass but supported by roots and fifths. The riff does receive support from a second guitar, which is shadowing the chord changes. Listen to the riff carefully to hear not only the contrasted tone of the guitars playing it, but also that it isn't a strictly one-note-at-a-time riff at all. Other adjacent strings within the chord are also hit and allowed to ring.

Artist	Free
Title	**'All Right Now'**
Writer	**Fraser/Rodgers**
Released	**single: Island (UK), A&M (US), 1970**
	album: *Fire And Water*, Island/A&M, 1970

Due to its use in TV commercials, 'All Right Now' has out-shone the rest of Free's output – which is a pity, if you know the quality of songs like 'Be My Friend', 'Mr Big', 'Little Bit Of Love', and 'My Brother Jake'. Free's blues-rock was particularly good at a slowish tempo, with Andy Fraser's nimble melodic bass and Paul Rodger's blues-inflected vocals.

Thanks to a brave arrangement decision, the verse riff of 'All Right Now' has no bass to support it – the bass only enters at the chorus. The main guitar riff is difficult to emulate, partly because its character is the combination of two guitars playing similar but not identical parts. The basic idea is an A chord with a Stones-ish double 'suspension' (D and F# coming on) – a chord idea that can also be thought of as a second inversion D major or A sus4/6. The Stones element is interesting because *Rolling Stone* magazine's reviewer said at the time it reminded him of 'Honky Tonk Women'.

After a suitably sexy gap the A is followed by a G5 and another D before a return to A. Paul Kossoff liked to beef up the A chord by doubling the open A-string at the fifth fret on the sixth string. The underlying chord change is A-G-D-A (the mixolydian chordal idea), as is the chorus, which simply finds another way of 'voicing' it.

Artist	**Bruce Springsteen**
Title	**'Born To Run'**
Writer	**Bruce Springsteen**
Released	**album: *Born To Run*, CBS/Columbia, 1975**
	single: CBS/Columbia, 1975

After two albums that had drawn (misplaced) comparisons with Dylan and Van Morrison, Springsteen had gained a reputation as a live act but had not made a commercial breakthrough. It came in 1975 with 'Born To Run', on which, flying in the face of the prevailing rock trends of the mid-1970s, he reached back in musical time to the late 1950s/early 1960s. Over the initial E-A-B chord changes Springsteen laid a riff that evoked the spirit of Duane Eddy: a low-string E major-derived figure that avoided the root note E over the E chord, opting instead to jump a minor seventh from B up to an A that functioned as a fleeting Esus4.

Sus4 chords can also be heard through the song's bridge section. On the album an Esus4 riff is also critical to 'She's The One', and another sus4 change dominates 'Night'. For a very different arpeggio approach to an E7sus4 chord, listen to the Smiths' 'The Headmaster Ritual'.

28. TRIAD-BASED RIFFS

The next two sub-sections look at other ways of writing chordal riffs. First, instead of using full chords why not experiment with triads? The theory of triads is simple: it only takes three notes to make a harmonically complete major or minor chord. Full guitar chords double or treble these notes in order to create more sound, but such doubling or trebling doesn't add anything harmonically.

The advantage of triads is that there are more of them on the fretboard, and they are usually easy to play and move around. They also permit you to experiment with chord progressions in which each note moves only a short distance to the nearest next note in the succeeding chord.

Have a look at this example:

Close-voiced triads

With common barre and open-string chord shapes it's often difficult to preserve such close movements within a chord-progression. Triads allow you to do this, and that can create riffs that have a sound all of their own. Triads will also 'sit' well over pedal notes, whether on the guitar or on another instrument.

You can hear triads (including suspended chords) on the verse of Van Halen's 'Dance The Night Away', and on The Who's 'Substitute', and throughout their instrumental 'Sparks', mostly over a D pedal. Angus Young puts triads over the main chords on the intro of 'For Those About To Rock'.

ZZ Top's 'A Fool For Your Stockings' makes excellent use of major triads that are turned into minor seven chords by the right bass notes, in a slow 12/8. Their track 'Beer Drinkers And Hell Raisers' puts minor triads over eighth-note basslines in a verse structure derived from a 12-bar. Ozzy Osbourne's 'Crazy Train' has E, D and A triads over an A pedal, similar to the Tom Robinson Band's '2-4-6-8 Motorway'. Pearl Jam's 'Not For You' puts second inversion E F and G triads over an E pedal.

Artist	**Argent**
Title	**'Hold Your Head Up'**
Writer	**Argent/White**
Released	**album: *All Together Now*, Epic, 1972**
	single: Epic, 1972

Having previously played in the 1960s group The Zombies (of 'She's Not There' fame), keyboard player Rod Argent formed Argent in 1970 with Russ Ballard on guitar – he of the shades and silver Fender Strat with a lot of holes in the body. 'Hold Your Head Up' is a great example of a chord riff based on triads on the top three strings while the bass plays a D pedal. The guitar chords are Dsus4-D-C at III-Csus2-Dsus4-D-G (III)-Cmaj7 (V)-Am (V). The pedal note in the bass adds to the harmonic richness. The steady slow rhythm and sustain allows the chords' sonority to be enjoyed.

**RIFF GALLERY:
triads**

Artist	Dire Straits
Title	'Sultans Of Swing'
Writer	Knopfler
Released	single: Vertigo/Warners, 1978
	album: *Dire Straits*, Vertigo/Warners, 1978

An unlikely guitar hero, Mark Knopfler found his own voice as a guitarist by back-tracking – looking past the flash excess of mid-1970s Marshall/Les Paul riffery, to a less distorted Fender 'twang' in which silvery bends seemed to have been corralled in from country rock and put to a new use. His sound was also influenced by a penchant for the Strat's so-called 'out-of-phase' pickup positions, and the fact that he didn't use a pick. The sound of thumb and fingers pulling at the strings makes a big difference.

This technique also influenced his composition because, when pulling three strings at a time, triads make perfect sense, rather than full chords. Part of what makes the 'Sultans' riff so memorable is the use of triads, most of which are second inversions (using strings four, three and two) and the way Knopfler slides them around. The riff is heard at the end of most of the verses and implies a Dm-Bb-C progression. This sequence is a rock staple (the chorus is the same chord sequence as 'Layla') but Knopfler found a different way of presenting it. He re-used the triads in 'Lady Writer'.

Artist	All About Eve
Title	'Tuesday's Child'
Writer	Bricheno/Cousin/Price/Regan
Released	album: *Scarlet And Other Stories*, Mercury/Phonogram, 1989

As well as having one of the best British female voices of the 1980s in Julianne Regan, the Eves had a guitarist, Tim Bricheno, with a flair for constructing riffs that had energy without going down the usual bare fifths route. A track like 'Flowers In Our Hair', ten years before its time, makes no bones about the D major-F# minor chords of the riff. Consequently, as a live act the Eves' could bang heads with an inimitable velvet elegance, as though Motorhead dressed in Laura Ashley and read Keats. Sadly a combination of business pressure and band relationships caused them to implode.

'Tuesday's Child' has all the virtues of the Eves' melodic rock. The verses are carried by twin-lead guitar fills and Bricheno's trademark filigree arpeggios. The triad riff comes in the chorus, with a fierce guitar part that has a standard A5 riff followed alternately by G and F, and Em and F triads. During the guitar break these arpeggiated triads occur again but with a couple of A pentatonic minor phrases crammed between them.

29. INVERTED CHORD RIFFS

A second resource for riffs is the use of inverted chords, where the order of notes in a chord is changed. First and second inversions can be spotted in printed guitar music by the presence of a 'slash' (/), provided the two letters are either a third or a fifth apart. A 'slash' chord is one with apparently two letter names, like C/E or C/G – the note on the left is the original root note, and the note after the slash is the new lowest pitched note resulting from the inversion. 'Slash chords' fall into three categories: inversions of simple major and minors, chords with a passing bass note, and complex (extended) chords. For riff purposes we'll just consider inversions.

Understanding inversions is easy. Changing the *order* of the notes in a major or minor chord makes a difference to the musical effect. In a simple major or minor chord there are three notes – for instance in C major we have C-E-G. If C is at the bottom we have a root position chord. Almost all guitar chords tend to be root position. But if we put the middle note (known as the third – here an E) at the bottom (in other words make it the lowest note) we have a 'first inversion'. If we put the top note (the fifth) at the bottom – here a G – we have a 'second inversion'. *The number of possible inversions is always one less than the number of notes in a chord.* So with a simple triad you can only have first and second inversions before you've exhausted the mathematical possibilities.

Here are inversions for C and G:

Inversions of C and G

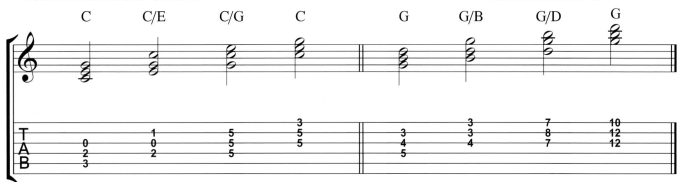

Compared to the root chord, a first inversion has a 'mobile' quality – it sounds like it wants to move. The bass note wants to either rise or fall a step. For this reason the most frequent use of first inversion chords is in descending chord progressions, linking the root chords, such as C-G/B-Am-G-D/F#-Em-D-A/C#-Bm (which would have the descending bassline C-B-A-G-F#-E-D-C#-B). You can also invert minor chords: if C minor is C-E♭-G, we make it a first inversion by putting E♭ as the lowest note, and a second inversion by making G the lowest note.

Second inversion chords don't sound as mobile as first inversions, but they can also feature in descending or ascending progressions. Try this one: C-G/B-Am-C/G-B/F#-Em. The second inversion has a dreamier, less focused effect. Surprisingly, it occurs in some of Nirvana's grungier numbers. Minor chords can have a second inversion too, but they're quite rare.

A chord progression with no root chords at all in it would sound unstable, not really anchored, but a few inversions inserted between root chords can make for more interesting music. You can hear combined second and first inversion chords on the intro to Jimi Hendrix's 'The Wind Cries Mary'. There are inversions in songs by the Stereophonics, such as 'Have A Nice Day', Muse, and Dire Straits. The riff in Queen's 'Tie Your Mother Down' ends with the chords G-D/F#-C-G/B, one on each beat. There are plenty in AC/DC's catalogue too: 'You Shook Me All Night Long' wouldn't be the same without the G/B chord on the chorus, and nor would 'Highway To Hell' without its D/F# chord in the mixolydian riff of A-G-D.

A whole major or minor scale can be harmonised with just inversions of chords I, IV and V (see stave at the top of page 104). Imagine a descending bassline: C-B-A-G-F-E-D-C. Using as many root major and minor chords as possible, we would normally harmonise it: C-G/B-Am-G-F-Em-Dm-C. The first inversion G/B takes care of chord VII, which is normally the awkward diminished triad. Using inversions you can limit yourself to a three-chord trick, and still keep the same bassline: C G/B, F/A, G, F, C/E, G/D, C. That uses only the chords of C major, F major and G major. If you're in a band, get your bassist to play the scale while you play suitable major chords. Play the chords in a sufficiently rhythmic way and you'll have a great riff...

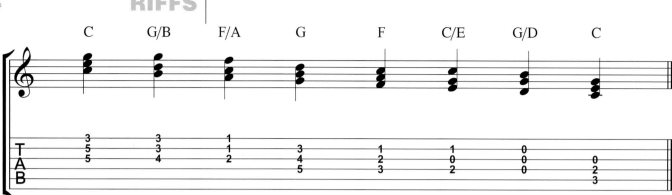

C major scale harmonised
with inversions

The most popular inversion shapes on guitar are G/B, D/F# and A/C#, because they are easy to play. The result is that only songs in certain keys on the guitar tend to employ inversions. If you play in a band and you want to explore inversions, just get your bass player to change his or her note. That's an easier way of doing it than trying to change the guitar chord. Say you've got a song based around a G-C-D progression. For a bit of variety, try inverting it by getting the bass to play B under G, E under C, and F# under D. That has quite a different sound from the root version.

RIFF GALLERY:
inverted chord riff

Artist	**Living Colour**
Title	**'Desperate People'**
Writer	**Reid/Glover/Calhoun/Skillings**
Released	**album: *Vivid*, Epic, 1988**

'Desperate People' shows off not only the band's musicianship but also an excellent grasp of song construction. It starts with feedback imitating a siren, and then plunges into a musical whirlwind of 16th-notes at a tempo of about 175bpm. It's in this intro section that inverted chords are used. The sequence goes E/B-B-G/B-D/A-A (twice) and then an ascending sequence of B-G#/B#-F#/C#-C#. This means the bass is moving up in semitones. The musical effect of these inversions is twofold. It gives the music an up-in-the-air quality which creates anticipation of the moment it will crash to earth (which it does at 0.55 with the main riff at a tempo of 103bpm). Second, it lends extra colour to the harmony. The band exploit the intro's inversions further by recycling them during the bridge at the slower tempo. Listen out for the shifting ways in which these bridge chords are accented.

30. UNUSUAL CHORD RIFFS

We've been looking at chord-based riffs which fit within the frame of a major, minor or mixolydian harmony. Another way of experimenting when writing riffs is to throw in the odd unusual chord. So what makes a chord count as 'unusual'?

Imagine a piece in the key of E major. The usual chords would be E, F#m, G#m, A, B and C#m. Chord VII in a major key is always a diminished triad – here D#dim – so in a rock riff the inclusion of that would sound unusual. If the piece has a hard rock/blues edge the chords G and D are likely to occur. Since minor chords are not so common in a blues-based hard rock song, even a chord like C#m, which is technically in key, might strike the ear as something out of the ordinary. Any other chords will probably sound unusual, to a degree. Inserting one or two in a standard chord sequence is a good way to make an out-of-the-ordinary riff.

A further refinement is either to add a note to a simple triad where it wouldn't be expected, turning a major chord into a sixth or a minor chord into a ninth, for example, or using the 'wrong' form of a more complex chord. Let's take sevenths as an instance. In the key of E, building the correct sevenths by taking the additional note only from the scale of E major, we get this sequence: Emaj7-F#m7-G#m7-Amaj7-B7-C#m7. Using an unexpected type of seventh (eg Bmaj7 instead of B7, thus introducing a note not in the key) will create an unusual chord. Turning minor chords into majors or moving them up or down a semitone will have similar effects. But remember that such chords must be used sparingly in a riff, otherwise they undermine the fundamental sense of key – after all, if there was no 'normal', how would you know what was strange?

Here is an example of a riff with unusual chords in it:

Unusual chord riff

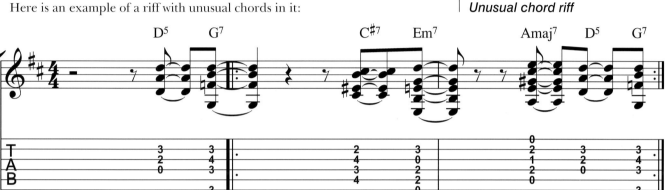

The key is D major. The first change is from D5 to G7, which gives a hard, bluesy start (chord IV would normally be Gmaj7, but G7 isn't so far out in a rock song). Then the riff moves to C#7 (instead of the usual C), Em7 (chord II in D), and Amaj7 instead of the 'correct' A7. Two of the five chords (D and Em7) are in key, two are 'off-key' by a single note (G7, Amaj7), and one is wholly off-key (C#7).

Artist	**Black Rebel Motorcycle Club**
Title	**'Red Eyes And Tears'**
Writer	**BRMC**
Released	**album: *Black Rebel Motorcycle Club*, Virgin America, 2001**

RIFF GALLERY: unusual chord riff

Along with The Hives, San Francisco three-piece Black Rebel Motorcycle Club have enjoyed success playing guitar rock, in their own way loosely based on the 'garage rock' of The Stooges and the MC5 – with elements of Television and the Velvet Underground. It's reaching an audience who don't like nu-metal and want a new take on some traditional rock virtues – like short songs and hooks.

'Red Eyes And Tears' is a fine example of a rock song given an exciting slant by the inclusion of an unusual chord riff. The verse features a C# octave riff which indicates an alternate tuning for the guitar. The unusual chords enter at 0.58 and 1.50, and at 2.14 during the guitar break. The riff consists of major thirds on the guitar – E-G# sliding down to D#-G (F double-sharp) and then to a phrase that implies C# minor. The bassline moves to B-A# and then back to C#.

The net result is a sense of an E-D#-C#m progression, and this is unusual because D# isn't usually found in C# minor. It's a dark, sleazy riff that gives the song a haunted quality reminiscent of The Smiths' 'How Soon Is Now', though coming from a West Coast band it isn't surprising that 'Red Eyes And Tears' also includes guitar phrases out of the 1960s 'raga-rock' book. Other unusual chord progressions occur in BRMC's 'Love Burns', with the E5-implied C#m-C5 over an E pedal during the verse, and also in their 'As Sure As The Sun'.

Techniques for playing RIFFS

So now we've surveyed our 30 types of riff – let's go on to have a look at some musical approaches and guitar techniques that will inspire you to write new riffs of your own, and do more with the riffs you already have.

REPETITION AND DEVELOPMENT

Possibly the greatest trap that writers of riffs can fall into is not realising the potential of the riffs they create. Rock music should be exciting – so don't bore your listener. It's always good to leave people wanting more. Repetition is essential, but always try to judge where the line is between hearing a riff too many times and hearing it too few. Err on the side of too few repetitions. If the listener hears your song and thinks, "That's a great riff, that song was over too soon", chances are they will play it again – which is exactly what you want.

A new riff will take shape in a certain key, with a given rhythmic feel, at a certain speed. Once these are sorted out, write your riff down and/or record it. With its initial form captured you can start to mess about with it. Most bands don't do enough such exploration. Do it too early and the original inspiration might get blurred or lost. But once the riff is on tape, disc, or paper, you are free to realise its potential. You can always go back to the original form if things don't work out.

Don't think of a riff as a finished entity when you get the first version preserved. Think of it instead as something that's maybe only showing one of its faces to you. You need to walk round it and have a look at its other sides. How is this 'walking round' done? Remember the RHM formula: rhythm-harmony-melody. Your riff has a rhythm facet, a harmonic facet, and a melodic facet. So why not try consciously altering them?

TEMPO

First, try changing the rhythm of some of the notes. Shorten some, lengthen others. Also check the tempo. If the riff is intended for a medium-to-up-tempo song, try speeding it up gradually and see how fast it will go before it loses its character (or your fingers fall off). What you're looking for is not the fastest tempo at which the riff could be played, but the fastest tempo the riff can be played *without losing its identity*. You can easily test this notion of a riff losing its identity: take any famous riff cited in this book and play it faster or slower than the original – there's always a point where it doesn't sound as good, where the riff loses something. The change in tempo eventually robs the riff of its character. To test the tempo of a slow riff, make it slower. At a certain point it becomes ineffective because there isn't enough forward momentum. An audience will get bored… and so might the band.

This principle of what happens when the tempo of a riff is changed was demonstrated dramatically to me many years ago when I heard a bootleg of Led Zeppelin's 1979 *Knebworth* performance. Either the show was recorded on a slow-running tape deck, or the vinyl pressing was cut at the wrong speed, but the consequence was that all the songs were faster than they should have been, and the guitar pitch was a whole semitone sharp. This made the fast songs sound silly, but the slower numbers sometimes gained: 'Kashmir' became even more relentless, and 'Ten Years Gone' was simply spectacular played with more drive. Jeff Buckley's amusing send-up of 'Kashmir' (on the *Live At Olympia* CD) shows what happens when the increase is too great. He pretends to be copying a 33rpm vinyl album turning at 45rpm. The 'Kashmir' riff suddenly loses its grandeur.

Many songwriters experience recording a song, as a demo or even something for release, only to find later that the song now sounds too slow to them. They ruefully reflect that it would have been better quicker. There is a natural, human reason why demos in particular often turn out too slow: they are generally recorded when the composer is still learning the song, still getting to grips with it. As a result, it's not surprising this should affect the tempo by keeping it a little below what it could be.

One further type of rhythmic variation involves shifting the accent on a riff. More complicated would be repeating a riff in a different time signature altogether, or re-writing an idea that initially comes as a 4/4 riff (it often seems that all rock riffs leave the Creator heading for you with a default of being in 4/4) as 5/4. We'll look at alternate time signatures in a few pages.

RE-HARMONISING

The next way of developing a riff would be to change the chords that go with it. Try turning major chords into their relative minors and vice versa. Remember that a relative minor is always three semitones below the major chord (C to Am, D to Bm, F to Dm etc). If you are playing a riff where there are only fifths or fourths, which is tonally neutral, you could put major chords behind some of its appearances and minor chords behind it on another section.

Otherwise, with a simple unison riff where guitar and bass are playing the same notes several octaves apart, you could change the bass note to imply different chords or even inversions of the same chords. First inversions are useful in this respect if you want to imply major and minor chords without actually playing them, and also to delay a root note unison riff, because the inversions will sound less 'grounded' than when the guitar and bass are simply playing the same notes at different octaves.

A good example of re-harmonising is Garbage's hit 'Androgyny'. Leaving aside the A pentatonic minor phrase that punctuates the verse and intro, the main riff in here comes at the chorus – an E pentatonic minor phrase with an octave leap from the bottom E to the E at the seventh fret on the fifth string. As such, it's a distant relative of riffs like 'Black Night' and 'How Many More Times'. But it's what Garbage *do* with this riff that is interesting. The predictable approach would have been to transpose the riff onto the same root note of each chord in turn. Instead, in the first bar of the chorus, the E pentatonic minor riff is played against an E minor

"there's always a point where a riff doesn't sound as good, where it loses something"

harmony, so it fits. But through the rest of the chorus the riff stays the same while we hear it against the chords of G, C and F. This causes tension, and makes the riff sound different even though it hasn't gone anywhere. Type O Negative's 'My Girlfriend's Girlfriend' uses a similar technique.

TRANSPOSING A RIFF

Another way of changing the harmony is to transpose a riff into a different key or onto a different root note. The term transposition usually implies that the actual shape of the riff stays the same – none of the internal musical relationships contained in it are changed. You simply raise or lower it in pitch.

There are three main ways of using transposition. The first is follow the structure of the song. One time-honoured way of developing a riff is to repeat it during a verse and move it up with the expected chord changes, while another is to transpose it several times at the bridge or for the guitar solo. Think of Blind Faith's 'Presence Of The Lord', which starts as a pentatonic minor riff on A, then gets transposed to D and then E. Hendrix uses this technique in the middle section of 'In From The Storm' where an A blues scale riff is transposed onto B and then C. Transposition comes into its own towards the end of a song because it can breathe new life into a riff that's already been heard many times, simply by re-pitching it.

A riff can be transposed by any interval. Within a 12-bar progression where the riff replaces overt, strummed chords, the transposition will be first onto the note a fourth higher, and then a fifth higher. The first type of transposition was developed in rock in the 1960s during the so-called British Blues Boom, when many songs were structured as 12-bar sequences with the expected chords and chord changes. In bands where there's only one guitarist, and no keyboard player, the guitar part could be a riff rather than the actual whole chord. So for a 12-bar in G that could mean a riff on G played four times; then at bar 5, when the music changes to a C chord, this riff would simply be transposed up a fourth so it started on the note C; and in bar 9, when the music reached a D chord, the riff would be transposed up a fifth from G to D. In this manner the entire 12-bar could be played without chords but with a single one-bar riff occurring in three different positions, as in this example:

Transposed riff

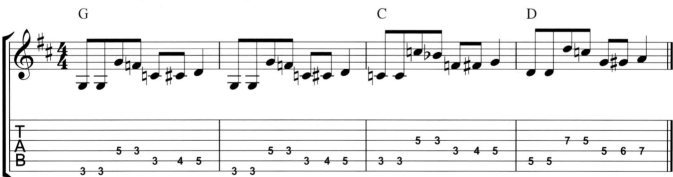

Very often in such an arrangement the guitar would play the riff with the bass doubling an octave or two lower. These kinds of transposition are easy on the guitar because if the initial riff is played on the lower three strings only, it can be moved up or down the neck, or across so the root is on the fifth string and retains the same pattern. The famous Jeff Beck/Rod Stewart track 'Rock My Plimsole' (1967) is a good example, along with Cream's 'Strange Brew', Free's 'Worry', Taste's 'Same Old Story', and Rory Gallagher's 'Messin' With The Kid' (in E mixolydian, with the riff crammed into eight bars). Basslines can also be transposed – as in James Brown's 'Papa's Got A Brand New Bag'.

The second type of transposition doesn't depend on supporting a preordained musical structure like a 12-bar. It involves transposing a riff to wherever you like, depending on which section of the song you're in. Probably the most common shift for a riff is up a tone. There is a formula in heavy rock where a riff is shifted up a tone after the second chorus for the guitar solo. Another favourite shift is the minor third, because of its relationship to the pentatonic minor scale (which has a minor third between the first two notes, ie A-C). In fact, you could transpose a riff on the basis of the pentatonic scale, so the first riff on A is shifted in turn onto C, D, E and G, these shifts being distributed through the song. For a more unsettling transposition, move up or down a semitone, or even by a tritone.

Free's 'Moonshine' has a single-note A pentatonic minor riff transposed to D in the verse. The bridge of Kiss' 'Detroit Rock City' has a C pentatonic minor riff that's then shifted up a tone. Hendrix's 'Izabella' has a verse riff transposed up a minor third, and 'Beginnings' has even more instances. In Led Zep's 'Heartbreaker' the main riff first appears on the note A, is then heard on B and then returns to A. After the second chorus, when the riff comes in again it appears on C, then D and finally on E. So in this song, one two-bar riff has appeared at five pitches. Transposition allows you to get the most out of a single riff. Also, transposing up in pitch is a good way of increasing a sense of excitement with the same musical material.

The only thing to be careful of is if the original riff uses open strings, as these will be lost through most transpositions. Chord-based riffs or riffs with inversions, and pedal/drone note riffs, tend to be susceptible in this regard. It may not be possible to find another open string to do the job of the old one in the initial riff. In which case you can either cheat (in the recording studio) by using a capo or even re-tuning the guitar and doing an overdub just for the transposed version of the riff. Or (probably more sensible, given live performance etc) take the transposition problem as an opportunity to write a variation of the riff. In other words, 'compose out' the problem of the untransposable open string – as in the example below.

The third transposition method involves deciding that an initial riff idea is not in the most effective key – whether for the singer's voice range or for the guitar itself. So what keys suit the guitar? Is there such a thing as a riff-friendly key?

When it comes to hard rock/heavy metal the number of keys is more limited since the style requires keys that are low in pitch with regard to the open strings. This means pre-eminently E and A. F# and B are also hard rock favourites because in both cases the open string a tone below the key note (E below F#, A below B) is the flattened seventh of the key scale, as is common in rock. To increase the 'heaviosity' of their riffs, many bands resort to detuning (which we'll come to in a moment – see page 111).

We could extend this and say that there are some keys in which the guitar simply sounds better. With some instruments the question of which key you play in is not vital. There might be a minor inconvenience of fingering, but not a substantial difference to the sound (on the piano, for instance). The guitar, though, is moderately key-sensitive. So what are the main factors that determine whether a key gets used on the guitar?

RIFF-FRIENDLY KEYS

The classic rock mixolydian chord riff of I-bVII-IV in a variety of keys:

Key		
I	bVII	IV
C#	B	F#
F#	E	B
(1) B	A	E
(2) E	D	A
(3) A	G	D
(4) D	C	G
(5) G	F	C
C	Bb	F
F	Eb	Bb
Bb	Ab	Eb
Eb	Db	Ab
Ab	Gb	Db
Db	Cb	Gb
Gb	Fb	Cb
Cb	Bbb	Fb

(1) 'Broad Daylight' *(Free)*
(2) 'Communication Breakdown' *(Led Zep)*
(3) 'Won't Get Fooled Again' *(The Who)*
(4) 'Freebird' *(Lynyrd Skynyrd)*
(5) 'Queen Bitch' *(David Bowie)*

All these are the same chord change merely at a different pitch. But that change of pitch has considerable implications for the guitar because the voicing of the chord – how many open strings it has, what is the lowest bass note, and so on – is critical to how it sounds.

Transposed riff with variations

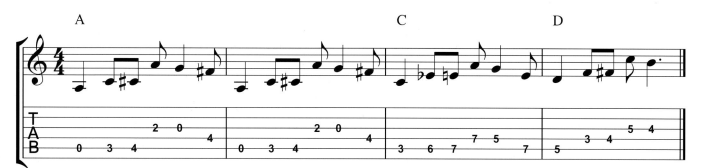

First, will the key allow open strings as notes on the major scale or natural minor? Actually, the majority of keys allow at least one open string, but it's more effective to have several (we won't get into the weird and wonderful world of using open strings as chromatic 'foreign' notes in a key). The more notes a key has that are open strings, the more likely you are to get open-string shapes that are resonant and easy to play. The six open strings, EADGBE, are present in the keys of C, G, D and their respective minors Am, Em and Bm. If we then allow ourselves a mixolydian A (A-B-C#-D-E-F#-G) – a major scale with a lowered seventh – all the open strings are still 'in key'.

Notice that these keys are on the 'sharp' side of C major. The guitar has a natural bias toward sharp keys and away from flat keys. For example, write a riff in F major, the first flat key, and the guitar 'loses' one of its open strings, B, which becomes B*b*. In some keys important notes of the desired scale will be open strings. The Yardbirds' 'Stroll On' makes much use of the chords G and A with the bass note dropping to the open E string. This would not work as well in any other key.

In rock music the usual harmony of a major key is often replaced by a hybrid based on the pentatonic minor for that note. The formula is: take a pentatonic minor scale and build major chords on each note. So, if A pentatonic minor is A-C-D-E-G and we think of it as a 'cut-down' version of the A minor scale, the chords that properly arise on that scale are Am,C, Dm, Em and G. For a hard rock song it would be more promising to make up a chord sequence using A, C, D, E and G majors. You can also throw in an F chord for good measure.

This formula/approach is heard on *White Blood Cells* by The White Stripes. The album has three songs centred on A, five on G, two on E minor, one on A minor, two on D, one on B and one on E. In each, chords occur which don't strictly belong in the major key on these notes but are chords built on these pentatonic minors. Another way to think of this is to take a major key and map out its seven primary chords. In E major: E, F#m, G#m, A, B, C#m, D# dim. Throw away the diminished (because this is rock'n'roll, not jazz) and throw away the three minor chords (because minor chords are for wimps, apparently). That leaves chords I, IV, and V – E, A and B – the good old 'three-chord trick'. Next, take notes three, six, and seven of the scale (G#, C# and D#), lower them all a semitone to G, C and D, and turn them into major chords. The result is a scheme of six major chords to play with for songwriting. Next, if you're The White Stripes, dump the bass player and get a strong colour scheme…

CHORD-SHAPES

The second factor in whether a key is 'guitar-friendly' concerns chord-shapes. The more open-string chords a key allows, the easier it is to play in, and the more sound comes from the instrument – especially on an acoustic guitar. This is one of the reasons for the appeal of open tunings, which increase the amount of open-string 'ring'. C major's primary chords for songs are C, Dm, Em, F, G and Am, and B diminished, the latter usually replaced with a B*b*. So, among the first six, there's only one barre chord – F. It would be easy to get rid of that by playing an Fmaj7 instead, which is why in guitar tutor books beginners are often taught to play Fmaj7 before F. Now compare the chords of C with those of E major, which are E F#m G#m A B C#m. Notice we have four barre chords. Using the hard rock formula outlined above we would get E, G, A, B, C, D – much easier. Or how about a key like B*b*? The main chords for songs are B*b*, Cm, Dm, E*b*, F and Gm – all except Dm are barre chords – and this is a key with only two flats. So it's clear that as soon as you move 'flat-ward' in the circle of keys, in come the barre chords.

This is why, if you are trying to work out a song from a record/CD and it appears to be in E*b*, always ask two things: first, has the artist detuned a semitone, so all the shapes and patterns and open strings are those in E, though the guitar is actually pitched lower by a half step? Second, are they using capos at the first fret (where E*b* is a D shape), or the third fret (where E*b* is a C shape). Detuning is common among rock bands, so if the song is a rock number, bear this in mind. If the song is a singer-songwriter number, suspect the presence of a capo: ringing open strings, descending basslines on the lower strings, and the use of easy inversions (like G/B and D/F#) are a give-away that there's a capo involved.

So the guitar-friendly keys are pretty much F, C, G, D, A and E, and the use of a capo simply puts a difficult flat or sharp key into the guise of one of those. One final point concerns riffs that start with an open A-string. With a 12-bar, three-chord format, if you put the song in A, each of the three riffs (A, D and E) should be transposable and still commence from an open string.

To see how choice of key can alter a riff, take Jimi Hendrix's 'Freedom', from the album *First Rays Of The New Rising Sun*. The opening riff is C# pentatonic minor. What is unusual about this riff is the way that, because the key is C#, the open bottom E becomes the flattened third of the scale. So Hendrix drops a sixth from the root note C# on the fifth string to the bottom E and then climbs up from there. This has the effect of making the E seem lower than it actually is (a technique exploited by bass players).

The effect is even more pronounced if the drop is to the major third of a chord, which in this key would have to be E#. Each time Hendrix comes back up to C# he hits a C#m7 (possibly C#7#9) chord on that note. I recommend the version of 'Freedom' recorded at the *Isle Of Wight Festival* in 1970, because it's full of brilliant guitar ideas – examples of how Hendrix's compositions were becoming more soul-influenced and more sophisticated toward the end of his life.

DETUNING FOR RIFFS

The simplest form of detuning is when the entire tuning of the guitar is lowered by one semitone to E*b*A*b*D*b*G*b*B*b*E*b*. Unlike a proper 'altered tuning', the chords and scale patterns you know remain the same; they are simply one semitone lower in pitch. Some players in the 1980s and 1990s have taken this even further by detuning by a tone or even a tone-and-a-half (where the lowest string is D*b*). This greatly increases the 'sludge' factor of riffs and very soon will make you feel neck-deep in cold mud... which for a death metal band may be the effect you're after.

Detuning by this amount has, shall we say, *interesting*, effects on a set of light-gauge '9' strings, because they go rather slack. This is fine for bending, but not so good for intonation, and they won't take kindly to being hit hard. Most players who use detuning compensate by shifting up a gauge in strings for every semitone they lower them. A '10' set for E*b* standard tuning will give better string tension and more tone. Experiment and find a combination you feel comfortable with.

Tracks that feature detuning include Linkin Park's 'One Step Closer', Limp Bizkit's 'Pollution' and 'Rollin', The Offspring's 'Americana', Dokken's 'Sunless Days', and Korn's 'All In The Family'. Tony Iommi was a pioneer of de-tuning. On Black Sabbath's third album, *Master Of Reality*, he succumbed to the evil lure of D*b* major by detuning down a tone-and-a-half on 'Children Of The Grave', 'Into The Void' and 'Lord Of This World', and used the same approach for the later 'Supernaut', 'Cornucopia', 'Snowblind', 'Sabbath Bloody Sabbath', 'A National Acrobat', and 'Killing Yourself To Live' (though the key centre there is G*b*). I'm not sure if these songs were just the sixth string down to D*b* or the whole lot down three semitones. Whichever, this was the true beginning of grunge.

Recent guitar design offers another possibility for players who want their riffs to sound heavier: get a seven-string guitar. The extra string is a B a fourth below standard bottom E. Korn tracks like 'Twist' and 'Swallow' feature seven-string

> "most players who use detuning compensate by moving up a gauge in strings for every semitone they lower them"

guitars tuned down a semitone, and on songs such as 'Porno Creep' and 'No Place To Hide' down a tone. The usual shapes for fifths, fourths and so on, remain intact, and for something really insane you could always put the seven-string into its equivalent of dropped D tuning with the bottom B down a tone to A, which provides a bowel-shocking low fifth on the bottom two strings. Mike Mushok of Staind has used BEADGB, which is standard tuning with a low B but no top string (like the lowest six strings of a seven-string guitar). Dropped D on this would be BDADGB. He has also used variations such as ADADGB, and AEADGB and AEBDGB. For examples of how bassists can get into five (and more)-string riffola read about John Paul Jones' recent bass riffs in the Masterclass Interview, Section Five.

If you don't want to get into all this detuning malarkey, there is a neat way of creating the *illusion* of a detuned riff – by playing fourths on the bottom two strings where fifths might have been expected. Hendrix did this in the verse of 'Spanish Castle Magic'. The effect is startling: it sounds as though he's fallen off the bottom of the Strat.

ALTERED TUNINGS IN ROCK

Another way of creating new riffs is to take detuning one step further. Instead of just detuning each string by the same amount and ending up in a version of standard tuning a semitone or a tone lower, you can move into a new tuning. Altered tunings offer the chance of coming up with a different type of riff – maybe with an unusual chord or run of notes. Although mainly used by instrumentalists and singer-songwriters, there's no reason why rock guitarists can't use altered tunings for their own heavier purposes, as bands like Sonic Youth have demonstrated.

Altered tunings found their way into rock music from two main sources. One was the blues, because blues slide-players often play in open A or open E, and blues has had a powerful influence on rock. Rock guitarists tried these open tunings for slide, got to grips with Elmore James' classic blues riff 'Dust My Broom' (a slide to a 12th-fret Em7 chord), and thought perhaps they could write other music in these tunings. The other source was the 1960s acoustic guitar style known as 'folk-baroque', pioneered by players such as Davy Graham, Bert Jansch, John Renbourn and Martin Carthy. They were interested in open tuning because it enabled a finger-style guitarist to play a melody, a bassline, and a harmony in the middle, all at once.

From the rock perspective it was highly significant that Jimmy Page chose to put his adaptation of Jansch's 'Blackwaterside' (see page 115) on the first Led Zeppelin album as 'Black Mountainside'. That album also featured a blues cover, 'You Shook Me', which Page probably played in open E for the slide. Page went on to use many other tunings, and, as Led Zeppelin's fame grew through the 1970s, more and more players were influenced by his example. Altered tunings can be divided into two main groups: those that make a simple major or minor chord, and those that don't. The former we can term 'open tunings'.

Open tunings

When it comes to rock riffs, the most significant open tuning is open G (DGDGBD). This tuning was adopted by Keith Richards in the late 1960s and became a cornerstone of the Stones' sound. Open G is what you're hearing on Stones classics like 'Brown Sugar', 'Tumbling Dice', and 'Start Me Up', and on Black Crowes tunes such as 'Hard To Handle' and 'Hotel Illness'.

The popular way to use this open tuning for riffs is to create sus4/6/9 additional notes to the major chord that results from a barre at any fret. The open tuning allows these on/off chord figures more effectively than standard tuning. Ronnie Wood has written similar riffs with open E (EBEG#BE).

> "altered tunings offer the chance of coming up with a different type of riff"

With any open major tuning, frets three, five, seven, ten and 12 are the crucial positions. These frets represent major chords on a pentatonic minor scale. If we are in open G tuning, fret three is B*b*, fret five is C, fret seven is D, fret ten is F and fret 12 is G (the octave above the open string chord). The notes G-B*b*-C-D-F make a G pentatonic minor scale, and these represent the root notes of chords I, *b*III, IV, V, and *b*VII in G.

This is the obvious way to use open G tuning, working in the key of G. Another way to use it would be to write a riff in the key of A in open G tuning. Fret two is now A, fret five is C, fret seven is D, fret nine is E, and fret 12 is G, which gives the notes of A pentatonic minor. In this key the open-string chord becomes the flattened seventh (*b*VII) blues chord in A. A third possibility is to write a riff in the key of C in open G tuning. Now the open strings and 12th fret are G (chord V), fret three is B*b* (*b*VII), C is at fret five (I), E*b* is at eight (*b*III) and F is at ten (IV). Other keys are easily obtained by using a capo. Billy Corgan tuned one of his guitars EGDGBE (giving an open Em7 tuning) for Smashing Pumpkins' 'Sweet Sweet'.

Non-open tunings

An altered tuning that doesn't form an open major or minor chord is DADGAD. This tuning originated with acoustic folk-blues guitar hero Davy Graham. Inspired by the music of Morocco, the story goes, Graham worked out the tuning in order to imitate the drones and pedals he heard in North African music. It was a kind of poetic/musical justice that the tuning's greatest moment in rock consequently came in the Led Zep epic 'Kashmir'. Page also used it for 'Midnight Moonlight' on The Firm's first album, and on the instrumental 'White Summer'. One of the appeals of DADGAD for the rock guitarist is that the three lowest-pitched strings, DAD, make a perfect fifth plus octave that can be played with a single first-finger barre.

'Dropped D' riffs

Something of the effect of altered tunings can be had by the simpler method of a single string alteration. The most popular is 'dropped D' tuning. The name is misleading because it isn't a D that's being dropped, it's the bottom E-string which has gone down a tone to D. It's a good way to experiment with altered tuning. Make this change either by comparing the open fourth D-string until the sixth is in tune an octave lower, or tune down until the seventh fret of the bottom string is in tune with the open A-string. Remember that for every semitone tuned down, the notes on a string move up a fret. Straightaway you'll find dropped D alters the guitar's standard tuning bias from E towards D. You can bend notes on this detuned bottom string more easily because of the decrease in string tension. Smashing Pumpkins' 'Hummer' and 'Jellybelly', Bon Jovi's 'Let It Rock', Led Zep's 'Moby Dick', and Guns N' Roses' 'The Garden' are examples of songs that use this tuning.

An intriguing variation on dropped D is 'double-dropped D', where the top and bottom E-strings are both tuned down a tone to D. This gives the tuning DADGBD, which is only one string away from open G. Neil Young used DADGBD to great effect in 'Cinnamon Girl' (see page 114).

If playing altered and open tunings with overdrive/fuzz you will find that, because of the increased resonance, sustain, and enhanced overtones, you may want to back off the distortion to less than normal. This is especially true for chords more complicated than fifths, and also with riffs that take advantage of one of the benefits in altered tuning: the ability to play notes on adjacent strings that are only a tone or semitone apart. This is tricky in standard tuning, but in altered tunings it's possible to get harp-like run of clustered notes. There's no reason why you can't use these in a riff, but they will sound better if the guitar is clean(ish).

When writing riffs in altered tunings, make sure you write them down on paper in some way – chord boxes will do. It can be frustrating years later to try to re-learn a riff written in a funny tuning – even if you remember what the tuning is – and find you can't remember the shapes and can't work them out from an audio source either. Chances are if you write a couple of riffs in altered tunings you will get to like them, and you'll soon find you've used a dozen different tunings and it's just too much to remember without notes.

Artist	The Move
Title	'Brontosaurus'
Writer	Wood
Released	single: Regal Zonophone (UK), A&M (US), 1970
	album: *Looking On*, Fly (UK), Capitol (US) 1970

This was one of the last Move singles before writer and multi-instrumentalist Roy Wood formed ELO then swiftly moved on to his glam-era band Wizzard. 'Brontosaurus' is a good example of what can be done by detuning the E-string to D. The riff is a slow climb up a D blues scale, three times, each time the bass supplying a different root note, with a descending phrase at the end to give balance and wind the whole thing up to repeat.

The main guitar riff is multi-tracked and partly doubled on one side by a synth. The last bar of the riff is heard frequently in the chorus at the end of the various lines. At about 2.35 the music goes into double-time and a new pentatonic major riff enters, changing on each chord. Notice the hint of piano on the last time of the slow riff, like a much slowed-down 'Lady Madonna'.

Artist	Neil Young
Title	'Cinnamon Girl'
Writer	Young
Released	album: *Everybody Knows This Is Nowhere*, Reprise, 1970
	single (US): Reprise, 1970

'Cinnamon Girl' is a wonderful example of 'double dropped D' tuning (DADGBD), recorded early in Neil Young's long, eventful career (and on his first outing with Crazy Horse). It sounds like a heavy rock band rehearsing in a barn somewhere in Arizona. The main riff is two bars long and has two phrases: the first is a C-D chord change followed by a descending run that goes down a D mixolydian scale to a flattened third (F) and then to the note G. The second bar repeats this but the run stops on that low bluesy bIII.

Listen for the way that most of time there is no percussion on the last off-beat of the 4/4 bar during the riff. This riff is possible in standard tuning, but would lack the low D and a couple of other notes.

Where the DADGBD tuning really comes into its own is in the verse, where it creates a resonant D5 (with a unison D on the top two strings), a beautiful Amadd4, a Cadd9, and a G, before culminating in a quick ascending phrase that moves in fifths up a D pentatonic minor (F-G-A-C-D) scale.

This track has a surprising and haunting erotic charge, caused in no small measure by the tuning.

Artist	The Faces
Title	'Stay With Me'
Writer	Wood/Stewart
Released	album: *A Nod's As Good As A Wink... To A Blind Horse*, Warners, 1971 single: Warners, 1971

Ron Wood remains one of the less appreciated rock rhythm guitarists – something not helped by his sterling work sharing rhythm duties with Keith Richards. Much of Wood's rhythm work is driven by fuzzy pungent dyads – pairs of notes or, even threesomes, where a note is hammered on or pulled off to create tension. Wood always had an astonishing tone, quite unlike anyone else, courtesy of a Zemaitis custom-made silver-body guitar shaped like a Les Paul, with a fuzz-box built in. Nothing captures this tone better than the opening seconds of 'Too Bad' – where Wood, probably in an open tuning, constructs a riff from a C to F chord change by hammering-on various notes and using the blues flattened third in both instances – or 'Miss Judy's Farm', or 'Stay With Me'.

'Stay With Me' uses open E tuning (the electric version of open D, which is favoured on acoustic guitar because the strings don't need to be tuned upwards) and the block on/off chords you would expect. What lifts it far above the run of this kind of boozy, good-time rock is the contrast in tempos and keys. It starts fast and frenetic in E, puts its verses and choruses in a half-time A major, and then reprises the intro for the wild coda.

Artist	Bert Jansch
Title	'Blackwaterside'
Writer	Trad arr Jansch
Released	album: *Jack Orion*, Transatlantic, 1966

Riffs don't only occur in *electric* guitar music. 'Folk baroque' is the label given to a complex style of acoustic guitar that flourished in the mid-1960s and influenced a generation of players. It was kick-started by Davy Graham, who wrote 'Anji', an attractive piece on a descending Am-G-F-E sequence that might also be considered a riff, and a version of the traditional tune 'She Moved Through The Fair'. Closely associated with Graham were John Renbourn and Bert Jansch, and the latter's album *Jack Orion* was a big influence on the young Jimmy Page.

The essence of folk-baroque is that it's a self-contained finger-style for steel-string acoustic. A typical Jansch or Renbourn instrumental will feature a melody with a bassline and supporting harmony. The bassline will often be an alternating octave played with the thumb. The other fingers play higher notes in a syncopated rhythm against this. A single piece may well contain marked breaks in this rhythm, where the player suddenly strikes all the strings by a flick of the finger. It's a style that encourages you to stop thinking in standard chord shapes. Instead, each string is almost a separate instrument and the finger-picking brings them together.

'Blackwaterside' was played in dropped D tuning (DADGBE) with a capo probably at the second fret. Its riff consists of an accented hammer-on/pull-off figure that Jansch uses in-between some of the lyric lines. He develops it too, adding extra pull-offs from time to time. The effect is hypnotic.

He played variations of the same riff in 'The First Time Ever I Saw Your Face' and 'The Gardener', and it was also the model for Jimmy Page's instrumental 'Black Mountainside'.

"riffs don't only occur in *electric* guitar music..."

FORM AND LENGTH OF RIFFS

An important part of the craft of writing good riffs is to understand their form. By form I don't mean specific musical elements like melody, harmony or rhythm. I mean how many times bits of the riff are repeated, how many bars a riff takes to play, and so on.

The simplest riff form is a single phrase that lasts one bar. But riffs can also last two, three and four bars. Three is less common because if repeated it gives a six-bar phrase, which runs against the tendency in rock for things to group in multiples of four. However, if you repeated this three-bar riff four times you would have 12 bars (a multiple of four). If you write a riff longer than four bars it's harder to make it sound as a single unit – though of course this depends on factors such as tempo and how many notes the riff has.

Let's call our one-bar riff 'a1'. A typical approach would be to repeat it in multiples of four with the arrangement changing around it:

a1   a1   a1   a1

Add interest to a simple riff like this by changing the bass guitar's part underneath with a pedal effect, or by making the bass note imply a different harmony. Imagine a one-bar riff that used the notes A, C and G. With a bass A underneath it would probably sound like A pentatonic minor, but the bass could enter with an F or a C and make it sound quite different.

The next variation on this riff form is to change the fourth bar. This gives us a 3 + 1 pattern: three riffs the same and then one with a slight variation ('a2'):

a1   a1   a1   a2

If we have eights bars to play with, instead of just repeating this idea we could make the repeat end with a third variation, so the eight bars would look like this:

a1   a1   a1   a2
a1   a1   a1   a3

If there were 16 bars, we would have another option, which would be to repeat the eight-bar form but add a fourth variation on the last time:

a1   a1   a1   a2
a1   a1   a1   a3
a1   a1   a1   a2
a1   a1   a1   a4

By this point we will have reached the limit of what can be done with the 'a' riff without something else happening, since in the 16-bar example the riff has occurred in its original form 12 times. The trick with getting a2, a3 and a4 to sound right is to make sure they work harmonically. You don't want a2 and a3 to sound more decisive and finished than a4, since a4 is the last in the whole block. So, if this riff is based on the chord of A major, it will sound more effective if the a2 and a3 variations end on a note that implies a D or E chord, or perhaps the bIII C chord or the bVII G chord.

Another approach would be to take the original 'a' riff and make a four-bar phrase from putting its variations one after another.

a1   a2   a3   a4

Whether the listener heard this as four riffs or a single one with four parts would depend on how similar the individual bars were to each other. Another popular variant on this is to make the riff in bars 2 and 4 an answer to the original riff:

a1   **a2**   **a1**   **a3**

Here's one slightly less common riff form where there's a single variation in bar 3:

a1   **a1**   **a3**   **a1**

So far we've assumed the riff is a one bar–phrase. Riffs can also be two bars long, in which case some of the forms above can be applied to a two-bar riff. Just treat 'a' as two bars instead of one.

There are many more variations to the form of riffs, but these basic patterns of repetition, answer, and variation are the most useful. Remember they can be expanded by combining them with the principles of rhythm, harmony and melody.

HOW RIFFS ARE USED IN SONGS

You may have a killer riff, but how impressive it seems will depend on the musical context in which it's placed. This depends on the genre of music.

In most styles of hard rock, heavy metal etc, the riff is at least as important as anything else in the song, including the chorus, which in traditional songs is supposed to be the 'hook', the most memorable part. In heavy rock the riff can be found as the intro and kept going during the verse with the vocalist singing over it.

If writing a song along these lines, where almost every part is accompanied by riffs and not chord progressions, then you will either need to write several riffs, or variations on the initial riff, for the different sections. There may also be a need to alter the way the riff is presented in terms of arrangement or dynamics. One way is to have the riff played at full volume by the guitars during the intro and chorus, but during the verse pull the guitars out of the mix and just have the bass play the riff. Another approach is to use a simplified version of the riff for the verse and keep a more complex one for the chorus or links. Otherwise, use the riff for the intro and as a link between the chorus and the verse. The same riff can then support the guitar solo, or lead out of the guitar solo, and occur again in the coda (the final section of a song). This is a more mainstream way of writing a rock song, where the vocal sections of verse and chorus are supported by chords.

A 'busy' riff can distract attention away from the vocal line. It can also be difficult to work out a melody over a riff – this is because a riff not only sets up competing melodic shapes and rhythms, but also doesn't offer the same harmonic support to the vocal melody as chords. If you want to fit a melody over a riff, strive to get the melody rhythm to fit with the riff's rhythm, and also choose notes which harmonise with the riff's notes. If the riff itself has lots of gaps in it you may be able to fit the melody in those gaps.

In a song that comprises a riff, or riffs, plus chord sequences, there are great possibilities for strong musical contrasts through mixing harmony. For example, a pentatonic minor or blues scale riff could be contrasted with a chord progression in a major or minor key. Robert Plant's 'Tie Dye The Highway' has a fierce A pentatonic minor riff using the notes A, C and G, but this contrasts with the more poignant Em-C chord change, the Em intensified by being voiced as a ninth. This song's arrangement also gains power from the fact that a drum machine provides the beat for about two-thirds of its duration, before real drums enter and step up the energy level. Pentatonic minor/blues scale-based sections can contrast powerfully with major key sections, as on the Levellers' 'Hope Street'.

"you may have a killer riff, but how impressive it sounds will depend on the musical context"

Riffs and rock music are almost synonymous, so it's easy to think that a riff has to be loud. This isn't the case. Riffs can be used just as effectively in quieter material. Take Tracy Chapman's hit 'Fast Car' (1988). During the verses and links a two-bar riff based on the chord progression IV-I-VI V (D-A-F#m-E) is played on an acoustic with a sparse backing. The repetitions of this riff express the lyric's theme of being trapped in life situations. On the choruses the lyric often talks about escape, so the riff is abandoned and full chords break out. This is a good example of the way a riff can connect with a lyric and a song's dynamics.

RHYTHM AND TIME SIGNATURES

The most popular time signature in rock is 4/4. The symmetry of this time signature has a universal appeal: the 'magic' number four is also present in rock in other structural details, such as the length of phrases, how many times something is repeated, how many chords there are in a phrase etc. So the majority of the riffs are in 4/4. Every now and again, however, you might feel like something different, or a riff may suggest a different time signature. So here's a quick guide to some other useful time signatures for riffs.

Simple time
Broadly speaking, simple time signatures are those in which the beat can be divided by an even number. For instance 3/4 (three quarter-notes, or crotchets, in a bar) is a time signature associated with the waltz. Even if you are not writing a song entirely in 3/4, single 3/4 bars can be used in a variety of ways in a song that is primarily 4/4. Imagine a four-bar intro in 4/4, 16 beats in total. Substitute a 3/4 bar for bar 4 and you have a touch of asymmetry. Now there are only 15 beats. This means the next section (presumably a verse) arrives one beat before the listener expects. Such a huge proportion of rock music during the past 50 years has been in 4/4 and dominated by fours of everything that as listeners we unconsciously expect things to happen in fours. Breaking with this is a nice way of creating a bit of the unexpected.

Think of it like this:

symmetry = beauty; asymmetry = drama

Another possibility would be to alternate 4/4 and 3/4 bars. This again would create an element of surprise, because either the two-bar riff would be one beat short or bar 1 repeated would lose a beat, or bar 3 would arrive a beat before the listener expects.

In 2/4 time bars tend to be too short for a riff to get going, but they can be used effectively at transition points between song sections to cut a phrase or riff by two beats or lengthen by two, or make the listener wait another two beats before the next section. 6/4 is quite an easy time signature to handle – sort of 4/4 with a bit more room, so you can fit in an extra couple of notes, or words. It offers intriguing possibilities for adding pauses to a riff, or shifting the accents of either a riff or a melody if they are written as though the bars were all 4/4. What then happens is that the start of a phrase will not always line up with the start of a bar, and since the first beat of the bar always carries a stronger emphasis than the other beats, that emphasis will fall in different places. But because 6/4 is an even number, every so often they will line up:

6/4 beats:	1 2 3 4 5 6	1 2 3 4 5 6	1 2 3 4 5 6	1 2 3 4 5 6
riff:	G C	D Em	G C	

There has been the occasional chart hit in 5/4 time, most famously Dave

"single 3/4 bars can be used in a variety of ways in a song that is primarily 4/4"

Brubeck's 1959 'cool jazz' classic, 'Take Five'. 5/4 is an asymmetrical time useful for giving relief from the steady beat of 4/4. Use it in a bridge section, for example, or under a guitar solo, or just for the intro, and then drop into 4/4 for the verses and choruses. Peter Buck of REM once said, "We count measures. It's a dumb trick, but if you're doing repetitions of four measures, repeat them three times instead of four … or five. The ear is going to hear if you're working in fours, but if you do three, to the ear things are changing faster. Or sometimes you'll add two beats to a bar." The same principle applies to beats and employing odd time signatures.

If you're intrigued by the whole business of odd time signatures, listen to Brubeck's albums *Time Out* and *Time Further Out*. Although it's jazz, not rock, you might pick up some great ideas for use in a rock song. Jazz-rock, fusion, and progressive rock also feature odd time signatures. Jethro Tull's 'Living In The Past' is a good example of the last genre. Led Zep's 'Four Sticks' makes use of 5/4, and 'Achilles Last Stand' has bars of 5/4.

To hear a witty use of an unusual time signature applied to a standard rock'n'roll shuffle rhythm figure, listen to the intro of 'Going For The One' by Yes. Pink Floyd's 'Money' uses a B pentatonic minor riff in 7/4. Led Zep's 'The Ocean' has bars of 7/8, which can be understood as a bar of 4/4 with the last off-beat missing (very good for emphasising the first notes of a riff). One staggering example of the use of strange time signatures is Jethro Tull's 'No Lullaby' which has 4/4, 5/8, 2/4, 7/8, 3/4, and 6/8, and a complex riff that starts as E pentatonic minor and ends in chromatic fashion.

Anything longer than 7/4 (the larger the first number, the more beats in a bar) would probably not be heard as such by the listener. It would take great skill on the part of the composer, and the musicians playing it, to write a riff in, say, 8/4 because the listener would almost certainly hear it as two bars of 4/4. Similarly, a 9/4 bar would be heard as 4/4 + 5/4. Even 7/4 has to be handled with care to stop it breaking down into 4/4 + 3/4. Time signatures with more than four beats have an inherent tendency to 'sag' in the middle, which becomes more pronounced at slower tempos.

You might wonder what the difference is between a 4/4 + 3/4 combination and a bar of 7/4, or 4/4 + 2/4 and a single bar of 6/4? This is where the understanding of the emphasised first beat is crucial. In 6/4 or 7/4 the strong beat only occurs once, and then you have to wait five or six beats for it to be felt again. With alternating bars of shorter number of beats like 4/4 and 3/4, a strong beat will be heard twice as frequently. So to ensure your 6/4 or 7/4 bar is really heard as such, emphasise the first beat (loud chord, cymbal crash, or whatever) and let the vulnerable beats in the middle of the bar go slightly under-emphasised.

Compound time signatures

Compound time signatures are those in which each beat of the bar is divisible by three. The commonest are those in which a quaver (eighth-note) forms the basic unit of the bar. In rock the most popular is undoubtedly 12/8, which has four dotted crotchets/quarter-note beats to a bar (just like 4/4) with each of them splitting into three quavers. The same rhythmic effect can be temporarily achieved by playing triplets on the beat in 4/4. 12/8 is a time signature used for blues shuffles, and similarly 'swung' songs. After 12/8 comes 6/8, which has just two (dotted crotchet) beats – use it instead of 12/8 if you want the feel of only two beats in each bar.

This, incidentally, is how to distinguish 6/8 from 3/4. At the right tempo it's easy to confuse the two, since a slow 6/8 would count as *one*-two-three, one-two-three – which might be mistaken for two bars of 3/4. In fact, the difference would be that in 6/8 only the first '*one*' would be stressed, whereas in 3/4 each of the 'ones' are stressed because both are at the start of a bar.

To introduce a little asymmetry into 12/8 or 6/8 sections, try adding a bar of 3/8 (which will be like adding one extra beat). For a rarer effect, try 9/8, with its three groups of three. Plenty of scope there for creating a whole song based on units of three instead of the usual four. Hendrix wrote 'Manic Depression' in 9/8, as discussed below.

Other rhythm effects

You can spice up the rhythmic effect of your riffs even without resorting to odd or changed time signatures. Stay in good old 4/4 and try one of the following methods.

First, put an accent during one of the repetitions of a riff, where there wasn't one before. Second, reverse one of the rhythmic components of the riff. If you have a dotted quaver/semiquaver combination on one beat, try reversing the time values (in this case put the semiquaver first). Try the classical composer's tools of augmentation and diminution: the former means increasing the time value of the riff, the latter decreasing it. This will work best if done uniformly, otherwise the riff will change its shape too much. Diminution is probably more useful in rock.

If you are getting towards the end of a track and want to increase the excitement, decrease the time values of a riff by 50 per cent. This would have the effect of reducing a four-bar riff to only two bars. To the listener it would seem as though the speed of the music has increased, though in fact it would be at the same tempo. This is closely related to approach known as half and double-time, which can be very effective if the switch is from 4/4 at one speed to a matching 12/8 at another (for breaking the monotony, quite apart from anything else).

Some bands have adapted rhythms from outside rock altogether. Led Zep's 'How Many More Times', Jeff Beck's 'Beck's Bolero', and Deep Purple's 'Child In Time' all use the rhythm known as 'Bolero', after the famous orchestral piece by Ravel. Hendrix even put a foxtrot rhythm into 'House Burning Down'.

And don't forget that one of your best musical friends is always silence. Listen to Robert Plant's 'Messin' With The Mekon' for the startling use of silence to add power to a bII-II-I riff. Other effects can result from changing what the rhythm section is doing. The Police used a G mixolydian riff on the chorus of 'Invisible Sun', but made it special by setting it without a standard rock drum rhythm. Listen for the heavily accented fourth beat of the second bar of the riff.

Syncopation

Another vital technique for making rock riffs rhythmically interesting is syncopation. This means working in some way *against* the beat by placing accented notes on off-beats, and sometimes letting them stretch *across* the beats and bar-lines. The drums will bring the beats through; the guitar and bass can play against them. One of the things that made the classic rock bands of the late 1960s /early 1970s sound as good as they did was the fact that their bassists, consciously or unconsciously, were often influenced by the syncopated bass heard on soul records. What syncopation gives straight away is that magical ingredient, the groove.

Often nowadays bands fill bar after bar with nothing but straight eighths in the bass. It sounds so much better to have some syncopation in a riff. The simplest way is to have a one-bar riff that repeats not from the first beat of bar 2 but from the last offbeat of the first bar (tied across to the next bar). This creates a distinctive 'pulling' effect.

The appearance of triplets in a riff in 4/4 will give a 'bounce' to it. Although eighth-note triplets are the most common, you can also have quarter-note triplets, where three quarter-notes are played across two beats, giving six notes in all. This produces a curious sense of the bar being stretched, with the music floating above it. It often occurs in Latin American-inspired music, so there are plenty of examples in the recordings of a band like Santana, such as 'Se A Cabo'.

Led Zeppelin were famous for adding unusual rhythmic effects to their riffs. People often think this indicates the presence of an uncommon time signature, but it isn't always the case. Coming out of the guitar solo in 'Over The Hills And Far

Away' there is a climbing figure played by guitar and bass over a steady drumbeat. The notes are grouped in threes. This means the beginning of each group of three notes is accented against different beats within 4/4: the accents fall in beat 1 bar 1, beat 4 bar 1, beat 2 bar 2, beat 1 bar 3, and so on.

Zep repeated this trick of three against 4/4 in the verse of 'Misty Mountain Hop' with the chromatic triad riff. For other riffs developed by shifting rhythmic accents listen to Metallica's 'The Thing That Should Not Be', Bon Jovi's 'Bad Medicine', and Jethro Tull's 'Aqualung'.

Another way of using a time signature with a riff is to simply take the riff and fit it into a new time signature without any change. If you fit a 4/4 riff into 3/4 you will lose whatever note was on the last beat. If you put a 4/4 riff into 7/8 you will lose that last eighth-note or chop an eighth-note's duration from the last quarter-note. Alternatively, fit a 4/4 riff into 5/4 and your riff has gained a beat's rest. What you do with that rest is up to your creativity. It could be a drum fill, a moment of silence, a new bass note, or the room for a chord.

Spaces and drumboxes

Thinking about time signatures should not blind us to one obvious factor which affects how a riff sounds: the rest. Many of the greatest riffs depend on a rest or two to punctuate them. Such rests allow the rhythm section to come through all the more forcefully – writing great riffs means being especially aware of what the bass and drums are doing. The two basic choices when it comes to writing with a rhythm section are to dovetail your notes into the drums or play at the same time. The two bits of the kit you need to be especially conscious of are the kick (bass) drum and the snare. You can work a riff off either, or leave a gap where one or the other will come through. A fine example of this is the pentatonic minor riff on the chorus of Deep Purple's 'Strange Kind Of Woman' (in 12/8) where the riff is punctuated by cymbal crashes. Another Purple track, 'Space Truckin', has an interesting rhythmic relation between the drums and the riff.

Rhythmically, the best riffs are often doubled by the bass and their rhythm patterns coincide with what the drums are doing. The vintage trick is to leave a gap where the snare drum is hit and play around that. That's why some of the best riffs will come when you play against a drum machine (or drummer). Hearing a rhythm is the best way to spark a good riff that has punch.

For this reason, one of the best aids for writing riffs is a drum machine of some kind. Some guitar effects units now come equipped with basic drum loops to help you work. It's amazing what a difference the presence of even a drum loop can make to the way you write. Without rhythmic accompaniment you are much more likely to try to generate excitement in the riff by concentrating on the harmonic or melodic elements. You'll try to make it memorable by making the notes an interesting shape or by working in some unusual harmonies.

There's nothing wrong with either – but since rock music is primarily about rhythm, and this is especially true of riffs, it's better to at least combine such aspirations with a strong rhythm. The simplest ideas can really take off with a drumbeat. Even a metronome that only provides the steady click of the tempo is better than nothing. If all else fails, tap your foot as you play and make the riff dance against the rhythm of that tap – the end result will be more rhythmic. Any harmonic or melodic twists you include will come across even better if they are welded to a great rhythm.

The final point about timing and rhythms in riffs is to do with speed. Some riffs will sound better at slower or faster speeds. By increasing or decreasing the tempo on a drum machine or metronome you will automatically change the nature of the riff you write because certain speeds will suggest certain riffs (sometimes because they will remind you of things you've already heard).

"hearing a rhythm is the best way to spark a good riff that has punch"

RIFF GALLERY:
different time signatures

Artist	**Jimi Hendrix**
Title	**'Manic Depression'**
Writer	**Hendrix**
Released	**album: *Are You Experienced*, Track/Reprise, 1967**

'Manic Depression' is possibly rock's most innovative use of 9/8 time (three beats, each split in three). The riff is a simple arpeggio on A and G, returning to A via D. Hendrix plays four before the verse, and each lasts a bar. After each of the first two lines of lyric in a verse, the riff comes back. Hendrix makes plentiful use of unison bends to fill in the spaces, singing in falsetto with them at the start of the solo. Some of these bends are wonderfully vocal, like the two 'moans' at the three-minute mark, before the whole thing collapses in a welter of bleeping guitar feedback.

Artist	**Jimi Hendrix**
Title	**'I Don't Live Today'**
Writer	**Hendrix**
Released	**album: *Are You Experienced*, Track/Reprise, 1967**

This song is in 4/4 but shows what can be done if you borrow a rhythm pattern from elsewhere. For the intro Hendrix uses a heavily accented eighth-note rhythm, which is distinctly American Indian, making hay with a high B7 chord before the fierce descending single-note riff on B pentatonic minor. The song features feedback at 0.35, and octaves in the rhythm guitar during the guitar solo before the second chorus at 1.52. There's great tremolo work at 0.41 and 2.08, where Hendrix seems to bang the back of the guitar as the pitch drops slowly until 2.22, producing his patented 'alien spaceship parking' effect. The frenetic coda has more feedback in the centre, with the solo off to the left. This fades out at 2.51 into a terrifying wail.

Artist	**Deep Purple**
Title	**'Black Night'**
Writer	**Lord/Blackmore/Gillan/Glover/Paice**
Released	**single: Harvest (UK), Warners (US), 1970** **album: *In Rock*, *Anniversary Issue*,** **Harvest/Warners, 1995**

What makes 'Black Night' work is the combination of 12/8 time and the E pentatonic minor riff played around the fifth fret position. It's unusual for heavy rock riffs to occur in 12/8, but it gives this riff real bounce. It consists of an initial phrase, a variation and then two contrasted approaches to the tonic E, one from below, one from above, so they 'answer' each other. The first two bars have a single phrase that ends in bar 3 with a tone shift from D to E, the key-note approached from the flattened seventh. The fourth bar approaches the key-note E from G (the *b*III) – a good example of how these two flat notes of the pentatonic minor can be contrasted. The riff has a lovely rhythmic contrast because bars 1-2 are flowing whereas bars 3 and 4 have long rests in the guitar part. Notice also that the guitar solo is supported by the D-E tone shift, and the organ solo by a G-A tone shift – an example of transposition. Toward the end of the verse a longer variation to this riff is developed with the vocal melody in unison.

Artist	**Soundgarden**
Title	**'Fell On Black Days'**
Writer	**Cornell**
Released	**album: *Superunknown*, A&M, 1994**
	single (UK): A&M, 1995

It's notoriously tricky to write good melodies over heavy riffs, yet 'Fell On Black Days', from Nineties Seattle grunge band Soundgarden, manages exactly this. Listen for the major7 chord at the end of each verse just before the chorus. Major 7s are rarely used in heavy rock because they are deemed too 'sweet'. When their emotive appeal is successfully linked up to the power of heavy rock the effect is tremendous. Listen also for the bass going down to the really low register from the first "how would I know?". The extreme wah-wah break and the singer's shift up to a higher range for "I sure don't mind a change" is another highlight, as is the guitar harmony line toward the end of the song. The 6/4 time signature also makes a pleasing change from rock's standard 4/4. Though Soundgarden's music has a line of ancestry that goes back to Black Sabbath, the slow-burn introverted feel of 'Fell On Black Days' is reminiscent of a heavier Free.

> "it's notoriously tricky to write good melodies over heavy riffs"

ARRANGING AND RECORDING GUITAR RIFFS

Let's imagine you've written a song with a good riff – now it's time to record and arrange it. You need to think about how best to set it out: this will depend on many factors, most of which could not be anticipated without knowing the precise intended effect of the song. But here are some general suggestions.

Some guitar effects devices can enable you to construct a riff out of the simplest musical material. Perhaps the best example of this in rock is the wah-wah pedal. Even on a single chord the EQ changes and the rhythm it can make with a single chord can be highly effective. Much of Isaac Hayes's 'Theme From Shaft' has as its foundation an almost continuous G octave on the guitar, played through a wah-wah. Korn's 'Pretty' uses a single chord for the riff but changes the EQ to make it work.

As anyone who's ever messed about with delay will know, echo boxes transform your playing. As soon as you go beyond the shorter, reverb-type delays all the habitual scales and licks sound messy and cluttered, and distorted notes aren't too brilliant either. Echo units make you feel like hearing only one or two notes at a time. They set you thinking straightaway about (the magic word) *texture*. You hear potential harmonies and chords you never heard before. Random clashes of notes as you change chord produce startling musical phrases. Echo units make space itself a positive quality that you can work with, not an absence. This is strongly felt in a Big Country song like 'Chance', and some of U2's lesser-known tracks, like 'Heartlands' and 'Walk To The Water'. What's more, in a three-piece with a singer, delay provides a fuller concert sound.

So it was with The Edge. U2's music up to *The Joshua Tree* is characterised by Edge's growing awareness of guitar textures using delay. The first live recordings released as *Under A Blood Red Sky* gave a good indication of how full this could be. On a song like '11 O'Clock Tick Tock' the guitar part is almost a counter-melody to the vocal, at the same time as sketching the harmony. His parts are often typified by open strings ('I Will Follow' and 'Gloria'), including solos ('Sunday Bloody Sunday'), moving up and down a string while hitting the adjacent one. 'Pride' has this too, along with effective harmonics and chords that hang while the bass part changes. Songs like 'Where The Streets Have No Name' and 'I Still Haven't Found What I'm Looking For' are classics of rhythmic playing with a delay, where the simple opening phrase is transformed by the notes bouncing back from the echo.

Multi-tracking a riff

The chance to multi-track raises the question of how many guitars should play the riff? In a power trio, or a group with just one guitar, or on four-track demos, the options will initially be limited. The easiest way to generate the illusion of two guitars playing a riff is to use a stereo delay, along with a little EQ to differentiate the channels. For example, the direct guitar signal can go to the left, and the signal that goes to the right has a short delay on it. This gives the illusion of two guitars. How short the delay needs to be will depend on the tempo. Too long a delay will make it sound as though the virtual guitarist over on the right is half-asleep and not keeping up. A variation on this is to add distortion only after the guitar signal has split. Live, this would mean using two amps, one set to overdrive and the other not; or keeping both amps clean but putting an overdrive pedal after the delay so one side is distorted. You don't have to have the delay itself switched in to have the signal split.

Some players prefer to double-track a riff in real time by recording it twice. Unless you are a robotically precise player who can duplicate every nuance of expression in the first pass, enough small differences of timing and volume creep in to make the two sound close but not exact, thus thickening the riff. You can, of course, deliberately play a bit sloppily to give it more 'feel' – it depends on the style of rock. If you're double-tracking a riff at the same pitch you will probably want to distinguish the tone of the guitars. This can be done by using different amps, different amp settings, different effect pedals, EQ, and varying amounts of reverb at the mixing stage; or with different pickups on the same guitar, or by taking the classic route of using different kinds of guitar. The favoured combination is a double-coil-pickup guitar versus a single-coil or a mini-humbucker – the traditional Gibson/Fender contrast. One guitar could be clean, one distorted. Or how about one with slight overdrive and the other with 1960s fuzz? There are many permutations.

Different instruments

Another route is to multi-track a riff with other instruments. In funk a riff might be doubled on a synth. In rock'n'roll it might be doubled by saxes. Good results can also be had by doubling the riff on strings, especially cello (think of the texture of 'Good Vibrations').

For an earthy, funky effect why not bring the riff in first on acoustic guitars – say two six-strings or even a six and a 12 – and then hammer it home with the electrics later on? Electric 12-string gives an unusual tone to a riff, especially with a little overdrive, since the electric 12-string is something we are more accustomed to hearing with a clean tone, in styles of rock that are more chordal than riff-based. If you use an electric 12-string to double an overdriven six-string playing the same riff, the 12-string can be mixed a little quieter so its higher octave strings add a feeling of overtones to the original. Have a listen to Led Zep's 'Living Loving Maid' from *Led Zeppelin II*.

Another consideration is what the bass might be doing. Think carefully about when you want the bass to come in if it's going to double a riff one or two octaves below. On the basis that a rock number shouldn't blow all its ammunition in the first minute, you may want to have the bass double the guitar riff only an octave down at first, and save the lower octave for a suitable moment later on in the song. Another possibility looked at in the pedal/drone sections was to have the bass play a pedal repeating note (usually the key-note) under the first repetitions of the riff and then go into a unison effect. Try letting the bass play the riff first and then bring the guitars in on top.

Once a riff is double or triple-tracked at the same pitch, the law of diminishing returns comes into action. Using an extravagant number of guitars to multi-track a riff doesn't make it sound necessarily bigger. The more distortion you use, the more

"once a riff is double or triple-tracked at the same pitch, the law of diminishing returns comes into action"

this is the case (paradoxical but true). After recording two or three tracks of the riff at one pitch, you may need to consider doubling the riff at a different pitch, which initially means an octave or so apart. What can be done with octave doubling will depend on where the riff is pitched in the first place. Normally, if the riff is down in first position, in the lowest octave on the guitar, then there will be two positions above where it could be played and doubled. The previous suggestions about mixing different guitar tones on such parts applies here as well.

If the riff is in fifths which change very quickly, they may be too quick for one guitarist to play cleanly. In this case, fast fifths can be played by two guitarists, each taking a single note. You can hear this on Kiss's 'Detroit Rock City'.

Harmonising a riff

A further refinement of this idea of doubling at a different pitch is to harmonise the riff. This doesn't mean you have to harmonise the whole riff, or the whole riff every time it occurs. Sometimes it's enough to add a little musical colour by putting a few notes at a suitable interval above part of the riff – say in the last bar. These touches of musical colour can be effective without disrupting the riff itself. They have a less drastic effect, for example, than transposing the riff to another note.

The most popular interval for harmonising a riff would be a third or an octave plus a third (a tenth); alternatively, use sixths, or an octave plus sixths. When you select the right octave for the harmony consider also where the vocal line is going to be pitched. Remember thirds and sixths bring in the major/minor colouring and can imply chords. With careful thought and musical dexterity it's possible to construct a riff which consists of a bassline, a guitar riff, and a harmonising part in thirds or sixths, with only three notes at any given moment, which would imply whole chords. To give the riff a typically 'hollow' sound and avoid a major/minor feel, fourths, fifths and octaves are the option. Feel free to vary the interval; you don't have to harmonise in the same way all through. Choosing thirds but ending on a fourth or fifth can imply a particular chord on which you might want to end.

Some of the riffs in Black Sabbath's 'Supernaut', 'A National Acrobat' and 'Electric Funeral' are harmonised. Have a listen to Ram Jam's 'Black Betty' (1977) for an instance of how effective a harmonised riff sounds (this one in thirds, with a strong major key feel) when it occurs several minutes into a track that has had several riffs on the B pentatonic minor and B blues scales.

If your riff is chord-based, then the obvious doubling trick is to have another guitar playing in a different position on the neck. There's also the use of fifths to toughen up and support a chord riff. Remember that fifths will go with a chord regardless of whether it's major or minor.

RIFFS AND THE BAND

The type of riffs you write can be influenced not only by your playing style and other creative pressures, they can also be influenced by the type of band you play in. In a power trio (guitar/bass/drums) or a quartet with a vocalist, you only have one chordal instrument to establish harmony, namely guitar. So to generate a bigger sound you may feel more inclined to write riffs that use at least two notes at any one time, rather than single-note riffs. Chord-based riffs will obviously be very attractive. If you have a second guitar in the band then harmonised-type riffs will sound better, and any single-note riffs can be doubled. If you have a keyboard player try single-note riffs that have more 'cut', because the keyboards will fill in much of the harmony. Part of the musical discipline in working with a keyboard player in a band playing riff-based rock is to get him/her to limit the number of notes they play for the sake of the riff. Look to a band like Deep Purple for arrangement examples.

Writing and playing classic RIFFS

A MASTERCLASS WITH **JOHN PAUL JONES**

With album sales second only to The Beatles, Led Zeppelin are now regarded by fans and critics alike as the definitive exponents of heavy rock. John Paul Jones not only played bass at the core of rock's great riff machine, he also composed some of those riffs. Led Zep's nine studio albums contain 81 tracks; Jones has a writing credit on 32 of them.

Jones came to Led Zeppelin with several years experience in the music business. As a child he'd toured in Variety theatre with his parents, picking up eclectic musical ideas; by 17 he was touring with Jet Harris and Tony Meehan (ex-Shadows), and before long began making a name for himself not only as a session bassist (for the likes of Dusty Springfield, Lulu, and Tom Jones) but also as an arranger, scoring the strings on The Stones' 'She's A Rainbow', arranging Donovan's 'Mellow Yellow' and 'Sunshine Superman', and Jeff Beck's 'Hi Ho Silver Lining'.

Eventually Jones found the session work was stifling his creativity, but the diversity of music he'd encountered was significant for the musical development of Led Zep. After 12 years in the world's greatest heavy rock band, Jones returned to the studio. Apart from the Diamanda Galas album *This Sporting Life* and the soundtrack *Scream For Help,* he's composed music for early music group Red Bird, synthesiser music for Eno's record label Opal, and produced bands like The Mission, REM, and The Butthole Surfers.

He is still writing heavy riffs, now for multi-string bass – as can be heard on his two recent solo albums, *Zooma* (1999) and *The Thunderthief* (2002). If anyone doubts how important Jones was to Zeppelin, these albums reinforce his contribution. He is also largely responsible for changing the musical vocabulary of the rock riff by using scales other than pentatonics – his fondness for the minor second coincidentally mirrors current interest among nu-metal bands in scales and modes like the phrygian and locrian...

So who better to provide a unique insight into the world of the riff? Jones is quoted here in conversation with the author:

ON INFLUENTIAL RIFFS

"I loved the classic 'Lucille' riff. Little Richard's original was too fast to register for me as a riff – what I mostly heard was the pounding piano part. The first time I really thought of it as a riff and went crazy was when I heard the Everly Brothers version on the B-side of 'Cathy's Clown'. Not only does it contain that riff pre-'Pretty Woman' (which had a slight difference – I didn't like that as much because the ninth softens it too much) but it also contains the thing that got me playing steel guitar, the solo, which I worked out and got off as a lap steel part. Some of the early riffs came from boogie-woogie piano, translated onto the guitar.

"The other one from that time, the reverse of that riff, was 'Shakin' All Over' which went downwards. Then there was [Duane Eddy's] 'Peter Gunn Theme', the ancestor of 'Grind' [from Jones's *Zooma*]. Again, not the original version from the film, which is much softer and uses a major third on its penultimate note. Duane Eddy flattens it – he changed the riff, made it more economic and harder. That to me was the riff of all riffs ... I was very affected by Duane Eddy in the old days – that whole low melody thing, as with Jet Harris.

"I had a pop upbringing as far as my session days were concerned. You could hear what was going to work and what wasn't, how the music took you through the bridge and into the hook or chorus ... the formula for why it

> "I was very affected by Duane Eddy ... that whole low melody thing"

"any Zep riffs
with chromatic
movement would
be mine"

works. You could almost lay the songs on top of one another. It's like a book, or film, or theatre, it always has these stages of development, tension, release. If you're aware of this you can do it on a micro or macro level. You have to tell a little story."

[*Jones was strongly influenced by the riffs in Motown records.*] "I had to play a lot of it in sessions when Motown was the fashion … They knew they could give me a chord chart and I could improvise a reasonably authentic Motown or Stax-sounding bassline, and they didn't have to worry. So I used to be playing those wonderful James Jamerson lines and re-making them as I went. Duck Dunn [MGs and Stax bassist] wasn't a riff player, but I got my soul stylings from him, and from the Phil Upchurch combo, and later from Willie Weeks. There was more riffing in jazz: with a riff, you don't have to worry about knowing a chord progression."

ON ZEPPELIN RIFFS

"You can always tell my riffs from Page's because mine have got lots of notes and are linear. His are chunkier and chordier: I like the riff in 'The Ocean', and 'Kashmir' is a great one. I was coming at it from another angle. 'In The Light', during the verse – that's a riff of mine. I leave the seventh ringing. Page doesn't do riffs like that. In fact, anything with chromatic movement would be mine.

"When Page starts soloing and goes up high there's a big gap, and you have the problem of filling it. We filled it with eight-string bass … Page complained bitterly when eight-string first appeared. – he said [grumpy voice], 'I'm not playing to *that*'. Then he realised how much sound it made and how it gave him a much better base to solo over … then he liked it. When Page came out with the first riff of 'Achilles' [Em-F#m] he said, 'What are we going to do with the rest of it?' I said, 'The eight-string bass'… It fitted perfectly.

"Both Page and I had a high degree of discipline in routining, and making sure things were right … Being able to turn your hand to anything, and to know authentically how it should be done. Every piece of music I listen to, every piece of music I play, influences the next thing I do … A lot of the problem with the bands who imitated us was they all listened to the same sort of music. In Zep, we had areas where our tastes would cross, but not that many. We were into completely different things a lot of the time."

ON SOLO RIFFS

"I often write my stuff away from instruments and then I work it out on them … Sometimes patterns will suggest a riff, but then I'll go away, walk around and think of how it starts, what it's going to be from then, how I would like to hear it if it were the next track of an album. Otherwise, I just end up playing and then I forget I'm writing something. I do that for arrangements as well ... literally while walking.

"When I write riffs in my head I can often hear the drums as well. So what I'll usually do is come back and write a drum part on the machine and just practise it, and I'll often fine-tune it – move a beat here or there, so the riff works best. If there's anything wrong with the riff, I fix it.

"The most common scale I use is (in E, coming down) E-D-C#-B, A#-G#-G-F. It's not a straight mode, though it's like the lydian. It's all through *Zooma* and *The Thunderthief* . It's based on tritones as well. In jazz it's the scale that links all 13th chords and augmented ninth chords, which are the reverse of each other. It's the universal scale over the lot – the one that links all keys. I learned it a very long time ago, in the 1960s.

"You've got the minor second in 'Angry Angry' from A to Bb, and in 'Tidal' from *Zooma*. A lot of the riffs really work the minor second. I like the tensions – it's a riff of two halves: you can superimpose one half on top of the other if you need to ... You can play so many different major scales over it, which will all fit in: in E you could play an E major scale or an F# major scale; a Db5 would probably fit on it as well. There are just so many things it links together ... so many tension spots.

"It's half a blues scale, because it has the flattened seventh, but it also has the major third. There's also a slight whole-tone feel about it as you move between them. It's got a lot going for it as a scale, it's very flexible – you can accentuate different aspects of it."

'B Fingers'
[*Clearly a riff from the man who dreamed up 'Black Dog', complete with trademark tricky bit.*] "There's an added beat to make a 5/4 bar, but it's not like, 'Oh I think I'll do a tricky 5/4 here'. That extra beat was crying out to be there, and it felt very natural. It must be governed by the music. There was a tendency for some of those [progressive 1970s] bands to be 'spot-the-beat'. You've got to be able to feel those things. In Mediterranean music they always have things like 9/4: Greek, Arab and Indian music always has those naturally – and they dance to it, so it must feel natural ... All my weird timings are melody led ... and if it happens to be a beat longer, then the time signature has to change to fit it in. It's like the cross-rhythm in the riff of [Led Zep's] 'Nobody's Fault But Mine' – I just started playing it like that. That was just me saying, 'What shall we do with this, chaps?'"

'Grind'
"I like the shifts from the stark fifths to the minor – that juxtaposition. It starts as a good-time rock'n'roll track, almost Stonesy in a strange,

"all my weird timings are melody led"

swaggering sort of way. Then it turns into a snake-like riff on the bottom of the 12-string bass. In fact that's the only one where I use the low B-string almost exclusively. To be honest, it's a big sub-Duane Eddy riff which I've wanted to do since I was 14.

"As for the texture of riff one, it's because I've always liked the 12-string guitar – the way you can do those passing notes, the classic Byrds arpeggio sequences. Multi-string basses allow me to do that. They're very guitary instruments – I can play them like a 12-string guitar. The octave strings bring out the melody lines; if you did that on a four, five or six-string bass it would all get lost in low harmonics."

'Freedom Song'
"The riff to 'Freedom Song' was me picking up the ukulele and playing a little African thing. I tuned it differently to a straight ukulele. That's the first take – it has a mistake in it, but why make it perfect? It had such a great feeling about it ... I've found that playing while watching meter levels is a brilliant idea because I find the half of my brain that usually interferes with my playing is involved in checking levels. So you just get on with it."

'Leafy Meadows'
"I didn't want it bluesy. I'd done a lot of blues-based riffs before on *Zooma*. I thought, well riffs don't have to be bluesy all the time. So it was intentional that I went for the major third. The second half is slightly more bluesy, but it's all based around the major third or the minor second.

"The time signature change in the second riff came because it just needed a little tag on the end of a phrase. It's almost a Zeppelin thing. They're all in 5/4, with a bar of 6/4, I think. Because it's in a strange time signature it sounds much more complicated than it actually is: you put in an extra beat and everybody throws their hands up. Actually it's rounding it off – it's making what should be in common time [5+5+6 = 16: the same number of beats as four bars of 4/4]. It rounds it off in the right place, which gives it a closure, and although you're not counting you feel the closure."

'Shibuya Bop'
'Shibuya is an area of Tokyo, full of kids and loud music and shops with pinball machines. Very vibrant. I was walking past this shop with a really hard techno track coming out. It was the very intense, claustrophobic feeling about the rhythm – it didn't let you go. I thought it would be interesting to write a rock riff that, just as you thought it was going to give up, turned a corner and carried on. It was incessant, fast, hard and not very bluesy.

"The rock'n'roll koto solo has more of a Spanish scale – the phrygian. But you can change the character of a scale by accentuating a different interval in the scale."

"riffs don't have to be bluesy all the time"

'The Thunderthief'

"That one's much more of a blues scale. It has a strong tritone going from the A to the E♭, with a C in-between. The riff is structured so as not to have it going on at the same time as the words. It's almost like a confirmation of the lyric – it's like, 'OK, think of the lyric for a bit while I play the riff'. Another example of this would be [Berry Gordy's] 'Money'."

ON PLAYING RIFFS IN A BAND

"I usually think of any riff in terms of the rhythm section – how it's going to sound with the drums. So occasionally, if I want the snare to be a feature – like an off-beat to pop out – I'll leave a space for it, and like-wise the kick-drum. Sometimes it's good to have the bass-drum kicking the riff along. Sometimes you can stop the riff and let the kick-drum go another beat. Or have an accent. It just gives texture to the riff and makes it much more interesting. Like [Led Zeppelin's] 'The Wanton Song', where the snare is isolated between the octaves – whereas in 'The Immigrant Song' there isn't a gap like that, because the whole point about the 'Immigrant' riff is the kick down: Dum da da *da* dum [*emphasising the second beat*]."

"You've got to think like an arranger, look at the whole picture. Think rhythmically and spatially ... Often I would stop in any complicated riff, work out what the dynamic of the riff is, and let the drums do it – otherwise, if you're both playing at the same time, the whole thing becomes weak. Which to me is where a lot of the metal bands go wrong, because if you're all playing at the same time, it's not heavier – it's weaker. It's much stronger to get constituent parts of a riff to work so the whole thing pushes and pulls, and the tensions are on a micro-level, not a macro-level. It's the same thinking that says you need a stack of guitar amplifiers when in fact you can get much more out of a small amp with good mikes. And the more times you multi-track a riff, the more you lose all the grain."

"Everybody's got to listen ... If you choose a note, there's got to be a reason for it. Does it help the harmony, does it help the rhythm? If you're just playing it for no reason, then you'd be better off not playing it."

RIFFS on the CD

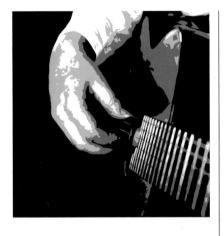

"the 30 tracks on the CD correspond to the 30 riff types in the book"

To illustrate the 30 types of riff described in the text, a specially-recorded CD is included with this book. The 30 tracks on the CD correspond, in sequence, to the 30 riff types listed on the Contents page and described in Sections One to Three.

In this section you'll find the music notation for these riffs, if you want to play along, and a commentary giving details about how each riff is constructed and some of the arrangement approaches used on the recording (as discussed in Section Four). Unless otherwise noted, each track has a four-beat count-in, and features a single-coil-pickup guitar on the left channel and a double-coil-pickup guitar on the right.

RIFFS GROUP ONE: USING INTERVALS

CD TRACK 1 semitone riff

Rather than use a traditional rock'n'roll or punk semitone riff, this track elects to do something less predictable by fretting the semitone below each of the open strings. Each semitone pair has a slightly different 'colour' because of the changing chords (especially as the G#m and Bm chords are unexpected in what sounds like a blues-inflected E major in the first two bars). The form of the riff is a1 a2 a3 b, where 'a' is the first eight quavers (eighth-notes) which have three different final phrases. For 'b' (bars 7-8) further use is made of the semitone by adding bends.

The arrangement has a single guitar track recorded in stereo.

CD TRACK 2 tone riff

Usually a tone riff will move on to the root note. Track 2 does this in bar 4, but in bars 1-3 it is moving off the root note. A 16th-note rhythm is used throughout, giving a rock/funk hybrid feel. Notice that bars 1-3 are not rhythmically identical; small variations make things more interesting (and keep players on their toes). This riff could also be described as having an a1 a2 a3 b form.

The arrangement features bass playing the riff, with the two guitars heard in bar 1 on the left and right. In bar 2 another guitar enters playing a third above, and in bar 3 a fourth guitar enters playing a fifth above the root notes. With all three parts sounding in bar 4, triad chords result.

CD TRACK 3 octave riff

Here's a typically 'bouncy' octave riff where the bass plays along with the guitar. Notice the semitone movement from the bottom E onto F in the middle of bars 1-3 (which could only sound like this in this key), and the powerful accented 16ths of bar 4. The attack of bar 4 complements the slinky quality of bars 1-3.

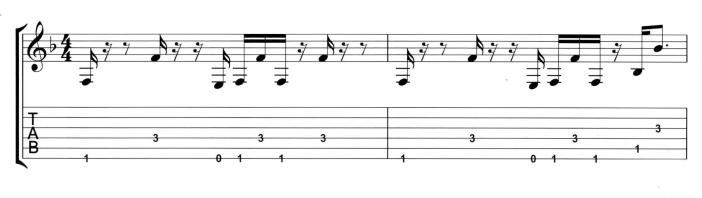

CD TRACK 4 fifth riff

This riff uses a descending run of fifths in G minor. The form is a1 (bars1-2) a2 (bars 3-4). There are small changes in the length of some of the notes, and the run at the end of each phrase is one note short in bar 2.

Listen for the sinister effect of the guitar on the right, which puts the riff through a wah-wah pedal. A piano sketches in the major and minor chords, which the bare guitar fifths don't make explicit.

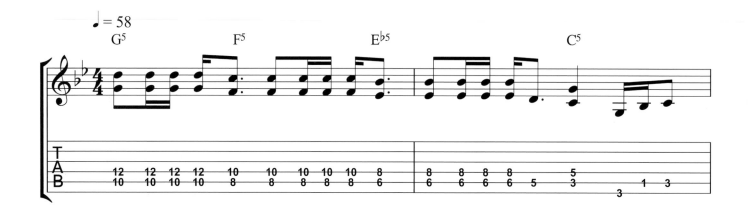

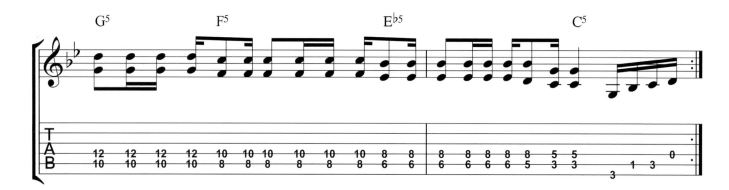

CD TRACK 5 fourth riff

Two bars of the so-called 'Hendrix' chord act as an intro for this riff, which uses fourths on the lower and middle strings in a two-bar phrase that falls and then rises. Notice the tie across the middle of bar 3 and the second quaver rest in bar 4 – both mean there are no notes on beat 3, creating a distinctive 'pull' in the riff. This riff would lend itself easily to transposition up the neck for variety.

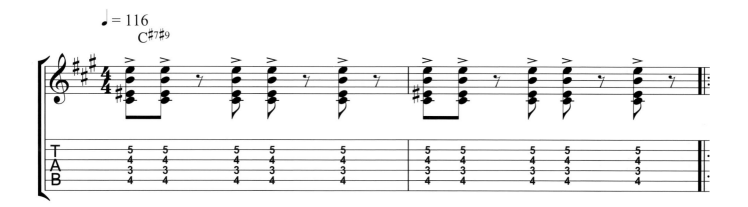

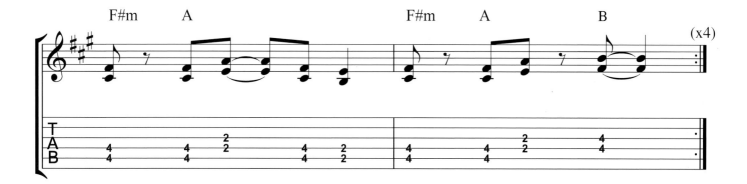

CD TRACK 6 tritone riff

Tritones often work best in a riff made of other elements. They function like the addition of hot spices to a meal. This riff uses 'dropped D' tuning (bottom E down a tone), a D mixolydian scale (D-E-F#-G-A-B-C) with the addition of F, the blues bIII (flattened third). Like the previous track, it's a two-bar form with different endings. In bar 1 a tritone can be heard on the last beat. The expected A5 (A-E) is replaced with a more unsettling tritone (A-Eb). A second tritone occurs in bar 2 as F-B. The B is bent up a semitone to C and momentarily the tritone becomes a fifth.

One arrangement trick to highlight different parts of a riff is to overdub guitars playing only part of the riff. On this track two guitars, left and right, play the whole riff. In the centre of the mix a third guitar doubles the tritones only, and on the third repeat a fourth guitar doubles the first-beat 16th-notes (of which there are four) an octave higher.

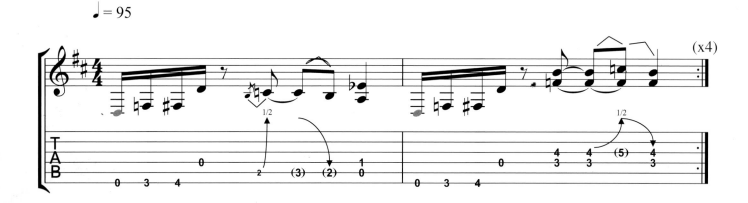

"try overdubbing guitars playing only part of the riff"

CD TRACK 7 riff in thirds

This riff brings out something of the 'sweet' sound of thirds over a major key sequence. Unlike a riff in fifths, thirds strongly emphasise the major/minor harmony. As is often the case, the thirds are combined with other intervals such as fourths, some coming from open string combinations. The form of the riff could be described as a four-bar phrase with two different endings (bars 4 and 8).

This type of riff requires less distortion on the guitars.

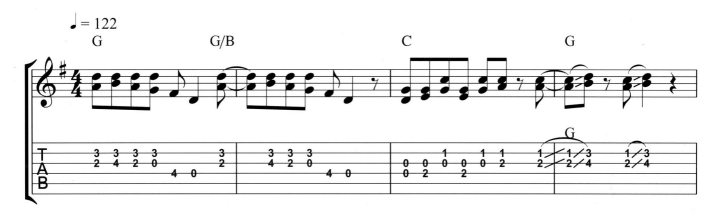

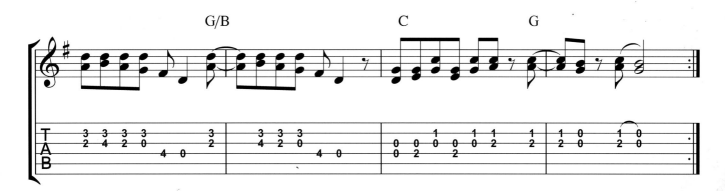

CD TRACK 8 riff in sixths

The structure of this riff in sixths is a1 (bars 1-2), a2 (3-4), b (5-6) and a3 (7-8). The 'a' sections each have a different final two beats. The purpose of section b is to create contrast, which it does by a change of rhythm and the unexpected introduction of a couple of fifths. Their 'bare' neutral quality contrasts with the harmonically explicit sixths. Another important feature is the fact that the a1 run of sixths is mostly heard over A minor, whereas a2 and a3 are heard over F. This shows that the same riff can be harmonised with more than one chord and will consequently sound different.

CD TRACK 9 mixed interval riff

This mixed interval riff combines sixths, fifths and fourths in bars 1-3 and 5. In bar 4 the fifth is supported by two open strings. Some of these fifths are not even built on the root note of the chord over which they are played; for example, in bar 1, G#-D# is sounded against an Emaj7 chord. This works because Emaj7 is E-G#-B-D#. Only in bar 5 does this fifth actually sit on the root note of the chord, which is then G#m.

This riff is a good example of asymmetry because it's five bars long, not the expected four, and bar 5 is rhythmically dramatic. The overall effect is of an unexpected and passionate outburst before the music can return to bar 1. The structure can be described as a, a, a, b, c.

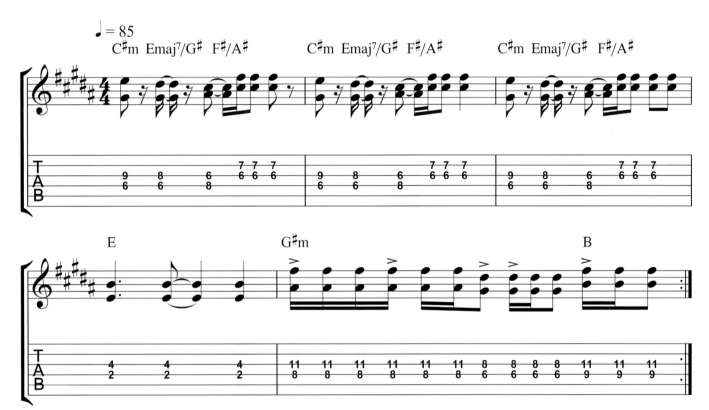

RIFFS GROUP TWO: USING SCALES

CD TRACK 10 pentatonic minor riff

Here's a typical pentatonic minor riff on C, with rock syncopations every other bar, a tone transposition in bar 5 (from C to D), and one additional passing note in the B and C# which occur in bars 2 and 6. Bass and guitar play the same notes. Listen for the guitar overdub second time through which doubles the riff an octave higher. Unlike Track 9, which is rich in chords, Track 10 has no supporting harmony (hence the NC, No Chords) – which partly accounts for its classic hard rock sound.

CD TRACK 11 blues scale riff

This riff draws on the E blues scale of E-G-A-B*b*-B-D. The blues flattened fifth (*b*V) makes its appearance in bar 2 in a traditional bend/pull-off figure. It wouldn't make sense to try to copy this on the bass because it's too fast, so the bass is free to play other ideas. This blues lick is replaced in bar 4 by a stark fourth (D-G) with a passing tritone (C#-G). The B-E fourth throughout is Fifties rock'n'roll or Seventies glam – however you hear it.

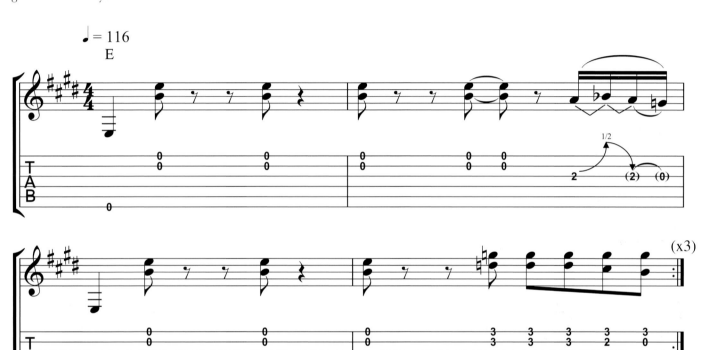

CD TRACK 12 pentatonic major riff

This two-bar riff is another 1950s-influenced idea, but with a twist. The main notes are taken from E pentatonic major (E-F#-G#-B-C#), but where G#m appears the note C# is bent a tone to D#. D# is one of the notes of G#m, and also the seventh note of the scale of E major – so on both accounts it fits perfectly. It's still a surprise, because that C# would normally be bent only a semitone to D, the blues bVII (as can be heard on Track 23).

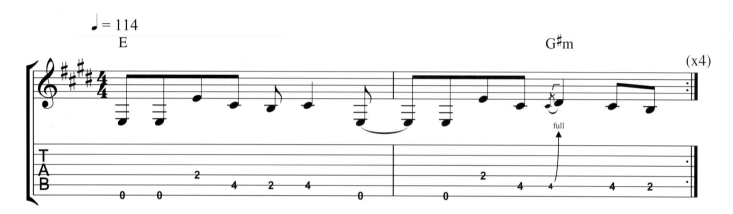

CD TRACK 13 major scale riff

The normal seventh of the major scale is also the determining factor in the riff here. This two-bar riff in G major is based on a common 1950s rock'n'roll idea: notice the flattened third (Bb) and natural third (B) next to each other – but with one significant difference. After the octave jump on G the riff falls not to the expected F natural (the blues bIII) but F# – the seventh of the major scale. Notice also that the bass guitar does not double the whole of the riff, but only the last five notes.

This idea of emphasising the usual seventh of a major key is then adapted for the verse section. Instead of putting the riff under the vocal, it is simplified into a rhythmic figure that implies Gmaj7 instead of the more usual G7. After four bars we get the predictable chord change to C – but it's Cmaj7, not C7. This verse has used eight-bars of a 12-bar blues sequence, but not the chords you would normally hear.

The swing feel of this track is created by using 12/8 time.

Continued on next page

Verse

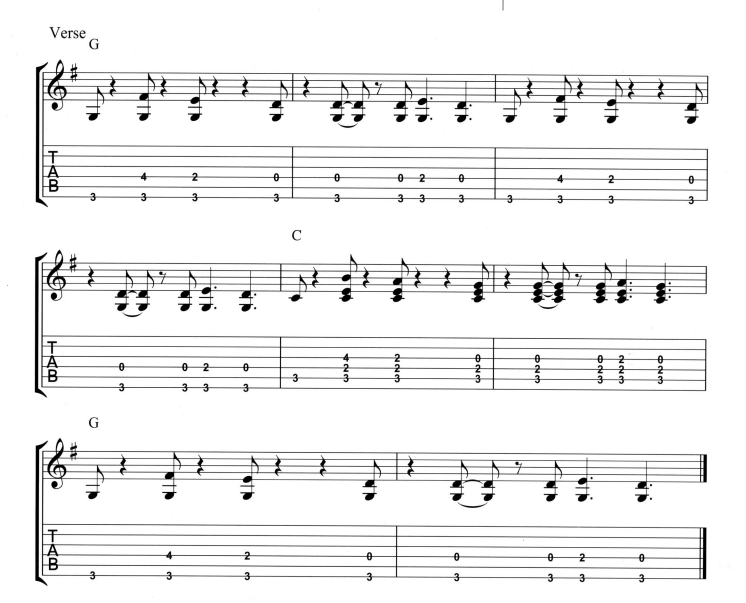

CD TRACK 14 mixolydian riff

This is the first of our examples to start with an incomplete bar, on the third off-beat. This shifts the rhythmic shape of the riff, which ends halfway through bar 7. C mixolydian (C-D-E-F-G-A-B*b*) supplies most of the notes. This is reinforced by the implied C7 chord of bars 1-2, and the B*b* *b*VII chord in bar 4. Notice how the rhythm pattern changes in bar 4. Bars 5-6 makes an unexpected shift of harmony to E*b* (a blues *b*III chord) and then to the exotic B*b*m. This chord change is linked by the transposition of bar 5 down a tone to bar 6. The predictable blues harmony of the mixolydian opening has been taken somewhere new. The sequence ends with a strong tone shift from C to B*b*.

Listen for the 12-string guitar (on the right) playing the riff throughout.

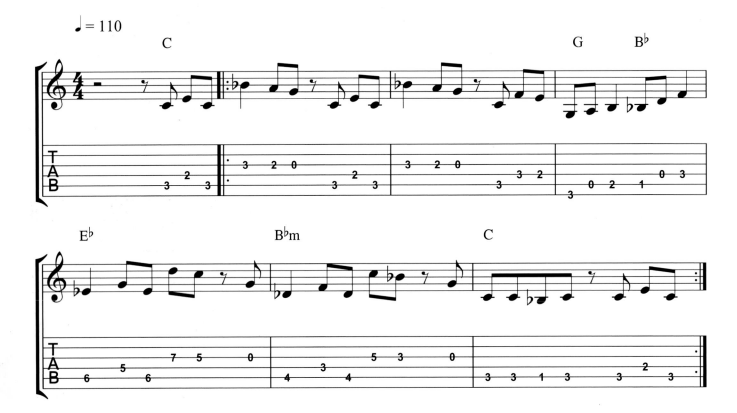

CD TRACK 15 minor/aeolian riff

Back to the swing of 12/8 but very, very slow. The E aeolian scale (E-F#-G-A-B-C-D) is pressed into doomy service for a clearly scale-based climbing riff. The form is a1, a2, with two contrasting endings to the two-bar phrase. In bar 2 a full Am7 contrasts dramatically with the single notes that surround it. In bar 4 the C-B notes are transformed by brief arpeggios based on the chords of C and G/B. Throughout, the bass guitar sticks to the basic scale and root notes.

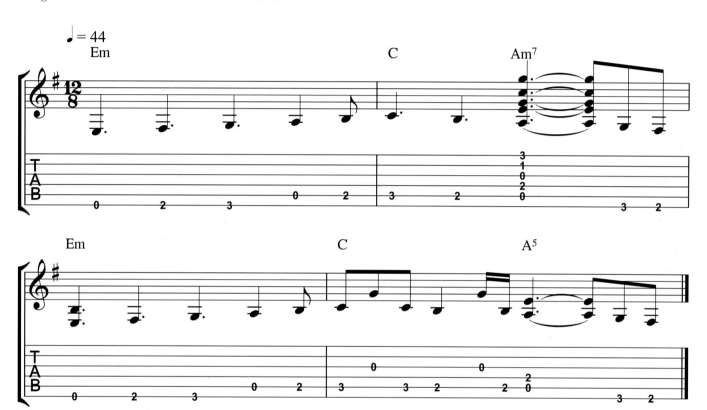

CD TRACK 16 dorian riff

This dorian riff in single notes is structured a1, a2, a3, b, each section lasting two bars. The scale of A dorian (A-B-C-D-E-F#-G) is supplemented by a flattened fifth (Eb) note in bar 7. The dorian flavour is created by the emphasis on F#. The first part of a1, a2 and a3 is a phrase that ends on this note. Notice how the riff uses rising and falling phrases. Listen for the guitar overdub in bars 5-8, which doubles the riff an octave higher.

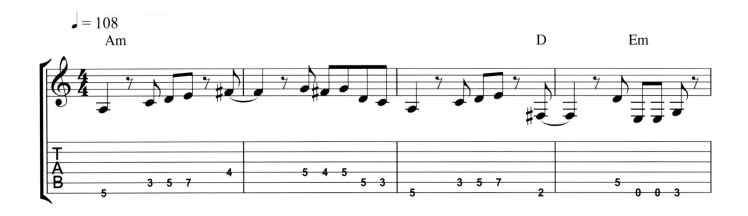

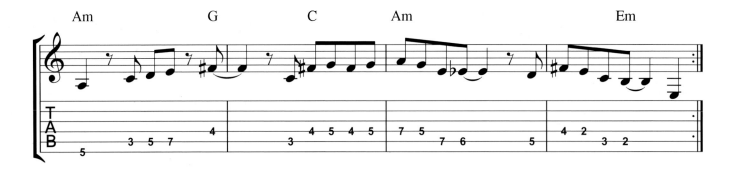

CD TRACK 17 phrygian riff

The 'signature' note of the phrygian mode on A is B*b*, the flattened second. This riff emphasises that note in the way Track 16 emphasised F#, the dorian sixth. The track begins on the fourth beat of the bar. An initial 16th-note phrase is played four times with variations. At bar 5 the riff turns into chords. The note B*b* is heard in the A7sus4/*b*9 chord (where it is the *b*9), in Gm and B*b*. Choice of chord helps to retain the flavour of the mode.

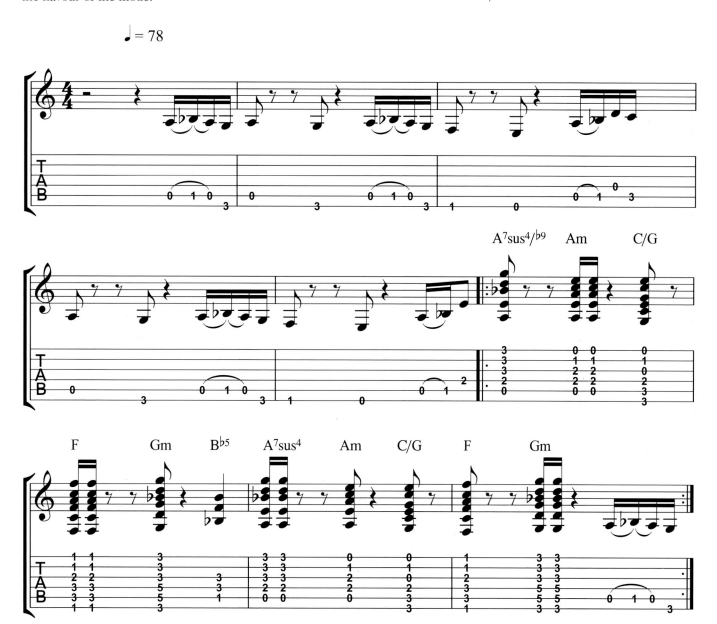

CD TRACK 18 lydian riff

F major normally has a B-flat in its scale (F-G-A-B*b*-C-D-E-F). This means that the chords G and Cmaj7 (both of which contain a B-natural) would not normally occur in this key. However the lydian mode on F gives F-G-A-B-C-D-E-F, and so the chords of G and Cmaj7 are possible. Apart from the scale-like passages in this riff there are also arpeggio-based ideas, as in bar 2. Listen for the 12-string guitar on the left side. Remember that a 12-string guitar overdub is an easy way of doubling the riff an octave higher.

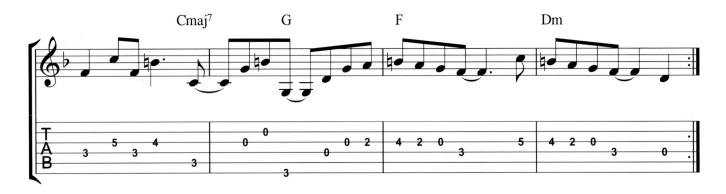

CD TRACK 19 locrian riff

This riff in F# locrian (F#-G-A-B-C-D-E) is played entirely in fifths, as might be expected in a heavy rock style. Of all the modes the locrian is the most asymmetrical, because of its flattened fifth note, C, resulting in chord I being a diminished triad, rather than major or minor. The asymmetry of the mode is enhanced by the use of an asymmetrical time signature – 5/4 – and the fact that 5/4 and 6/4 bars alternate. The absence of a regular pulse has almost as unsettling an effect as the mode itself.

♩ = 97

CD TRACK 20 chromatic riff

Chromatic riffs are characterised by step-wise movement, as Track 20 illustrates in a funky style. The key is D major (D-E-F#-G-A-B-C#) but to these notes are added F, C, E*b* and B*b*. Bar 2 transposes bar 1 down a tone, so the riff structure is a1, a2, b1, b2. Listen for the creeping movement back to the key-note in bar 4. The bass plays the same notes as the guitars. Notice the 'jumpy' effect of the dotted eighth-note/16th-note pairing in bars 1-3.

♩ = 106

RIFFS GROUP THREE: USING CHORDS

CD TRACK 21 pedal-note riff

The pedal note itself is D and the scale played on the third string is D mixolydian (obvious because of the Cs instead of C#). Notice the semitone bend in bar 2. A 12-string guitar plays the riff on the right. The significant element to this riff is the arrangement: the first time, the riff is supported by slight percussion; the second time, the drums enter properly; on the third time through, bass and organ clearly change chords, altering the sound of the riff even though the riff is the same. Remember that new light can be cast on a riff by re-harmonising it.

$\quad$ = 110

CD TRACK 22 drone-note riff

To play this riff a new tuning is required: E-A-D-F#-B-C#, with alterations to the first and third strings. All the played strings are allowed to ring, so be careful not to accidentally damp them. It looks complicated on paper but it's based on the shape of a fifth, moving up the lower strings. The drone notes are the top three strings. Listen for the entry of the 12-string guitar overdub. A further overdub has a guitar in standard tuning just playing fifths, to strengthen the bass frequencies.

Notice also that this riff is grouped in three four-bar phrases instead of the more common four. Four repeats give a 12-bar verse instead of the usual 16-bar verse.

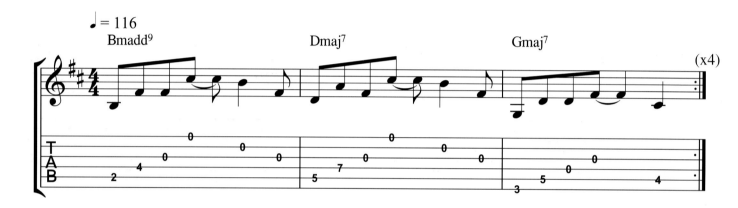

CD TRACK 23 arpeggio riff

Back to the Fifties swing feel of 12/8 time for this riff in E, which uses some traditional arpeggio figures on E7 and A7. As before, a twist is given to the ideas by the semitone bend from C# to D (implying a tritone against the G blues chord), which is harmonised in sixths on its second and third appearances. The same thing happens to the A7 riff: when the C chord appears in the last bar, another tritone (F#) is created against it by the off-key sixths.

Continued on next page

CD TRACK 24 major chord riff

Here's a typically meaty chord riff in E major, using a I-IV-V-IV-*b*VII sequence, and then the same with the last chord replaced by a *b*III G. Although all the chords except the Dsus2 are straight majors, the scale degrees of *b*VII and *b*III (D and G) complicate the picture slightly, giving a harder, blues edge. Even with only two guitars playing there isn't much room left in the sonic picture for more rhythm overdubs.

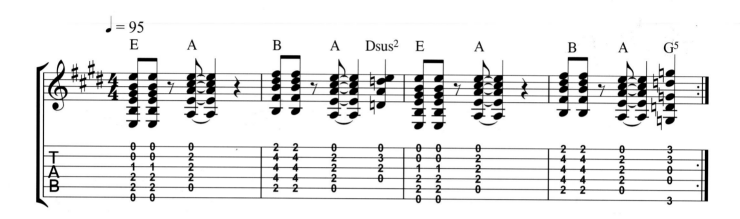

CD TRACK 25 mixolydian chord riff

Sometimes a riff can be created simply by holding a chord and lifting a finger on and off a string. The chord in question here is a familiar D7, but made to yield a rock riff by taking the fingers off the first and third strings to get the sense of something happening. The 'dominant seventh' chord – here formed on the first of the scale, D, in true blues fashion – naturally occurs as chord I of the mixolydian mode. The *b*VII of that mode is also heard in the descending run which ends each of the riff's phrases, though one has an F and the other an F#. Notice how the single notes of the riff's ending contrast with its chordal bars.

Continued on next page

CD TRACK 26 minor chord riff

Minor chord riffs lend themselves to less rocky material. In B minor the three main chords would be Bm, Em and F#m. They are supplemented here by the more exotic Gm6. On the arrangement, one cleanish electric guitar is joined by an acoustic guitar.

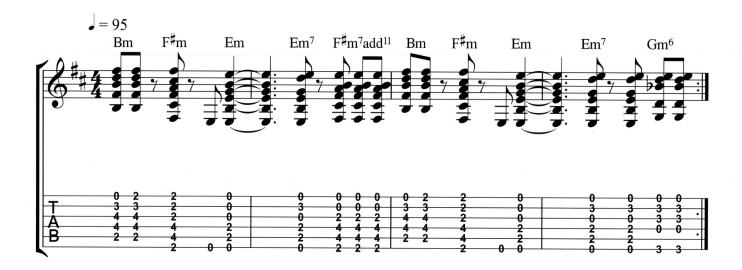

CD TRACK 27 suspended chord riff

The tension of a suspended chord is exploited in Track 27 by the heavy accenting of A7sus4, G7sus4, Esus4, and Fsus2 chords. Notice the unexpected Chuck Berry-ish double-stop bend in bar 1 and 3, and the shift to a higher resister for the G7sus4 up at the seventh fret. The structure of the riff is a1, a2 (on A), b (on E).

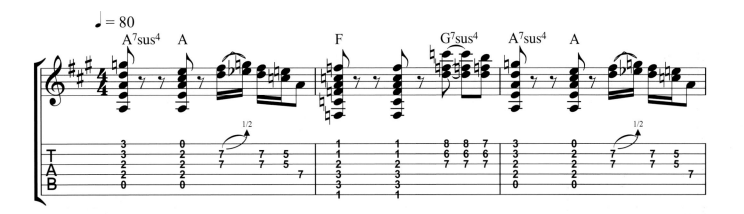

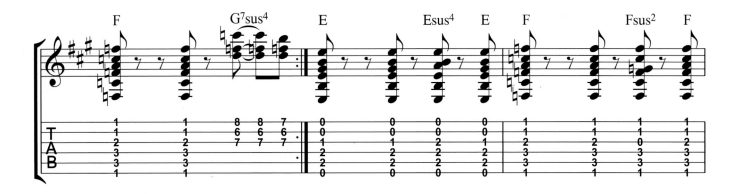

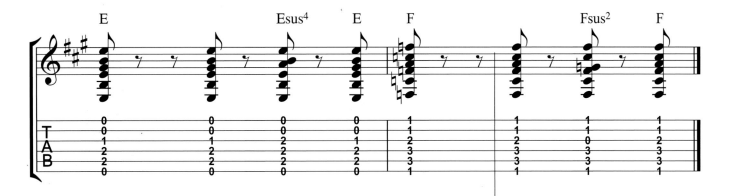

RIFFS

CD TRACK 28 triad riff

This triad riff has a slight soul feel because of the 16th-note rhythm patterns. The triads are in D and moving up the top three strings. Extra harmonic colour is created by additional tones such as the sus4 in bar 2, the add9 in bar 3, and the minor add9 in bar 4. Notice how the rhythm pattern is fairly constant in each bar, and the chords change against this.

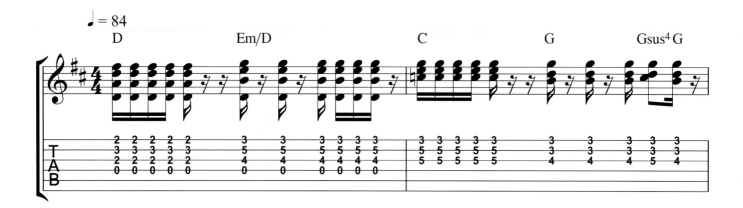

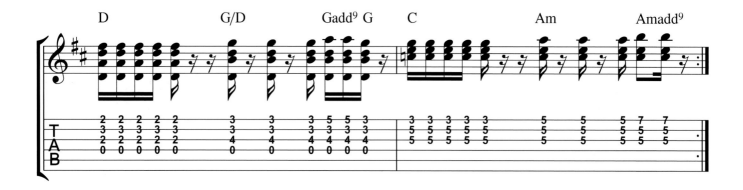

CD TRACK 29 inverted chord riff

The logical way to make a riff with inverted chords is to construct them on a bassline that is moving in steps up or down. Track 29 features a rising bassline of E-F#-G-A-B-C-D-E. After the initial root E, those bass notes are harmonised with a sequence of inversions that goes: first, second, second, first, first, first, culminating in another root E. The bass guitar strengthens the sound of the inversions by also following this line – if it played the root note of each chord the effect of the guitar inversions would be weaker. In bars 8-9 two more inversions appear, putting a new slant on an old chord progression.

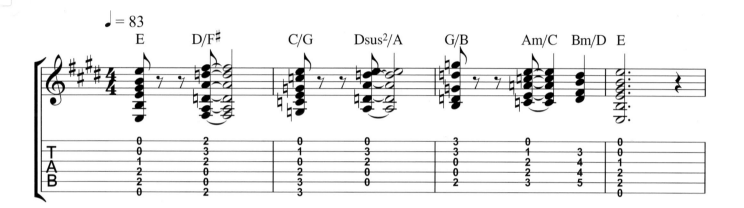

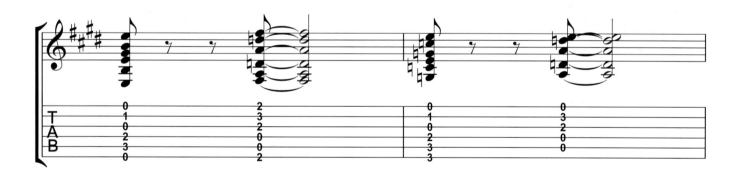

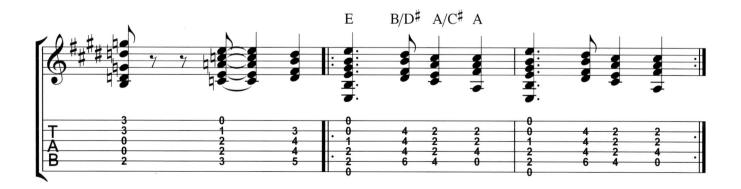

CD TRACK 30 unusual chord riff

To finish, here's a riff that brings together several musical elements... The asymmetrical, unsettling effect of the 5/4 time signature is enhanced by the unusual chords. The tone-shift first beat of bar 1 would not normally be followed by an Am6 chord (Am is foreign to the key of B major); the F#7 chord would not normally have an add11 in it, and such a hard rock riff would be unlikely to have a G#m chord...

The riff is then developed. In bars 3-6 the music goes into 4/4. The first beat is retained but a more common bIII chord (Dsus2) and IV (E5) are added – only to then be trumped by the wholly unexpected Gm6 and first inversion Dmaj9. A climbing low bass phrase leads to a further development of the opening riff, which is in 6/4, and dropped a tone to be based around A (although it is not an exact transposition).

In the song from which this example is taken, the 6/4 riff did not occur until a verse and chorus had passed. In a real musical context it would be too much to put these three riffs next to each other, but this has been done here for the sake of illustration. Remember that development is a technique hardly used in rock, so there's an opportunity here to do something out-of-the-ordinary now and again. Instead of repeating the same riff throughout a track, why not write a variation on it that can be slipped in at certain points to add extra interest?

Track 30 shows how a single idea can mutate in and out of different time signatures and pitches.

"instead of repeating the same riff, why not write a variation on it"

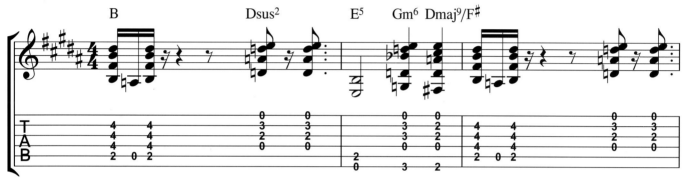

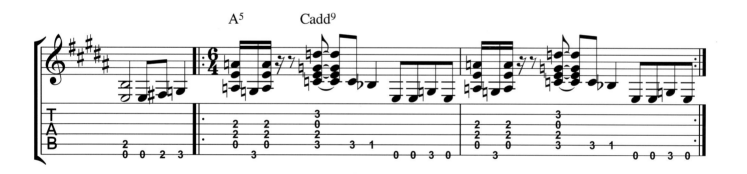

Index of artists

Page numbers in **bold** indicate a
detailed analysis of particular tracks
in the Riff Galleries.

Index of songs

Page numbers in **bold** indicate a
detailed analysis of particular tracks
in the Riff Galleries.

M

N

O

ACKNOWLEDGEMENTS

ABOUT THE AUTHOR

Rikky Rooksby is a guitar teacher, songwriter/composer, and writer on popular music. He is the author of *How To Write Songs On Guitar* (2000) and *Inside Classic Rock Tracks* (2001), and contributed to *Classic Guitars Of The Fifties* and *Guitar: A Complete Guide For The Player*. He has also written *The Complete Guide To The Music Of Fleetwood Mac* and *The Complete Guide To The Music Of Madonna*, 14 Fastforward guitar tutor books, and four in the *First Guitar* series. He has transcribed and arranged over 30 chord songbooks, including Bob Dylan, Bob Marley, The Stone Roses, David Bowie, Eric Clapton, Travis and *The Complete Beatles*, and co-authored *100 Years 100 Songs*. He has written a number of articles on rock musicians for the new *Dictionary Of National Biography* (OUP), as well as contributing interviews, reviews, articles and transcriptions to magazines such as *Guitar Techniques*, *Total Guitar*, *Guitarist*, *Bassist*, *The Band*, *Music Collector*, *Encore*, *Sound On Sound*, and *Making Music*. He is a member of the Guild of International Songwriters & Composers and the Vaughan Williams Society. Visit his website at *www.rikkyrooksby.com*

ACKNOWLEDGEMENTS

For their involvement in the preparation of this book I would like to thank Nigel Osborne, Tony Bacon, Holly Willis, Paul Quinn, Phil Richardson, Paul Cooper and Stephen Bishop. Thanks to Tim Turan for mastering the CD, and also to Rupert Winchester and Roger Dalrymple who suggested riffs for inclusion. **RR**

PICTURE CREDITS

Artist pictures supplied by Redfern's, London. Playing pictures selected from the Balafon Image Bank.

"*Dun-dun-da, dun-dun DA-DA.*" Deep Purple, 1972.